Library and Information Sciences

Chuanfu Chen • Ronald Larsen
Editors

Library and Information Sciences

Trends and Research

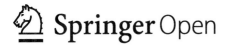

Editors
Chuanfu Chen
School of Information Management
Wuhan University
Wuhan
China

Ronald Larsen
School of Information Sciences
University of Pittsburgh
Pittsburgh, Pennsylvania
USA

ISBN 978-3-642-54811-6   ISBN 978-3-642-54812-3 (eBook)
DOI 10.1007/978-3-642-54812-3
Springer Heidelberg Dordrecht London New York

Library of Congress Control Number: 2014940283

© The Editor(s) (if applicable) and the Author(s) 2014. The book is published with open access at SpringerLink.com.
Open Access This book is distributed under the terms of the Creative Commons Attribution Noncommercial License which permits any noncommercial use, distribution, and reproduction in any medium, provided the original author(s) and source are credited.
All commercial rights are reserved by the Publisher, whether the whole or part of the material is concerned, specifically the rights of translation, reprinting, re-use of illustrations, recitation, broadcasting, reproduction on microfilms or in any other way, and storage in data banks. Duplication of this publication or parts thereof is permitted only under the provisions of the Copyright Law of the Publisher's location, in its current version, and permission for commercial use must always be obtained from Springer. Permissions for commercial use may be obtained through RightsLink at the Copyright Clearance Center. Violations are liable to prosecution under the respective Copyright Law.
The use of general descriptive names, registered names, trademarks, service marks, etc. in this publication does not imply, even in the absence of a specific statement, that such names are exempt from the relevant protective laws and regulations and therefore free for general use.
While the advice and information in this book are believed to be true and accurate at the date of publication, neither the authors nor the editors nor the publisher can accept any legal responsibility for any errors or omissions that may be made. The publisher makes no warranty, express or implied, with respect to the material contained herein.

Printed on acid-free paper

Springer is part of Springer Science+Business Media (www.springer.com)

Preface

From Boone Library School to School of Information Management (SIM), an iSchool at Wuhan University, the teaching and research in library and information science (LIS) has been a century-old tradition of this university. The journal, *Documentation, Information & Knowledge (DIK)* launched by SIM in 1983, has been making great efforts to identify quality academic papers in LIS areas and gradually developed into a premium LIS journal in China.

Since China's reform and opening-up initiative was introduced, the exchange between Chinese and international LIS community has become more frequent. Stepping into the twenty-first century, the global information environment has changed rapidly and digital native has emerged. People's information needs, information literacy competency, and information search behavior are constantly changing, which poses challenges and at the same time, brings opportunities to LIS profession. In order to explore these challenges and opportunities, and further develop LIS education, Wuhan University established the National Key Discipline Forum on LIS in 2008. This Forum puts emphasis on the past, present, and future of LIS education and theories. Quite a few established experts, educators and theorists have been invited to the forum, providing valuable insights in the development, trends and research of LIS areas.

Our readers have witnessed the steady efforts of the DIK, developing from China to the world, and from Chinese version to English version, and some other language versions, in the past 30 years. The speeches and presentations delivered by experts and scholars on at the Forum and Wuhan University's joining iSchools has created favorable conditions for the development and progresses.

The publication of *Library and Information Sciences: Trends and Research* is undoubtedly a great challenge for us. I am pleased that each of the articles contained in this book is based on cutting-age studies of authors. This book is divided into five parts. In the first chapter, Dr. Forest Woody Horton introduces the opportunities and challenges faced by library and information literacy profession in the society, followed by Dr. Alease J. Wright's contribution on the key role of librarians in the future information literacy education. The last chapter of this part is featured with a discussion panel at which seven authors present their thoughts on information literacy. In the second part Professor Elizabeth D. Liddy discusses the trends in

LIS education by examining the vision of the iSchool movement and detailing its practice in Syracuse University. In the third part, Professor Jin Zhang et al. first uses visual data mining technology to detect the relationship and pattern between terms on Q&A site. Next, Professor David Nicholas et al. consolidates the reliability of Google Analytics using as information search and research data source through empirical study on the multimedia website. Dr. Tingting Jiang then conducts a critical analysis of the theoretical foundations, systems features, and research trends of exploratory search. The fourth part starts with Professor Peter Ingwersen's contribution in which he stresses the importance of building an academic accreditation framework for scientific datasets, studies its metrological characteristics, and proposes the dataset usage indicator as an indicator of dataset management framework. After that, Professor Feicheng Ma, et al. present their findings in knowledge discovery of complex networks research literatures. This part ends with Professor Ruth A. Pagell's explorations on the relationship between bibliometrics and university rankings. The fifth part includes an article by Mr. Eugene Wu, detailing the birth and development process of East Asian Library in North America.

This book is co-edited by SIM, the Center for the Studies of Information Resources of Wuhan University, and DIK. I am very grateful to Dr. Forest Woody Horton and other authors for their contributions to this book. I'd like to express special thanks to Professor Ronald Larsen for accepting our invitation to serve as the Co-editor in Chief. I would also like to thank Dr. Daqing He of Pittsburgh iSchool. I am particularly grateful to my colleagues Liming Zhou, Xiaojuan Zhang, Yuan Yu, Jie Xu et al. for their hard work for compiling this book. Thank Dr. Niels Peter Thomas and Editor Emmie Yang at Springer Publishing Group for their enthusiastic support, and thank the National Social Science Foundation of China for their journal publishing fund (12QKB073) support.

Well begun is half done. I hope the publication of this book can be a good start, lay a solid foundation for future studies, and thus facilitate the global development of LIS in the digital age.

26 Feb. 2014   Chuanfu Chen

Advisory Board

Feizhang Peng Professor, School of Information Management, Wuhan University
Changzhu Huang Professor, Member of Chinese Academy of Social Sciences
Guangjun Meng Professor, Chinese Academy of Sciences
Weici Wu Professor, School of Information Management, Beijing University
Zhanping Liang Professor, China Institute of Science and Technology Information
Feicheng Ma Professor, School of Information Management, Wuhan University
Changping Hu Professor, School of Information Management, Wuhan University
Junping Qiu Professor, School of Information Management, Wuhan University
Qing Fang Dean and Professor, School of Information Management, Wuhan University

Editorial Board

Editors in Chief

Chuanfu Chen Editor in Chief, Documentation, Information & Knowledge Professor, School of Information Management, Wuhan University

Ronald Larsen Professor, School of Information Sciences, University of Pittsburgh

Executive Editors

Ruhua Huang Professor, School of Information Management, Wuhan University

Liming Zhou Deputy Editor in Chief, Documentation, Information & Konwledge

Project Editors

Xiaojuan Zhang Professor, School of Information Management, Wuhan University

Jie Xu Lecturer, School of Information Management, Wuhan University

English Associate Editors

Daqing He Associate Professor, School of Information Sciences, University of Pittsburgh

Lihong Zhou Associate Professor, School of Information Management, Wuhan University

Yuan Yu Lecturer, School of Information Management, Wuhan University

Contents

Part I   Information Profession and Information Literacy

Career and Professional Opportunities and Challenges for Librarians and Other Information Professionals Specializing in Information Literacy and Lifelong Learning 3
Forest Woody Horton

So What's the Big Deal With Information Literacy in the United States? 9
Alease J. Wright

A Group Discussion on Information Literacy 21
Jason Phelps, Steve Van Tuyl, Gladys Joy E., Martin Julius V. Perez, Joseph M. Yap, Lihong Zhou, Yiwei Wang and Han Jiang

Part II   Trends of Library and Information Sciences Education

iSchools & the iSchool at Syracuse University 31
Elizabeth D. Liddy

Part III   Information Seeking and Retrieval

Visual Data Mining in a Q&A Based Social Media Website 41
Jin Zhang and Yiming Zhao

Information Seeking Behaviour and Usage on a Multi-media Platform: Case Study Europeana 57
David Nicholas and David Clark

Exploratory Search: A Critical Analysis of the Theoretical Foundations, System Features, and Research Trends 79
Tingting Jiang

xi

Part IV Informatics

Scientific Datasets: Informetric Characteristics and Social Utility Metrics for Biodiversity Data Sources 107
Peter Ingwersen

Knowledge Discovery of Complex Networks Research Literatures 119
Fei-cheng Ma, Peng-hui Lyu and Xiaoguang Wang

Bibliometrics and University Research Rankings Demystified for Librarians 137
Ruth A. Pagell

Part V Development of World Libraries

The Development of East Asian Libraries in North America 163
Eugene W. Wu

Contributors

David Clark CIBER Research Ltd., Newbury, UK

Forest Woody Horton International Information Management Consultant, USA

Peter Ingwersen Royal School of Library and Information Science, University of Copenhage, Copenhagen, Denmark

Han Jiang School of Information Management, Wuhan University, Wuhan, China

Tingting Jiang School of Information Management, Wuhan University, Wuhan, China

Gladys Joy E. University of the Philippines—Diliman, Quezon City, Philippines

Elizabeth D. Liddy Syracuse University, Syracuse, USA

Peng-Hui Lyu Centre for the Studies of Information Resources, Wuhan University, Wuhan, China

Fei-Cheng Ma Centre for the Studies of Information Resources, Wuhan University, Wuhan, China

David Nicholas College of Communication and Information Studies, University of Tennessee, Knoxville, USA

CIBER Research Ltd., Newbury, UK

Ruth A. Pagell University of Hawaii, Honolulu, USA

Martin Julius V. Perez School of Library and Information Studies, University of the Philippines—Diliman, Quezon City, Philippines

Jason Phelps Information School, University of Washington, Seattle, USA

Steve Van Tuyl University of Pittsburgh, Pittsburgh, USA

Xiao-Guang Wang School of Information Management, Wuhan University, Wuhan, China

Yiwei Wang School of Information Management, Wuhan University, Wuhan, China

Alease J. Wright Springdale, MD, USA

Eugene W. Wu Harvard-Yenching Library, Harvard University, Cambridge, USA

Joseph M. Yap School of Library and Information Studies, University of the Philippines—Diliman, Quezon City, Philippines

Jin Zhang University of Wisconsin-Milwaukee, Milwaukee, USA

Yiming Zhao Wuhan University, Wuhan, China

Lihong Zhou Department of Information Studies, the University of Sheffield, Sheffield, UK

Part I
Information Profession and Information Literacy

Career and Professional Opportunities and Challenges for Librarians and Other Information Professionals Specializing in Information Literacy and Lifelong Learning

Forest Woody Horton

Abstract This article reviews the new career and occupational opportunities for librarians and other information professionals as a result of dramatic and pervasive developments in IT technologies in the last several decades. In particular, a case is made for a new information counsellor position which would be analogous to financial counsellors but operating in the information arena. Traditional library and information positions are being very widely expanded by new challenges which every social and economic sector, both public and private, is experiencing as they confront the twenty first century's rise in Google search engines, mobile devices like smart phones, and the spread of broadband and the Internet.

Keywords Careers · Occupations · Counsellors

You will be hearing a great deal about information literacy and lifelong learning at this workshop today and tomorrow. I have the honour to serve as UNESCO's facilitator for a series of 11 workshops being held throughout this year in all of the regions of the world. Six are now completed, and I would like to share with you today some of the career and professional opportunities, as well as challenges, that have been highlighted and discussed by both the expert presenters and participants at those first six workshops.

First the career and professional opportunities.

I hope when you come away from these three workshop days here at Wuhan University you will be convinced that you have selected a bright and promising future for yourselves in a field that has emerged as a critical twenty first Century skill requirement. The opportunities, both tangible and intangible, both quantifiable and non-quantifiable, are numerous, growing by leaps and bounds every day, and are already, and will continue to be realized by all sectors and by all professions. For

---

Remarks delivered at the UNESCO "Training-the-Trainers" in Information Literacy Workshop, Wuhan University, Wuhan China, October 21, 2008. It has been updated, with a postscript, for republication here.

F. W. Horton (✉)
International Information Management Consultant, USA
e-mail: f.w.hortonjr@att.net

C. Chen, R. Larsen (eds.), *Library and Information Sciences,*
DOI 10.1007/978-3-642-54812-3_1, © The Author(s) 2014

example, with a more highly information literate workforce, private sector companies can expect that their workers will work smarter at whatever they do, and therefore produce at a higher rate–whatever the products and services involved–than ever before. But I want to concentrate on librarians and information professionals because most of you are in that career area already, and I therefore want to try to address your needs and expectations, and try to deal with some of your fears and misgivings–real or imagined.

To begin with, you are going to be in great demand for your knowledge and skills because you can expect that your superiors, colleagues, peers and subordinates, not to mention your family and friends, will have been reading about information literacy and asking many questions–what is it, why is it important to me, how can I learn about it, and how can I practice it so as to improve my life, do my job better, and help my family resolve their problems? They will begin to look to you for the answers to those questions–perhaps from the moment you arrive back home and go back to your jobs on the first day. They will need training, which is why this workshop is designed to help "train the trainers." So the first opportunity I'm addressing is that you are in a new and still-emerging profession, the members of which will be expected to have acquired, both in formal schooling, in special workshop opportunities such as this one, as well as in practice, on-the-job, information literacy knowledge and skills. Whether you respond to this demand for your expertise and talents is, of course, entirely up to you. Some of you may be timid, and believe that you have not learned enough to call yourselves information literacy experts. That is understandable. Sometimes titles are not all that important. But, hopefully, many, if not most of you, will, slowly but surely, rise to this demand for your talents, whatever your current job title, and, however modestly, and however carefully you begin to respond to that demand, you will, eventually, be looked up to in your organization as one of the, if not THE information literacy expert! Many professionals are in stable or even declining fields and careers. But yours is a field that is ascendant–rising fast–and the demand will not lessen for years to come. I personally happen to believe it is rising exponentially!

Secondly, as the benefits of a more information literate faculty, student body, office worker, laboratory worker, factory worker, and managerial level becomes more visible, quantifiable, transferable and sustainable, inevitably your job opportunities will proliferate and salary levels and other kinds of benefits can be expected to increase commensurately. Do not sell yourself cheaply! Perhaps you may need to transfer, moving to another unit, or even an entirely different organization, to take advantage of new opportunities that are arising. Do not be bashful or hesitant to consider such offers and opportunities. In short, the price tag you command should increase proportionately to correspond with the level of expertise you acquire as you learn more and more about information theory concepts and practices. Like all fields, you start as a beginner, then advance to an intermediate level, and then, sooner or later, go on to an advanced level. Be sure to keep your resume and C.V. up to date to reflect your information literacy expertise and learning. For example, include workshops of this kind in your C.V. so that when a more lucrative and challenging job offer becomes available, you will have a job portfolio that reflects accurately your training as well as on-the-job experience.

Thirdly, consultancy opportunities. Whether you are currently working for a library in some other kind of information job at a university, a government agency, a private company, an NGO, or somewhere in the Civil Society, and whether in a regular line or staff position, with a regular career progression ladder, inevitably new consultancy opportunities will appear for you. Perhaps you are already largely satisfied with the career ladder in front of you. That is, the salary levels at each step on the ladder, the intellectual satisfaction, the working environment, your peers, and so on. But I can predict that, as your information literacy expertise increases, and becomes more widely known in your community, sooner or later you will be called upon to provide advice and assistance to organizations beyond your own. Consistent with your current legal and ethical job demands and employment rules, you may well be able to benefit from such offers, and, in many cases, monetarily benefit. Perhaps if such requests come from close friends and colleagues you may decide to provide your expert advice and assistance gratis–free of charge–recovering just expenses. But do keep in mind that experts normally charge a fee for their knowledge and expertise–they do not often give it away free!

Finally, even if you choose to remain in your present job, without risking any significant requests to change your job descriptions and position duties, you still will have considerable professional opportunities to share your information literacy expertise with your colleagues, both inside and outside of your present organizations. What I mean here is that as it gradually becomes known that not only are you a librarian, or an information professional of some kind (whatever your exact job title may be), inevitably your colleagues, and even strangers, will begin to approach you and ask for your advice and assistance. In short you will become recognized as a person who possesses knowledge and skills that are extremely timely, and very valuable. You must decide, then, how to handle that kind of opportunity. Obviously there is also some risk that unless you obtain at least implicit permission from your superiors to spend at least some time offering information literacy advice to those seeking it from you, your superiors may come to believe you are extending yourselves beyond your assigned duties and responsibilities. So you must be careful to address this risk. But, having said that, I believe that the benefits and values of deliberately expanding your skill portfolio to beyond your "classic" academic training, to embrace the new skill sets possessed by an information literacy expert, outweigh the costs and burdens. But each of you will have to make that decision for yourself.

Now let's go on to the challenges of becoming an information literacy expert.

First, the challenge of adopting lifelong learning attitudes and behaviors. I list this as a challenge because information literacy, although an exciting new career and professional opportunity, carries with it, implicitly, the demand that you keep up with new advancements in the field. After all, relatively speaking, information literacy has only been with us as a discipline in its own right for less than two decades. That is a very small amount of time compared with the traditional disciplines of, for example, teachers, doctors and nurses, accountants, lawyers, and so on. This means that you need to refresh your knowledge and skill portfolio regularly, not just periodically or intermittently. Every day, virtually, there are new and updated ideas, approaches, strategies, and so on, that are being advanced by both information literacy theorists and practitioners. You need to keep abreast of what these are, and decide whether any of them have relevance to you and your organization and your information literacy practice. If they do, then you need investigate them carefully, and decide how you will adapt and adopt them into your organization and your programs and projects.

Next, the risk arising from a failure to understand and grasp related concept inter-relationships with information literacy. What I mean here is that at this early stage of information literacy theory experimentation, and promising 'best practices' development, inevitably there are already, and will continue to be many differences of opinion among the experts. That is perfectly normal and to be expected. For example, there is still a difference of opinion on exactly what information literacy is, and how it should be defined. And there are many different terms and words being used to describe what is essentially the same concept–such as information competency, information fluency, digital literacy, and so on. And then there is the challenge of inter-relating information literacy to various closely related fields and disciplines. For example, media literacy and information literacy, ideally, should go "hand in hand," which means they should be pursued in a complementary fashion, not independently. But there are distinct differences between media literacy and information literacy, and you must be able to explain those distinctions clearly, and how they can work in harness together, and in simple enough terms to be understood by people outside of the librarianship and information fields. And then there is distance education. While distance education is very important in the context of information literacy, it is a separate field, and, once again, you must be able to articulate the inter-relationships between the two areas. In sum, you must have a certain tolerance for dealing in a world that is proliferating many new disciplines and technologies and tools, and how they relate to each other is an integral part of the information literacy challenge.

Next the burdens and costs of establishing and maintaining a higher level of peer social networking. Information literacy is not like a physical or biological science where you and perhaps one or two colleagues and assistants can work in isolation in a laboratory for years and years, and perhaps neither see nor talk to professionals outside of your immediate team, even if they are employed in the same laboratory and on very closely related challenges. Instead, you must establish and network with information literacy colleagues who share your special interests, needs and desires, so that you can rely on them to provide you with advice and assistance, or perhaps just informal consultation and the testing of new ideas. This need puts a premium on what is now called 'social networking,' which is a mode of collegial interaction that employs Webcasting, online learning, and similar approaches to maintaining close ties with kindred colleagues.

In this short time I have tried to stimulate your thinking about very personal decisions you will have to make, given the new knowledge and skills you are acquiring. I cannot stress enough that every one of you will have to make his or her own personal decision–there are no standards or ironclad guidelines that I can give to you. But I believe that the career and professional opportunities now being presented to you are indeed very substantial, and I urge you to think carefully now about whether or not, how, and when to make your next career and professional moves so as to enhance your personal futures.

Postscript

Since the author wrote the above words, science and technology have revolutionized information handling so we need to "fast forward" to the twenty first century and review some of the many career risks, challenges, and opportunities confronting librarians now.

First, incredibly fast search engines have revolutionized the ability of ordinary people to search for information which they need themselves, whether at a desktop home, a laptop in the workplace, using a smart phone or tablet while traveling between locations, and so on.

But, like a student first entering library school, ordinary people very soon discover that, while searching for some kinds of information such as the weather, sports news, stock market reports, and the daily news headlines, is, indeed, relatively easy and fast, more complex searches require learning more detailed methods, techniques, concepts, best practices and "tricks."

Suppose, for example, you are looking for a job, or trying to solve a personal or family health problem, or applying for admission to a college? How do you even begin to search for that kind of information, efficiently and effectively, without wasting an inordinate amount of time and effort? Or falling prey to fraudulent misinformation or disinformation or "infotainment?"

There are, of course tutorials online that allow you to self-teach yourself some of these concepts, methods and tricks but almost all of them require some basic knowledge of the very fundamental building blocks of librarianship knowledge.

What is a "tag?" What is an index and how does it differ from a table of contents? What is a citation? What is a bibliography? What is a directory? And so on.

Soon the novice searcher, no matter how proficient with computer hardware and software, or with cell phone texting and apps, or with social media networking, discovers that just because the information universe is becoming digitized does not mean that they automatically can learn to become skilled in being able to find just the right information needed at the right time and in the right place.

Librarians discover very early in library school that learning how to go about finding and retrieving information—from whom, from where, when, and how, is the essence of their craft and they must learn those things thoroughly and proficiently if they are to succeed in their careers.

The discovery by ordinary people that search and retrieval does not come "naturally" like breathing, eating or sleeping, may come sooner than later, but inevitably it does come to everybody, and when it does, people have a choice: continue ploughing ahead, blindly trying to self-teach themselves the basic elements of librarianship, or, in desperation, go to a library and ask for the help of a librarian.

Which leads us to the present context?

Much timely, detailed and relevant material has already and is currently being written about the transformation of the traditional bricks and mortar library into the ultra modern digital library. So, instead of discussing here how the "analog librarian" job is being retooled to the "digital librarian" job, we prefer to concentrate on only one very important brand new career opportunity—the Information Counsellor.

Previously the specific domain or "turf" which I want to talk about now was usually called the job of the "reference librarian." Or the job of the librarian involved in "user instruction." Or sometimes we have seen the terms "Solo Librarian" or "Paraprofessional librarian."

We have had Financial Counsellors, Health. Counsellors, Employment Counsellors and many other kinds of counsellors for a very long time.

Now, with the twenty first century and the dawning of the Global Information Society, we are finally, and very clearly, seeing an emerging, critical need for an Information Counsellor (IC).

Credit for the IC idea, historically, must be shared among many LIS professionals. But one whom I remember, especially, is Professor Marta Dosa who for many years taught at Syracuse University in New York State in the USA.

Professor Dosa presciently forecasted the need for this new occupational category in the 1950s.

She foresaw a wide array of specialties under that umbrella category. Here are a few illustrations.

First, an IC at the top end of the occupation who would do theoretical research to advance the IC concept and to train ICs to learn best practices.

Second, an IC who would specialize in a certain field, sector or area like Heath, Employment, Small Business, Education, Citizenship, etc. Thus we would have, for example, a Health Information Counsellor.

Third, she said we should have ICs who team with "sister" Counsellors like those in the finance area, so that the team, operating together, would be stronger than each performing independently.

Fourth, ICs should specialize by audiences served. Thus we should have Immigration Information Counsellors.

And so on. Here are some other key aspects of the IC job and role.

For one, ICs would perform in both the public and private sectors.

For another, ICs would operate at all levels of organizations and institutions—at the very top, at the middle levels and at the lower levels.

ICs should also not exclusively limit their advice to their clients on traditional librarianship matters. Their domain must extend to media, telecommunications, communication, problem solving, analytical thinking, brainstorming, and other areas.

And ICs must be skilled in Information Literacy, Media Literacy, Computer Literacy, Digital Literacy, and the other so-called twenty first century literacies.

Finally we foresee a range of IC firm sizes emerging that offer primarily IC products and services, from, at the one end, independent proprietorships, to small firms, medium ones, large and then very large at the other end.

In summary we hope that a significant number of library and information school graduates enter this exciting new field! Some may be solo entrepreneurs. Some may team with colleagues to form small businesses. And some will join large companies.

Open Access This chapter is distributed under the terms of the Creative Commons Attribution Noncommercial License, which permits any noncommercial use, distribution, and reproduction in any medium, provided the original author(s) and source are credited.

So What's the Big Deal With Information Literacy in the United States?

Alease J. Wright

Abstract Today's researchers have access to vast information, whether within the library or any place that provides access to the Internet, and frequently the access is free of charge. Such places can include school, home, office, restaurants or coffee houses. Access to information is available from smart and handheld devices such as Smartphones, as well. But now, more than ever a researcher must have a discerning sense of authoritative information. Information seeking has become a rapidly growing trend across society. And as technology continues to evolve, how we seek information and determine its authenticity will present challenges for teaching users how to remain information literate. Additionally, one cannot be information literate without the development of related skills such as critical thinking. Since the United States Department of Labor's well-know SCANS report (Secretary's Commission on Achieving Necessary Skills) published in 1991, other organizations have emphasized the need for information literate workers. Such organizations include the National Forum on Information Literacy and Project Information Literacy

Keywords United States · Information Literacy · Critical thinking · Business needs

A speech delivered at the seminar during the International University Student Information Literacy Competency Invitational Contest, which was, as a part of 1st Wuhan University Student Organization International Exchange Summer Camp, hosted by SIM, Wuhan University, July 13, 2010. It has been updated, with the author's article entitled "Big Deal with Information Literacy in the United States", for republication here.

Alease J. Wright: MLS, Ed.D, Springdale, MD, USA. An IBM retiree, former librarian and adjunct professor at Prince George's Community College in Maryland, has worked extensively with first year college students. Her re-search interests involve preparing academic librarians how to teach, and teaching and learning concepts. Comments and questions can be sent to: ajchristy@hotmail.com

A. J. Wright (✉)
Springdale, MD, USA
e-mail: ajchristy@hotmail.com

C. Chen, R. Larsen (eds.), *Library and Information Sciences,*
DOI 10.1007/978-3-642-54812-3_2, © The Author(s) 2014

Background and History

Libraries in the United States have undergone extensive change in the past 25 years. Prior to the 1980's research was performed primarily using printed sources such as books, maps, and indexes to periodicals. Online research existed during that era, but only by librarians, and usually at a cost per search. Librarian-student interaction either involved giving directions, or conducting library tours (Mercado 1999; Branch and Gilchrist 1996).

But all of that changed with the expansion of technology and its infusion into the library's walls. Today, information users now have access to vast amounts of information within the walls of the library, as well as outside of the building. Enter the Internet, that conglomeration of special telecommunication protocols using telephony, connecting computer servers from anywhere in the world to everywhere in the world, allowing access to various kinds of information, and by anybody who knows how to navigate the World Wide Web. Twenty-eight years ago, John Naisbitt (1982) author of *Megatrends*, predicted such effects of the information explosion.

Students can easily retrieve information for their research purposes. But easy access does not always mean retrieval of *authoritative* information. The American Library Association (ALA) recognized this dilemma and in1989 convened a committee that produced a presidential report and proclamation deeming information literacy one of the key skills for the twenty first century. Information literacy is a set of abilities requiring individuals to "recognize when information is needed and have the ability to locate, evaluate, and use effectively the needed information" (American Library Association, Presidential Report 1989).

Soon after the proclamation and the publishing of the report, and as a response to the presidential committee's recommendations on information literacy, Patricia Senn Breivik founded the National Forum on Information Literacy. The organization's web site describes how education, library and business leaders agreed that "no other change in American society has offered greater challenges than the emergence of the Information Age."

The Association of College and Research Libraries (ACRL) followed up on the ALA's 1989 proclamation by developing a set of standards for higher education. The five standards address the need for an information literate student to determine, access, evaluate, incorporate and use information effectively, ethically and legally (ACRL 2000).

Why Information Literacy is so Important

In 1990, the United States Department of Labor called for an examination of the skills required for the workplace by the twenty first century. What emerged was a report known as the SCANS report, or Secretary's Commission on Achieving Necessary Skills, *What Work Requires of Schools for Americans 2000*. To create the report, researchers on the commission held discussions with "business owners, public employers, unions, workers, and supervisors in plants, shops, and stores"

(Department of Labor 1992). The commission reported that upon "graduation from high school, students must have a new set of competencies and foundation skills... to make their way in the world" (p. i). The report identified eight competencies, one of which deals with the use of information, that is, "acquiring and evaluating data, organizing and maintaining files, interpreting and communicating, and using computers to process information..." (p. iii).

Sharon Weiner, NFIL co-chair, professor and W. Wayne Booker chair in Information Literacy at Purdue University recently wrote in an *Educause* article that "college students think of information seeking as a rote process and tend to use a small set of resources no matter the problem. Collaborative efforts between faculty, librarian, technology professionals and others can develop students who graduate with information literacy competency." Weiner concludes that being information literate empowers individuals and is a skill that can be used throughout their life (Weiner 2010).

Information literacy is not meant to be an independently defined skill. One cannot be or become information literate without the development of other related skills such as critical thinking. The Partnership for the twenty first century (P21) is a national organization that advocates for twenty first century readiness. One such "readiness" skill it defines as a core competency skill is critical thinking. P21 issued a press release announcing that executives are looking for more skilled workers. Executives want to hire workers who are critical thinkers, problem solvers, workers who can collaborate, create and be innovative. The press release was the result of a recent survey conducted by the American Management Association.

Finally, the Educational Testing Service (ETS), known for administering college placement tests such as the SAT, GRE and the tests to assess English speaking and writing proficiency as a second language, created a panel in 2009 to develop a cut-score indicating good critical thinking skills. As a member of the panel made up of over 20 educators and librarians from around the United States, this author found the task to define a reasonable cut-score challenging and quite intense. Nevertheless, upon the completion of our efforts, the ETS issued the following statement as it introduced the new certification tool, *iCritical Thinking™*, late last year: "To succeed in today's digital world, students and workers need to think critically and solve problems using a full range of information and communication technology (ICT) literacy skills" (Educational Testing Service 2009).

We can see how the need for information literacy has evolved and has become a critical skill for the twenty first century. This skill transcends academic requirements and is a skill, along with critical thinking and problem solving, valued by the workplace. In fact, information literacy is a lifelong learning skill.

Thus, we have arrived to today, in the second decade of the twenty first century, where embracing the need for information literacy and critical thinking are an integral part of the First Wuhan University's International Exchange Camp. As an information literacy advocate, it is heartwarming to see that the focus of this event is not only the management of information, but the development of information literate awareness as well. The academy has a large responsibility in creating such awareness and much of the efforts in the United States are being undertaken by academic librarians. In fact, the emergence of information literacy has created a shift for academic librarians, from custodians and retrievers of information, to the role of teacher, teaching students how to become information literate (Wright 2007). As far back as 1905, Melvil Dewey predicted this new role when he described librarians as "teachers in the highest sense" (Vann 1978).

How Information Literacy has Affected Librarians' Role

The first part of this presentation has provided you with a background and history of information literacy. The next part of this presentation will emphasize the impact that information literacy has had in academic libraries in the United States. Part of this next section will demonstrate such impact through interaction with you. As undergraduate or graduate students, it might be safe to assume that you feel fairly competent in navigating the various sources for information retrieval in order to solve a problem, but let's find out how much you already know.

When you want to find an answer to a question how many of you use the popular search engines Google, Yahoo, and Bing? In the United States, Google has actually become a conversational verb whereby it is common to hear someone say "Google it!" when there is an information need. First year college students are cautioned by this author about using Google as their first resource. With the exception of Google Scholar, much of what is listed in the results may sound factual but can be misleading. Students are also warned about using Wikipedia. While Wikipedia is a good source to get general information about a topic or a person, it is not considered authoritative when it comes to doing academic research. The message here is simply to be discerning about the sources you use when you are doing academic writing. Authoritative sources such as the sources found on library web sites or within the library walls are best as your first selection. When you need articles, use the library's subscription databases. These contain thousands of articles from magazines, newspapers and journals about all sorts of topics. If you must use a search engine, try not to use web sites with the.com domain. Many of these sites are selling an idea, opinion, or product. To become information literate you must understand that one of the tenets of information literacy is to always honor copyright licenses which will help you avoid plagiarism.

What's Your Information Literacy Aptitude?

Let's see what you already know. Suppose you are taking a history class and you need to write a five-page paper on a famous war. Let's say you are given the following choices for sources to use during your research: encyclopedia, magazine and/or newspaper articles, text book, Atlas. Which ones would be appropriate to use? If you selected all of the choices, you would be on your way to writing a good paper. All of these sources are good secondary sources. You could also consider other possibilities such as interviewing someone who served in that war or any war to provide a soldier's perspective. Other creative approaches could be attending an historian's lecture on the subject, watching a TV documentary or listening to a radio program. The point I am hoping to get across is that doing a research project requires you to actively do several things: 1) determine you need information; 2) make a decision about the sources you could use; and 3) use and access the sources. These actions relate to several of the ACRL Standards for Information Literacy for Higher Education: Standard 1—Determine the need; Standard 2—Accessed information; and Standard 5—Used information effectively (ACRL 2000).

The problem we just discussed was a very basic research assignment. We will now try one a little more advanced. You have an assignment to write a paper for your Psychology class. You can select the topic. The paper must be five pages and you must use eight peer-reviewed sources to support your thesis. At the end of your five-page paper there should be an APA reference list. Your choices for resources are: text book, library databases, magazine and newspapers, encyclopedia, dictionary, APA Style Guide. Which source(s) would you *not* use?

If you chose not to use magazines and newspapers you would be on your way to being even more information literate. For this problem or assignment, you were asked to use peer-reviewed sources, or in other words, sources that are research-based and have been reviewed by others in the discipline. Magazine and newspapers are not considered peer-reviewed sources. It is also important to mention here that when you are searching databases you may see other terminology indicating research-based and factual data such as "refereed" or "scholarly." Sometimes the word databases use is as simple as "academic." Your assignment required that you use the American Psychological Association (APA) style guide to list your sources on a reference page. This action keeps you honest indicating that the information used in your paper is not yours.

Taking a look at what information literate actions you demonstrated, you exercised the same three as in the basic problem, but in this problem you evaluated your choices a little more and you were ethical and legal with their use. Again, these actions relate to the ACRL Standards 1 and 2 as indicated above, and would include Standard 3- Evaluated sources critically, and another aspect of Standard 5 – Understood ethical and legal use.

Thus, you have been involved in an information literacy instruction session conducted by an academic librarian who has worked in the United States. In solving your research questions (using the two problems we discussed) we were engaged in a teaching and learning session. Rather than retrieve the information for you, you and I, through a different kind of librarian-student interaction, placed more focus on developing you as an independent researcher, a new role for the academic librarian.

The new academic librarian is also involved with designing the library's web site such that tutorials are available for assisting students as they work to become information literate. Librarians are teaching students how to think critically and how to construct search strategies for finding articles in subscription databases. The use of Boolean operators is an essential part to this latter activity, and is quite integrated in the task of identifying key concepts in a research problem. For example, consider the following research question: What effect does global warming have on the world's climate? In this question are key words or concepts that must be addressed in the articles a student would like to retrieve. Librarians ask students to think about which key words would they use. Once these are identified, the idea of using AND, OR, NOT as Boolean operators helps students narrow or broaden the results generated by their search. Other controlling characters such as parentheses and quotation marks can be used to suggest order of operation and to indicate special phrases. Once these practices feel comfortable for students they begin to realize how they might be able to reduce their frustration and often, the time it takes for them to do good research.

Equally as important as teaching students how to do research is the need for librarians to assess how much learning has taken place. In addition to using pre- and post tests as discussed by Hufford (2010), librarians are beginning to create other tools of assessment. For example, at Prince George's Community College, librarian Imogene Zachery (2008) developed an assessment tool based on the popular quiz show, Jeopardy! Her version of the game is called "Psychology 101 Jeopardy!" During a research instruction class, and after preliminary information has been disseminated, Professor/librarian Zachery asks students to pick a category from which a question is posed. When a student responds correctly, Zachery not only reinforces their learning but encourages everyone to participate in the assessment by presenting the person with the correct answer with a prize.

In 2006 this author developed a research instruction quiz that attempted to assess the primary elements of doing good research. Each student in a research instruction session was given the quiz at the beginning of the session so that they could become familiar with what would be covered. Additionally, they were told to listen attentively because they might hear the answers during the course of the session. They could choose to record their responses during the session or could wait until the last five minutes when everyone would be given a chance to record and review their answers. Examples of quiz questions and the correct answers follow.

Q: When identifying that you need articles from databases with scholarly journals what other terminology may you see? Please list them.
A: Refereed, Peer-reviewed, Academic
Q: Which are the best Internet domains to get factual information? Circle the correct answer(s).
A: .edu.gov.org (All of these domains would be circled)
Q: What must I do to avoid plagiarism?
A: Always cite my sources

You may recall hearing these topics discussed during this presentation and perhaps you were able to respond with the correct answers because of your attentiveness. You have just participated in a form of self-assessment.

The assessment experience has been a rewarding one for this author for not only have areas where more teaching emphasis were identified based on students' response and comprehension calling for continuous revisions to the quiz, but observations of students' reactions have indicated that they might be able to leave the session with some degree of mastery of the research process using online resources. Such are the results that academic librarians hope to produce. In addition to the assessment tool, students in this author's research instruction sessions are usually given a list of tips for doing a research assignment to use as a reference point for current and future research projects. Although you are far beyond the first year, the list can be useful for your future assignments as well (See Appendix 1).

You may benefit from more advanced information regarding doing research and so the following are suggestions you might add to the list in Appendix 1: (1) Never use an in-text citation without appropriate reference information; (2) Always cross-check your references; (3) When using databases, remember that the reference list should include the date when the information was accessed; (4) Regardless of the citation style you are required to use, be sure to follow the structure meticulously; and finally, (5) When in doubt during any step of the research process, check with a librarian.

Summary

While the technology explosion has made information easier to access, the challenge has come in determining what is deemed "good" or authoritative information. There are many organizations that are advocating for increasing the awareness and need for information literacy. In the United States, this need has brought forth a more active teaching role for librarians. Both Dewey and Simmons (2000) predicted this role, though Simmons has had the benefit of being around during the information technology explosion. Information literacy not only applies for the college student but has become a valuable skill sought by employers in the workplace as well.

It may be easier to give a student the information he or she needs, but teaching them how to find the information is akin to the old adage, "Give a man a fish and feed him for a day; teach him how to fish and you feed him for life" (Anonymous). The role for academic librarians can be summed up similarly. The task for the student is to understand the importance of becoming or being information literate, to learn the tenets and the tools, and to use them in every aspect of their life.

The Big Deal with Information Literacy in the United States

In the summer of 2010, the author presented and published a paper at Wuhan University's First Ever Information Literacy Competition, giving a personal view and status of information literacy practices in the United States. The following article represents an update.

Libraries in the United States have undergone extensive change, especially in the last three decades of the twentieth century. Prior to that time information was solely found in books, indexes to periodicals, and maps. Any information stored in databases was accessed solely by librarians, and usually at a cost per search. Librarian-student interaction either involved giving directions, or conducting library tours (Mercado 1999; Branch and Gilchrist 1996). Technology infiltrated the walls of the library and since then, they have never been the same. Information was now available in formats easily accessible by any user.

The American Library Association's presidential committee produced a report in 1989 proclaiming information literacy to be a key skill for the twenty first century (American Library Association, Presidential Report 1989). Equally as prescient was John Naisbitt (1982) who predicted in *Megatrends* such effects of this information explosion. Shortly after the ALA's proclamation, Patricia Senn Breivik founded the National Forum on Information Literacy. The organization's web site describes how education, library and business leaders agreed that "no other change in American society has offered greater challenges than the emergence of the Information Age" (www.infolit.org).

Today's researchers have access to vast information, whether within the library or any place that provides access to the Internet, and frequently the access is free of charge. Such places can include school, home, office, restaurants or coffee houses. Access to information is available from smart devices such as smartphones, as well. But now, more than ever a researcher must have a discerning sense of authoritative information.

At the beginning of the twenty first century, the Association of College and Research Libraries (ACRL) developed and published five standards to address the need for an information literate person. The Standards for Information Literacy addressed when to determine the need for information, how to access, evaluate, incorporate and use information effectively, ethically, and legally (ACRL 2000).

Since the United States Department of Labor's well-know SCANS report (Secretary's Commission on Achieving Necessary Skills) published in 1991, other organizations have emphasized the need for information literate workers. The National Institute for Literacy (2001), in their publication regarding the competency of adults for the 21st Century, states that "…information and knowledge are growing at a far more rapid rate than ever before in the history of humankind" (p. 1). Sharon Weiner, NFIL co-chair, professor and W. Wayne Booker chair in Information Literacy at Purdue University wrote in an *Educause* article that being information literate empowers individuals and is a skill that can be used throughout their life (Weiner 2010). However, a recent study conducted by the Project on Information Literacy revealed that recent college graduates need a more comprehensive and varied approach to finding information required by their workplace environment. Students continue to rely solely on computer-related research skills learned in college rather than finding a way to integrate basic information tools such as the telephone (Head 2012).

Additionally, one cannot be information literate without the development of related skills such as critical thinking. The Partnership for the twenty first century (P21) advocates for twenty first century readiness. P21 issued a press release, the result of a survey conducted by the American Management Association, announcing that executives are looking to hire workers who are critical thinkers, problem solvers, as well as workers who can collaborate, create and be innovative. The Educational Testing Service, known for administering college placement tests such as the SAT, GRE and the tests to assess English speaking and writing proficiency as a second language, determined in 2009 a cut-score indicating good critical thinking skills. In their report they stated, "To succeed in today's world, students and workers need to think critically and solve problems using a full range of information and communication technology (ICT) literacy skills" (Educational Testing Service, iCritical Thinking, 2009).

Such is the evolution and demand for information literacy along with its companion skills, critical thinking and problem solving. No longer is the need for information tied to the libraries and the academy. Information seeking has becoming a rapidly growing trend across society. And as technology continues to rapidly evolve, how we seek information and determine its authenticity will present challenges for teaching users how to remain information literate.

Librarians in the Academy

To determine if library schools were preparing academic librarians for teaching information literacy, this author performed a study in 2007. Graduate school curriculums on web sites in the Middle States Commission Accrediting Region were examined to determine the emphasis on teaching skills. What the study revealed was that curriculums included course work related to information literacy but unlike the preparation for K-12 librarians, they did not require a demonstration of teaching skills (Wright 2007). A similar study was conducted a few years later when Bailey (2010) reviewed web sites and syllabi of 49 graduate schools. He concluded that for business information courses, more emphasis was placed on the theory of business information literacy than the practice of teaching users how to become information literate.

Practicing librarians are beginning to use active learning strategies. They develop information literacy games to assess how well students learn after a one-shot instruction session. One such librarian at a community college in Maryland created an information literacy Jeopardy!© game. Students pick a category from which a question is posed. A correct response from a student makes them eligible for a prize (Zachery 2008). In *Get in the Game*, Smale (2012) describes how she developed a game called Quality Counts. Students are asked to critically examine websites and compare them to criteria listed in a quality model based on ACRL Information Literacy Standard 3: "The information literate student evaluates information and its sources critically". Points are awarded for determining and using sites meeting the criteria. Librarians continue to develop interesting and interactive methods for teaching information literacy.

Ever Changing Role for Librarians

The movie *Avatar*, a blockbuster movie in 2010, was inspirational in ways inconceivable. Hao-Chang et al. (2011) envision librarians as avatars providing virtual world information services. They describe how important it is for librarians to continually blend traditional library services and resources with today's popular science fiction concepts. They use the term "Second Life librarians" to emphasize the new role and the importance to evolve as quickly as technology expands. Second life is a virtual environment where characters are created much live avatars (Secondlife). Tehrani (2008) suggests there is an advantage to virtual world searching for information. You can "find it faster and easier compared to navigating a Web site" (p. 8).

Finding information faster and easier is now available with the use of handheld devices such as smartphones/iphones/ipads. These are wonderful devices that allow us to get information at anytime, anywhere. You can even connect to the library from them. With such finger-tip access to information we need to become information literate users now more than ever.

Other Progress

Organizations are taking a stronger position on promoting information literacy awareness and workforce readiness skills. The National Forum on Information Literacy (NFIL) embarked on a campaign in 2012 for statewide awareness. The goal is to get each state in the United States to proclaim the importance of information literacy. At the writing of this article, the NFIL web site lists some 22 states and 1 territory that have issued such proclamation. Another 17 states have proclamation requests in the works (www.infolit.org). The Partnership for twenty first century Skills continues to nationally promote readiness and critical thinking. It currently has 19 states working toward "standards and practices for twenty first century education to prepare students to graduate ready for the challenges of an interconnected global workforce" (www.pil.org). Other research focuses on preparing future employees for the business world. Two Educational Testing Services researchers examined business schools' curriculum for evidence of information literacy. Ali and Katz found limited integration of information and computer technology (ICT) skills. The authors' work places the importance of infusing ICT in the curriculum (Ali and Katz 2010), proof that pre-service training must prepare future employees for the workplace.

Summary

It is evident that information literacy has begun to emerge as an important skill. Organizations are promoting the awareness of such a need nationwide. Academic librarians are creatively seeking ways to get students to become information literate, integrating twenty first concepts as stimulators for learning. Companies continue to demand a level of readiness that include information literacy and integrated

So What's the Big Deal With Information Literacy in the United States? 19

ICT skills. Clearly, as technology continues to permeate our lives through handheld smart devices, the access to information will continue the demand that information seekers become information literate users. Perhaps the United States will lead the world in making this demand.

Open Access This chapter is distributed under the terms of the Creative Commons Attribution Noncommercial License, which permits any noncommercial use, distribution, and reproduction in any medium, provided the original author(s) and source are credited.

References

Ali R, Katz IR (2010) Information and communication technology literacy: what do businesses expect and what do business schools teach? Research Report. www.ets.org/research/contact.html

American Library Association, Presidential Committee on Information Literacy (1989) Final Report. Chicago: American Library Association. Accessed 30 Jun 2013

Association of College and Research Libraries (2000) Standards for information literacy. www.ala.org/acrl/standards

Bailey EC Jr (2010) Educating future academic librarians: an analysis of courses in academic librarianship. J Educ Libr Inf Sci 51(1):30-42. http://ezproxy.pgcc.edu/login?url=http://search.proquest.com/docview/203240096?accountid=13315. Accessed 15 Aug 2013

Branch K, Gilchrist D (1996) Library instruction and information literacy in community and technical colleges. RQ 34(4):476–482. Retrieved October 12, 2006, from Education Full-text

Department of Labor (1992) Secretary's commission on achieving necessary skills. http://wdr.doleta.gov/SCANS/. Accessed 6 Aug 2013

Educational Testing Service (2009) iCritical thinking certification. www.ets.org. Accessed 16 Aug 2013

Hao-Chang S, Chen K, Tseng C, Wen-Hui T (2011) Role changing for librarians in the new information technology era. New Libr World 112(7):321–333. doi:http://dx.doi.org/10.1108/03074801111150459

Head A (2012). Learning curve. Project Information Literacy. Research Report, October 16, 2012. www.pil.org

Hufford JR (March 2010) What are they learning? Pre- and post-assessment surveys for LIBR 1100. Introd Libr Res 71(2):139–158

Mercardo H (1999) Library instruction and online database searching. Res Serv Rev 27:259–265. Retrieved February 14, 2004 from ProQuest Research Library

Naisbitt J (1982) Megatrends: ten new directions for transforming our lives. Warner Books, New York

National Forum on Information Literacy, www.infolit.org

Partnership for the 21st Century. Press release, April 25, 2010. www.p21.org

Secondlife. Secondlife.com

Simmons HL (2000) Librarians as teachers: a personal view. In Bahr AH (ed) Future teaching roles for academic librarians. The Haywood Press, Inc., Binghamton, pp 41–44

Smale MA (2012) Get in the game: developing an information literacy classroom game. J Libr Innov 3(1):126. http://go.galegroup.com.ezproxy.pgcc.edu/ps/i.do?id=GALE%7CA28853830 8&v=2.1&u=pgcc_main&it=r&p=AONE&sw=w. Accessed 6 Aug 2013

Tehrani R (2008) Virtual customer interactions. Customer 26(5):8, 10 (inter@ction solutions)

Vann SK (1978) ed. Melvil Dewey, his enduring presence in librarianship. Libraries Unlimited, Inc., Littleton

Weiner SL (2010) Information literacy: a neglected core competency. Educause 33(1)

Wright AJ (2007) Preservice preparation programs for academic librarians for teaching information literacy. Dissertation. Morgan State University

Zachery I (2008) Psychology 101 Jeopardy!. izachery@pgcc.edu

A Group Discussion on Information Literacy

Jason Phelps, Steve Van Tuyl, Gladys Joy E., Martin Julius V. Perez, Joseph M. Yap, Lihong Zhou, Yiwei Wang and Han Jiang

Abstract Main ideas presented in the information literacy seminar held in Wuhan University was reviewed. Core thoughts of the group discussion was manifested by seven leading speakers. Primary conclusions deducted from the discussion are: information literacy brings more efficient organizations; data curation should be highlighted in information literacy; librarians shall undertake the duty of teaching information literacy; the related education needs reform especially the curriculum set; deductively test existing theories and inductively generate concepts are two orientations for future China information literacy research.

Keywords Information Literacy · Data Curation · Information Literacy Education · Library 2.0 · Learning Organization

---

Note: The author ranking is based on the presentation order.

A group discussion at the seminar during the International University Student Information Literacy Competency Invitational Contest, which was, as a part of 1st Wuhan University Student Organization International Exchange Summer Camp, hosted by SIM, Wuhan University, July 13, 2010. It first appeared in the journal of *Document, Information & Knowledge*, no. 5, 2010.

J. Phelps (✉)
Information School, University of Washington, Seattle, USA
e-mail: Phelpsj2@uw.edu

S. V. Tuyl
University of Pittsburgh, Pittsburgh, USA
e-mail: steve.vantuyl@gmail.com

G. Joy E.
University of the Philippines—Diliman, Quezon City, Philippines
e-mail: gladys.entico@gmail.com

M. J. V. Perez · J. M. Yap
School of Library and Information Studies, University of the Philippines—Diliman, Quezon City, Philippines
e-mail: martjulps@yahoo.com

J. M. Yap
e-mail: joseph.yap@up.edu.ph

C. Chen, R. Larsen (eds.), *Library and Information Sciences,*
DOI 10.1007/978-3-642-54812-3_3, © The Author(s) 2014

During the Information Literacy (IL) seminar held in Wuhan University, professionals as well as amateurs who are interested in information literacy had demonstrated their thoughts on the topic, which showed the charming facets and practical usage of information literacy on people's daily life, business, education and individual well being. Despite the various illustration, the discussion can be well manifested by the following seven parts.

Jason Phelps's View: Information Literacy Makes More Efficient Organization

After graduating 3 years ago with my MBA, I now find myself back in the academic world trying to solve a major problem that I have encountered throughout my career. This major problem is the lack of Information Literacy, and even more important, professional information leadership in the business world.

I quite often hear from people that a business man like me should not worry about information management and let the IT folks handle IT. The problem is that IT departments have lost focus on the information side of the profession and are just technology professionals. Today's IT people are only the "T" in IT and we need to find the "I" in order to complete the organization.

I currently manage a factory for a fortune 500 company. When I came to this multi-billion dollar Hi-Tech company I did not think that information would ever be an issue. The sad truth is that I see a lack of information literacy and professional information leadership on a daily basis. Today we need people that are information literate in order to drive the company to make proper decisions in the most efficient manner. In today's world of globalization, companies more than ever need timely, accurate and relevant information in all aspects of business. Competition has grown a great deal and customers have grown into educated consumers. Businesses also need to grow and must develop into learning organizations in order to compete in the ever changing information age.

Today companies need people from i-schools like Wuhan University and the University of Washington in order to compete at the highest level. Today's employees need to quickly turn data into information by applying context, and information into knowledge in order to take action and make proper data driven decisions. These

L. Zhou
Department of Information Studies, the University of Sheffield, Sheffield, UK
e-mail: l.zhou@sheffield.ac.uk

Y. Wang · H. Jiang
School of Information Management, Wuhan University, Wuhan, China
e-mail: viantangtang@126.com

H. Jiang
e-mail: jh88992008@yahoo.cn

same people also need the capability to quickly share this knowledge as data with others in the organization in order to speed up the data to knowledge transfer.

This is where we, as current and future information professionals come into the picture. We, as a collective diverse worldwide group, are positioning ourselves as the future leaders of organizations. We will lead by providing the knowledge and skills in information management to help our colleagues of other disciplines grow their information literacy. We will provide leadership to make proper data driven decisions that will drive the most efficient organizations the world has ever seen.

Steve Van Tuyl's Insight: Data Curation is Crucial in Information Literacy

We create information when we conduct research, and when that information is used to generate transferrable data (e.g. publications, datasets, images) we find ourselves in the position of caretakers. Given that the data we assimilate to create new information (and data) has been preserved by and provided to us by someone, the only fair turn one can conceive of is to preserve and provide this newly birthed data for others. I propose that we need to append to the information acquisition models (e.g. Big Six) the additional step of information curation. The process of preserving and disseminating newly created information for others to use should be integrated into the information literacy education curriculum in order that responsibly created data, information, and knowledge can be shared with others in a responsible way.

According to information literacy theory, when we gather data we create information and knowledge. This information and knowledge can be converted back into data and conveyed to others in many forms (as text, audio, images, etc.). That data has been filtered through our information and knowledge gathering processes and in return carries with it the signature of our unique analyses and biases. These are useful signatures both to the original searcher and to other searchers and is part of the collective learning experience that we have come to see as an important component of the information age.

What we do with our data, then, is important to the continuing function of the information culture in which we live and as responsible members of that culture we must take responsibility for ensuring that our data is properly cared for and made available, whenever appropriate, to other users. This process of data curation can take many forms depending on the peculiarities of the situation at hand. Indeed, casual researchers and academic researchers have very different data curation needs, but the need is still there - to share our collective information in a way that allows access for others for the lifecyle of the information therein.

Gladys Joy E.'s Thought: Librarians' Duty on Teaching Information Literacy

As Melvil Dewey (1876) said, "The library is a school and the librarian is in the highest sense a teacher." Wilson (1987) said that the abilities, skills, and professional knowledge of librarians are needed in the teaching and promoting of the library's resources and services to the clients. The focus on literacy and on strategies necessary for creating competitive literate communities permeates the research literature related to all types of libraries (Lingren 1981). Information literacy has been in the field of library and information science since 1970's, but it was just in 1990's that information professionals become interested with it. Liesener (1985) stresses the value of teaching critical thinking and problem solving "throughout the learner's school experience," because "the cumulative effect of many of these kinds of experiences is what leads to the development of a self-directed learner able and motivated for lifelong learning."

From conducting library orientation and library tour, the roles of librarians have evolved to providing library instruction and bibliographic instruction, and finally teaching information literacy among its library users.

Information literacy, as defined by the American Library Association (1989), is the skill to recognize when information is needed and should have the ability to locate, evaluate, and use the needed information effectively. There are key skills involved in information literacy. These are skill to recognize the need for information, skill to find and evaluate information, skill to think critically to synthesize and assimilate information, skill to communicate information effectively, skill to comfortably use the necessary tools and technologies, and skill to understand and apply ethical principles (Lapuz 2008).

The teaching function of librarians is on a working plan. Professional teaching competencies should be developed so that librarians can become efficient and therefore knowledgeable enough to pass through this new phase in the fields of library and information science. This needs reengineering and redesigning of LIS (library and information science) curriculum emphasizing the inclusion of IL (information literacy) education to prepare the librarians for the teaching role (Batiancila 2010).

Martin Julius Perez's Analysis: Factors that Must be Included in Information Literacy Education

Information, as we all know, is vital to man's existence. It plays an important role in human life in the aspect of learning, working, surviving, etc. As we begin the twenty first century, people experience 'information explosion', wherein vast amounts of information is available almost anywhere and anytime across different formats for free. In the case of the students, 'information anxiety' and 'misinformation' are some common problems they encounter. People facing information anxiety panic and can't manage the abundant information present. Misinformation, on the other hand, leads people to be wrongly informed due to the abundant information present. To address such problems, one of the objectives of higher education is to make the students 'lifelong learners', wherein it enables them to be equipped with the right and necessary skills to make relevant, effective and responsible use of information. To this end, in the academe, information literacy is then integrated to the curriculum for the development of these students. Information literacy programs in the higher education suggest a positive output on the students' development for lifelong learning and competitive competencies. Kasowitz-Scheer and Pasqualoni (2002) listed some specific characteristics of successful information literacy instruction programs from the literature review: *the use of student-centered, active, and collaborative learning methods (from Wilson), *the adherence to instructional design principles during planning (from Hinchliffe & Woodard), *the relevance to particular course goals and, ultimately, the overall curriculum (from Breivik, & Dewald), *the formation of partnerships between library, faculty, and other campus departments (from Stoffle), *the support of faculty learning and development (from Wilson), and, *the scalability for large numbers of students (from Stoffle). Satisfying these characteristics, one successful information literacy instruction program is an information literacy course integrated on the curriculum. In the development of an information literacy course, several factors are being considered and should be focused into. From the collected information from the literature and the experience of the researcher, the different factors/elements to consider in developing or designing an information literacy course in the higher education can be drawn. It includes the following: (1) Need for the course, (2) Target audiences, (3) Nature of the course, (4) Course handlers, (5) Pedagogy/Teaching style for the course, (6) Course title, (7) Course objectives, (8) Course outline or topics to include, (9) Requirements of the course, (10) References/Reading list for the course. These factors are then extended to the development and proposal of an information literacy course for the University of the Philippines-Diliman.

Joseph M. Yap's Prediction: Library 2.0 Tools' Role in Academic Service

Library 2.0 tools have helped the librarians by marketing the services and programs of the library and also by sharing and spreading knowledge even if the student or faculty member is off-campus. Libraries use these tools for communication, interactivity, sharing and storing information. The increasing use of social media sites particularly social networking services and microblogging sites such as Twitter, make information dissemination collaborative and flexible. The way university libraries deal with their users in this contemporary age and time is a sign that we are concerned with our users learning and knowledge acquisition as expressed in the online environment. Academic libraries exhaust this kind of service to promote interactivity and easy communication with their clients. It's been said that today's users are impatient when it comes to getting information rapidly. In order not to sacrifice the loss of misused and abused information and by preserving the students' information literacy skills, this paper discusses Library 2.0 tools, its principles and practical usage in the Philippine academic setting. There were three examples enumerated in this paper as to how they practically manage to conduct information-reference services and include information literacy. These academic libraries utilize social networking sites, blogs and instant messengers to communicate with their patrons. It all boils down that to be librarians, one should be user and service-centered and that one should implement ways on how to best communicate with their users. Lastly, these tools improve the interaction between the librarian and its users. It gives a way to provide an effective and efficient service that the library can offer. Librarians continue the knowledge sharing and extending e-learning services in the realm of online environment, thus, incorporating and enhancing media and digital literacy skills as well.

Lihong Zhou and Yiwei Wang's Research: Two Orientations of China Information Literacy Framework

Since the 1970s, Information Literacy (IL) has been an area of increasing interest to information professionals and researchers from various disciplines. However, in China, IL is still a relatively new topic and not very well developed.

Many researchers have attempted to establish nation-wide IL frameworks that are deemed to be compatible to Chinese specific social characteristics (Zhang 2008). However, these initial works have not yet been widely accepted or well implemented, not only because these frameworks are probably not very well established, but also these frameworks are established at a general level and are highly conceptualised. In fact, there is a lack of substantive theories targeted at substantive contexts.

These two issues hinder IL implementation and cause inconsistencies in current research. Therefore, future IL research can be undertaken following two main orientations:

- Deductively test existing theories and identify insufficiencies. Future research studies can aim at testing existing frameworks, including those well-established in the West and those developed domestically, in the Chinese environment by using the deductive approach and quantitative methods. In this case, problems and insufficiencies in these frameworks can be identified and revised.
- Inductively generate concepts and frameworks for substantive research contexts. In this approach, existing frameworks can be adopted as theoretical foundations to generate substantive theories which are only applicable to specific contexts and which can be easily transformed into practical IL strategies.

Although great needs are needed for research in both orientations, the second orientation is probably more suited to the current needs of IL implementation in China, as demanded by *Information Literacy Standards for Student Learning: Standards and Indicators*: "The standards and indicators are written at a general level so that library media specialists and others in individual states, districts, and sites can tailor the statements to meet local needs" (AASL and AECT 1998, p. 1). Therefore, greater attention should be paid to tailoring or translating the high level IL frameworks into substantive theories according to specific social, economical, and political conditions, and the actual needs of people.

Han Jiang's Experience: Information Literacy is Basic yet Need Improved

To my understanding, information literacy we are discussing involves the transformation from data to information and the training of it is a sort of general education for all the undergraduate students which is essential regardless of major. If we want to extract knowledge from information, we need to use specific and corresponding methodologies in different disciplines. As for me, I'm interested in the behavioral research; thereby statistics and data mining may be my choice. But information literacy, what we utilize in searching for information, is basic but of paramount importance.

As defined by the ACRL, information literacy is a set of abilities requiring individuals to "recognize when information is needed and have the ability to locate, evaluate, and use effectively the needed information." I believe the most important term in the definition is "abilities". By stating this, I mean the information literacy is not just a few theories and principles that undergraduate students are required to grasp, but how to apply them in solving problems from their real studies and research.

After hearing lectures in this summer program, I read more materials concerning information literacy. Carefully I examined myself according to the indicators and outcomes articulated by the Information Literacy Competency Standards for Higher Education. The result turned to be typical, I supposed, within most Chinese students that I have already acquired some of the skills, but still on the way of improvement. For instance, I sometimes get confused when start to work on an assignment and cannot clearly define what kind of information is needed. And entering the retrieval stage, I usually face the dilemma of how to implement effective search strategies while taking into account the time and the cost. Maybe it supports a motif of UNESCO's information literacy project—life-long learning.

Open Access This chapter is distributed under the terms of the Creative Commons Attribution Noncommercial License, which permits any noncommercial use, distribution, and reproduction in any medium, provided the original author(s) and source are credited.

References

American Association of School Librarians and Association for Educational Communications and Technology (1998) Information Literacy Standards for Student Learning: Standard and Indicators. Chicago: American Library Association

American Library Association and Presidential Committee on Information Literacy (1989) Final Report. Chicago: American Library Association

Batiancila MR (2010) Raising the librarians' teaching identity through lifelong learning modules and porfolios. Presented at the PAARL-ABAP Forum 2010. Pasig City, Philippines

Dewey M (1876) The profession. Am Libr J 1:5–6

Kasowitz-Scheer A, Pasqualoni M (2002) Information Literacy Instruction in Higher Education: Trends and Issues. Library and Librarians' Publication. Paper 34. http://surface.syr.edu/sul/34. Accessed 15 Sep 2013

Lapuz E (2008) Information literacy and library 2.0. Proceedings of the School of Library and Information Studies Lecture Series. Philippines: University of the Philippines—Diliman

Liesener JW (1985) Learning at risk: school library media programs in an information world. Sch Libr Media Q 14(1):11–20

Lingren J (1981) Toward Libr Literacy. RQ 20(3):233–235

Wilson LA (1987) Education for bibliographic instruction: combining practice and theory. J Educ Libr Inf Sci 28(17)

Zhang M (2008) Review of the progress of the information literacy research in China and Abroad. Shanxi Sci Techno 4:94–96

Part II
Trends of Library and Information Sciences Education

iSchools & the iSchool at Syracuse University

Elizabeth D. Liddy

Abstract An overview of the origin, development, and current status of the iSchool movement—both the organization which began as the iSchool Caucus, which now leads the much larger iSchool Organization, as well as the profile of one particular iSchool—the School of Information Studies at Syracuse University, in Syracuse, New York. As the rate of change in who, how, when, and where information is being sought and produced is both evolving and accelerating, along with the need for reliable, high quality information, the demands on the information professions are both challenging and exciting. Today, the iSchool Organization is comprised of 55 leading iSchools, from 17 countries, spanning 4 continents, and is actively working with additional top-ranked Schools of Library and/or Information Science in multiple other universities and countries who are interested in joining. The iSchool at Syracuse, which was one of the original members of "Gang of Three" that conceived of a membership organization to promote the information profession, is presented with detail on programs, particularly their most recent focuses on social media, data science, and information entrepreneurship.

Keywords iSchool Caucus · iSchools · Syracuse University · School of Information Studies

It is a truly exciting time for those involved in the library and information science fields, as it is increasingly recognized in every quarter how important the information professions are. The rate of change in all endeavors is accelerating, along with the reliance on high quality information, and as a result, the demands on our profession are both challenging and exciting.

Elizabeth D. Liddy is Dean and Trustee Professor in the iSchool at Syracuse University. Liddy is the founding president of TextWise LLC, and founding Director of the Center for Natural Language Processing. Liddy has led 70 re-search projects, authored more than 110 research papers, and is the holder of 8 software patents. Liddy was the 2012–2013 Chair of the iSchool Caucus. Email: liddy@syr.edu

---

E. D. Liddy (✉)
Syracuse University, Syracuse, USA
e-mail: liddy@syr.edu

C. Chen, R. Larsen (eds.), *Library and Information Sciences,*
DOI 10.1007/978-3-642-54812-3_4, © The Author(s) 2014

In this era of rising prominence, it is important that we in the education of library and information science professionals share our experiences from around the world—that we learn from each other—so that we can respond in optimal ways to increasingly global demands, and further raise the recognition of the world's overwhelming reliance on information and the information professions.

The iSchool Movement

An initial and natural response to this need for cooperation has been what is termed the 'iSchool Movement' which began in the late 1980s when deans of schools in United States universities who offer degrees in library and/or information science started meeting informally for the purpose of building a strong, unified coalition of schools that are interested in strengthening the relationships between information, technology, and people. This group of deans has since come to be called the "iSchool Caucus" (caucus is defined as a meeting of people with the same goal of bringing about organizational change) and formally adopted its charter in July, 2005. Today, the iCaucus consists of 55 leading iSchools, from 17 countries, spanning 4 continents, and is now actively working with top-ranked Schools of Library and/or Information Science in multiple other countries who are interested in joining. Member schools must have substantial sponsored research activity, be engaged in the training of future researchers via Ph.D. programs, and be visionary in their views of the role of information in the world of the future.

The iSchool Caucus has enabled its member schools to jointly create a common image and message, which is particularly needed by schools which have an undergraduate program that students enter at the age of 18, when they themselves are not yet really sure what career they want to pursue, and do not necessarily think of the information field as a profession. On the other hand, Masters students entering the graduate programs recognize the importance of information and know what they want to be when they graduate—either librarians of one type or another, or managers of the Information Technology (IT) infrastructure in a large organization, or perhaps managers of large telecommunication projects.

The current members of the iSchool Organization, which includes the iCaucus are: Carnegie Mellon University, Charles Sturt University, Drexel University, Florida State University, Georgia Tech, Humboldt University, Indiana University, Michigan State University, Nanjing University, Northumbria University, NOVA University, Open University of Catalonia, Pennsylvania State University, Polytechnic University of Valencia, Rutgers, Seoul National University, Singapore Management University, Sungkyunkwan University, Syracuse University, Télécom Bretagne, University College Dublin, University College London, University of Amsterdam, University of Boras, University of British Columbia, UC Berkeley, UC Irvine, UCLA, University College: Oslo and Akershus University of Copenhagen, University of Glasgow, University of Illinois, University of Kentucky, University of Maryland-College Park, University of Maryland-Baltimore County, University of Melbourne, University of Michigan, University of Missouri, University of North Carolina, University of North Texas, University of Pittsburgh, University of Porto, University of Sheffield, University of Siegen, University of South Australia, University of Strathclyde, University of Tampere, University of Tennessee, University of Texas-Austin, University of Toronto, University of Tsukuba, University of Washington, University of Wisconsin-Madison, University of Wisconsin-Milwaukee, and Wuhan University.

Some iSchools grew out of Library Science Schools, some out of Computer Science Schools, some have merged with Communication Departments, some have merged with Management—but the telling characteristic of each is that they are interdisciplinary and all share the same goal—to enable their graduates to become successful professionals based on their combined expertise in information, technology, and management. As the figure here shows, graduates of the iSchools are prepared to assume positions in organizations in professional roles spanning both the technical and managerial aspects of information provision.

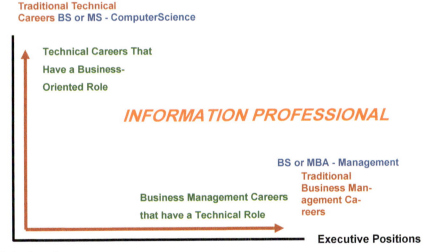

Presented quite broadly, the goals of the iCaucus are to work on behalf of its member schools to raise awareness of the Information Field amongst student prospects, the business community, the media, funders of research, and users of information. Members of the iCaucus are able to broaden their course offerings to students via distance education courses available through the WISE Consortium, wherein students can take courses offered at other member schools while paying their own local tuition and receiving credit at their home university.

In addition, the iCaucus sponsors an annual iConference that is open to all schools, faculty, and students, not just iCaucus members, and provides opportunities for presentation and sharing of research and teaching in the field of information. The 9th iConference was held in Berlin, Germany in March, 2014. Ongoing sessions of interest at the iConference include how the iSchool Movement is expanding internationally.

The iSchool at Syracuse

We now move from the topic of the field of iSchools to focus on how one particular school—the iSchool at Syracuse University—fulfills the iSchool mission. The iSchool at Syracuse University was founded in 1896 as the *School of Library Science*, and the school focused on educating students in librarianship for its first 78 years. Then, in 1974, Dean Robert Taylor changed the name to the *School of Information Studies*. Syracuse was the first school to recognize that information was of significance in organizations other than libraries, was the first to adopt 'Information' in its name, and is therefore rightfully called *The Original Information School*™ and has served over time as a model for an increasing number of emerging iSchools.

The iSchool at Syracuse is guided by the core values articulated by our faculty that emanate from our visionary goal *"To expand human capabilities through information."* Our beliefs are that *"Through information we transform individuals, organizations, and society."* And *"We recognize that information technology and management processes are means and not ends."*

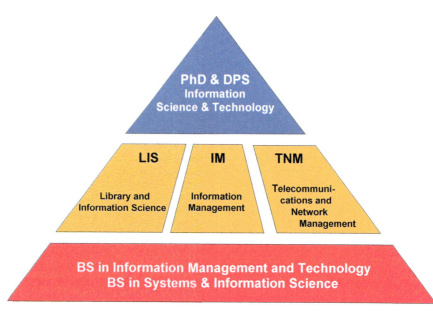

iSchools & the iSchool at Syracuse University   35

The iSchool at Syracuse currently has 7 degree programs—a unique combination of academic offerings and research foci that provide diversity—but a unified diversity. The three masters programs reflect the rich, complex range of capabilities our students learn—Library & Information Science, Information Management, and Telecommunications & Network Management. These degrees are offered via both onsite and online delivery modes, having been teaching online for 20 years, with 30% to 40% of the masters degrees now being earned online. The Doctor of Professional Studies in Information Science and Technology is now available for information professionals seeking to earn the next level degree, without the need to leave their current position, while receiving credit for the learnings they have gained from their professional experiences. This new offering fits with the iSchool at Syracuse's commitment to life-long learning and meeting the evolving needs of students at various stages of their professional careers.

Currently, the iSchool at Syracuse has approximately 670 undergraduate students, 700 masters students, and 70 doctoral students. Our students are of the highest quality and many are attracted to the iSchool at Syracuse by the high national rankings of our programs. The standard reference for masters programs is the *U.S. News & World Report*, which ranks Syracuse as #1 in Information Systems, #2 in Digital Libraries, #3 in Library and Information Science schools, and #4 in School Media.

Faculty of One Overview

The iSchool has a balanced commitment to scholarship, teaching, and research that attracts the finest scholars in the world. Our interdisciplinary faculty of 53 full-time members collaborate with colleagues across fields of study and readily partner with global communities of experts to expand the boundaries of exploration in the information field.

Faculty members consider themselves a "faculty of one," with no traditional departments dividing their interactions or their teaching and research activities. The school's collegial atmosphere encourages intellectual inquiry and lifelong learning among faculty and students. Our faculty serve as role models for students and challenge them to develop into independent thinkers, problem solvers, and architects of a better world.

Three Recent Focuses at Syracuse's iSchool

Information Entrepreneurship

The culture at the School of Information Studies is steeped in entrepreneurship, which at the iSchool encompasses both the traditional goal of creating startups and the forward-thinking skills to implement social change. From entrepreneurial faculty to student startups, the environment encourages students to explore their entrepreneurial spirit through several programs and curriculum opportunities.

In the classroom, two courses, *What's the Big Idea* and *Idea to Startup*, provide a framework for students to acquire the basic knowledge and skills required to run a successful business. Students also learn how to develop and refine new ideas—and turn those ideas into a viable venture.

The iSchool is a sponsor of the Syracuse Student Sandbox, a unique business incubator that gives aspiring student entrepreneurs the resources to make their visions a reality. The Sandbox's goal is to accelerate the process of ideation, development, and deployment through mentoring and coaching. Through a 12-week, experiential-based program, participants are expected to reach an end goal of producing revenue generating entities or investment-ready firms. Culminating in a "Demo Day," the Student Sandbox Program provides coaching, mentoring, educational programming, physical space, access to subject matter experts, and investors. A full-time entrepreneur-in-residence guides teams through the program and serves as a coach and conduit to the entrepreneurship community.

Data Science

As the amount of data in the world grows in variety, volume, and velocity, organizations need professionals who can collect, manage, curate, analyze, and visualize data to make better decisions and add value to their organizations. Experts predict a major skills gap over the next five to 10 years in data science and the Syracuse iSchool is preparing students to meet this critical, professional demand.

In 2011, the iSchool began offering the first New York State-approved Certificate of Advanced Study (CAS) in Data Science. The iSchool's interdisciplinary faculty developed an industry-relevant curriculum that allows graduate students from a wide array of educational and professional backgrounds to learn to bridge the gap between technical specialists who work directly with IT infrastructure and senior leadership who use data to lead organizations.

With a foundation in information management, digital curation, visualization, and analytics, the certificate in Data Science provides students with a comprehensive understanding of the full data lifecycle. While technical skills are an important component of the curriculum, graduates are also equipped with communication and leadership skills that will carry them far beyond the rise and fall of any one data analysis technology.

Social Media/Emerging Technologies

Social media and emerging technologies (such as Internet-connected devices and location-based technology) make it possible for people to access and share information in real time with their networks. This development has shifted how organizations of all types leverage information internally and externally. In some cases, this reality has introduced entirely new information challenges, thereby creating a need for professionals who understand social media technologies, their capabilities, and their applications in the enterprise.

Through new coursework and the development of the New Explorations in Information and Science (NEXIS) laboratory at the iSchool, students have the opportunity to learn first-hand how to manage information in the enterprise, and build tools and solutions to curate information and data from various sources, in real time.

Conclusion

As can be seen from the details above, both the status of the iSchools Organization as a whole, and the iSchool at Syracuse University in particular, our professional field has flourished and is poised for even greater growth and prominence—particularly as our international partnerships increase. As many have said, for a good number of years now, this is the Information Age, and the iSchools stand ready to lead in both the research essential for the advancement of the field, and in the education of information professionals to provide leadership.

Open Access This chapter is distributed under the terms of the Creative Commons Attribution Noncommercial License, which permits any noncommercial use, distribution, and reproduction in any medium, provided the original author(s) and source are credited.

Part III
Information Seeking and Retrieval

Visual Data Mining in a Q&A Based Social Media Website

Jin Zhang and Yiming Zhao

Abstract Data mining methods and technologies have been applied to different social media environments but seldom applied to narrative information based Q&A sites. This paper aimed to employ visual data mining techniques to address health care consumer terms use behavior in the Yahoo!Answers. Three months of data on the topic of diabetes in the health category of Yahoo!Answers were collected and analyzed. Terms from the collected data set were processed, validated, and classified. Both Multi-dimensional Scaling and Social Network Analysis visualization methods were employed to visualize the relationships of terms from related categories ('Complication & Related Disease' and 'Medication'; 'Complication & Related Disease' and 'Sign & Symptom'). Patterns and knowledge were revealed and discovered from the mapping of terms such as "acarbose might cause a side effect of hives", "antidepressant may increase the risk of developing diabetes", "there is a connection between imbalance and birthdefects", etc. The results of this study can be of benefit to both health consumers and medical professionals.

Keywords Data mining · Social media · Social Q&A · Term analysis · Visual analysis

---

Dr. Jin Zhang is full professor at the School of Information Studies, University of Wisconsin-Milwaukee. He has published extensively in prominent journals in the field of information science. His book "*Visualization for Information Retrieval*" was published in the *Information Retrieval Series* by Springer in 2008. His research interests primarily focus on information retrieval.
Phone: 414-229-2712
Email: jzhang@uwm.edu

Dr. Yiming Zhao is a post doc in the Wuhan University. He studied as visiting student one year at the University of Wisconsin Milwaukee. His research interests include knowledge organization and visualization; consumer health informatics
Phone: +86-18942901531
Email: zym_0418@qq.com

J. Zhang (✉)
University of Wisconsin-Milwaukee, Milwaukee, USA
e-mail: jzhang@uwm.edu

Y. Zhao
Wuhan University, Wuhan, China
e-mail: zym_0418@qq.com

C. Chen, R. Larsen (eds.), *Library and Information Sciences,*
DOI 10.1007/978-3-642-54812-3_5, © The Author(s) 2014

Introduction

Data mining is a knowledge discovery process that reveals hidden patterns and trends from an investigated data set, illustrates relationships among involved objects, and analyzes data in a holistic way. It is widely used in business, health, information sciences and other disciplines.

Information visualization techniques can project abstract and invisible items or objects in a data set onto a visual and observable space where relationships among the projected objects are displayed and people can explore and interact with them. Information visualization and data mining have a natural connection because they share a common purpose. Information visualization can be employed as an effective means for data mining.

Social media provides an interactive online environment where people can create groups of interests, post and share opinions and ideas, discuss issues and concerns, and exchange relevant information in a variety of formats and ways. Social media not only provides users with an interactive environment but also offers dynamic, rich, and open datasets for researchers to utilize. Social media data has been applied to various domains and it is no surprise that researchers use visual data mining techniques to address a domain problem in a social media environment.

With the development of Web 2.0, people seek information from social media instead of completely relying on experts in the Internet. This phenomenon is so widespread that no one can negate its existence and influence. For instance, Yahoo!Answers is the most popular Internet reference site in America (Alexa 2013) and 16.64% users in Yahoo are using Yahoo! Answers.

Yahoo! Answers is a social Question & Answer (Q&A) site, in which questions are categorized and broadcasted to the community. Any user can answer any question. Visitors to Q&A sites are increasingly seeking answers to a wide variety of questions that are organized under topical categories. Questions and answers from users are organized, archived, and searchable for other users (Rosenbaum and Shachaf 2010). Because of these unique characteristics and natural advantages of social Q&A sites, online Q&A sites are fertile ground for future studies in many aspects (Harper et al. 2008).

Social media has become one of the most popular textual and visual data sources for studying individual behavior and dispersive information. Data mining methods and technologies have been applied to different social media collections such as Flickr, YouTube, Twitter, Facebook, etc. but they have seldom been applied to narrative information based Q&A sites.

There are many technologies and tools to do data mining in social media. Applying some of these social network data mining techniques generates very complex models that are hard to analyze and understand (Ferreira and Alves 2012). Visual data mapping, however, is a simple, efficient, and effective mining technique which can present, understand, and explore complex abstract information by using computing techniques (Robertson et al. 1989). Visualization mapping is often employed to reveal connections and relationships among investigated objects, to do data analysis, to explore information, to explain information, to predict trends, and to detect patterns (Zhang 2008). This study employed two visualization mapping methods to mine social media data.

The astonishing size of social media communities and great diversity of information exchanged within them make these sites a valuable research setting for understanding the general public's online information seeking (Kim and Oh 2009). The interactions between users and social media include various user behaviors (Liu et al. 2012). Consumer health informatics is supposed to analyze and understand consumer behaviors and contained knowledge. Social media provides data generated by consumers for researchers to investigate the consumers themselves.

This paper will use data mining technologies, especially the information visualization techniques, to address health consumer terms use behavior. Two visual data mining techniques, Multi-dimensional Scaling (MDS) and Social Network Analysis (SNA), were employed to visually analyze the subject terms and their relationships under the topic of "Complication & Related Disease" of diabetes and its related topics in order to discover underlying patterns. Findings of this study can be used to better understand health consumer term usage behavior and provide a new research method to conduct similar research in consumer health informatics.

Related Work

Social media is a group of Internet-based applications that build on the ideological and technological foundations of Web 2.0 to allow the creation and exchange of User Generated Content (Kaplan and Haenlein 2010). A classification of social media is offered by Kerpen (2013) which includes communication channels such as blogging and social networking, collaboration channels like wikis, multimedia channels like video sharing, reviews/opinions channels like community Q&A forums, etc. A social media platform, which attracts so many users to seek information and which archives the information, is a rich and huge treasure for researchers to conduct data mine research. Evans et al. (2009) distinguished information seeking in social media into public asking and targeted asking. Social Q&A sites are typical public asking platforms and have become some of the most popular destinations for online information seeking (Shah et al. 2008). Most research studies on social Q&A sites focus on user-generated and algorithmic question categorization, answer classification and quality assessment, studies of user satisfaction, reward structures, motivation for participation, and mechanisms of trust and expertise from social Q&A sites (Gazan 2011).

Social Q&A websites have been studied in the domain of health information. Kim et al. (2008) investigated evaluation criteria people use with regard to online health information in the context of social Q&A forums. Zhang (2010) explored contextual factors of consumer health information searching by analyzing health-related questions that people posted on Yahoo! Answers, a mainstream social Q&A site. A recent paper investigated term usage of consumers' diabetes based on a log from the Yahoo!Answers via visualization analysis, and ascertained characteristics and relationships among terms related to diabetes from the consumers' perspective (Zhang and Zhao 2013).

One of the consequences of widespread use of social media is that a new form of labor that arises: the mining of social media data (Kennedy 2012). The emergence of new systems and services of social media has created a number of novel social and ubiquitous environments for mining information, data, and knowledge (Atzmueller 2012). Textual information has been mined for topic prediction, topic discovery, preference recognition and analysis (Kim et al. 2012), sentiment detection (Zhang et al. 2012), community detection and networks identification (Comar et al. 2012), characterization of real-world events and evaluation of the event relatedness (Lee 2012), and other natural language processing tasks. In addition, sentiment analysis is another interesting dimension of social media data mining. It uses linguistic and textual assessment, such as Natural Language Processing, to analyze word use, word order, and word combinations and thus to classify them into the categories of positive, negative, or neutral (Kennedy 2012). Visual data like picture and video in social media have been used to detect and discover emerging topics (Hashimoto et al. 2012). Liu et al. (2012) constructed a generative probabilistic graphic model to study and explore topics and user preference in large-scale multimedia data from Flickr for photos and YouTube for videos. Wang and Yang (2012) used data from community-contributed media as corpus to construct visual-word based image representation. Data from social media were also compared with mainstream media to determine trending topic predictions in video recommendations (Lobzhanidze et al. 2013).

Data mining via social media has been adopted by many businesses such as tourism and the pizza industry. Majid et al. (2013) obtained user-specific travel preferences from geo-tagged metadata in Flickr to recommend tourist locations relevant to users. He et al. (2013) applied a text mining method to analyze unstructured text content on Facebook and Twitter sites in order to do a competitive analysis in the pizza industry. Other interesting social media data mining research studies include: stock pick decisions based on user-generated stock pick votes; download predictions from YouTube video ratings; and the popularity prediction of a story on Digg (Hill and Ready-Campbell 2011).

The boom of social media also brings many data mining opportunities in politics. Wegrzyn-Wolskaand Bougueroua (2012) discussed a variety of issues and challenges surrounding the use of SNA and Text Mining methods with political applications. They surveyed the French presidential election trends using Twitter's discussions.

Due to the popularity of data mining in public social media platforms, an abundance of opportunities have become available in health research (Culotta 2010). Mining social media can provide insight to abnormal patterns of disease and aid in predicting disease outbreaks (Guy et al. 2012). Akay et al. (2013) used self-organizing maps to generate a word list that correlated certain positive and negative word cluster groups with medical drugs and devices. Bian et al. (2012) analyzed the

Visual Data Mining in a Q&A Based Social Media Website 45

content of Twitter messages to facilitate early detection of potential adverse events related to drugs.

After data are collected from social media, information visualization techniques like the MDS method can be used to effectively find relations within the data. MDS illustrates the relationships among abstract objects and demonstrate emerging clusters in a data set which is free of any data distributional assumptions (Zhang and Zhao 2013). MDS has been used to: analyze relationships among sports-related keywords in addition to traditional hierarchical clustering methods (Zhang et al. 2009); to investigate obesity-related queries from a public health portal (Health Link) transaction log (Zhang and Wolfram 2009); and to analyze frequently used medical-topic terms in queries submitted to a Web-based consumer health information system (Zhang et al. 2008).

In the MDS space, distances between words indicate their relatedness or strength even if the links between words are invisible. SNA can visualize these links and serve as a supplementary method. It uses the same data as MDS.

In summary, social media data mining has been applied to multiple disciplines, including natural language process, sociology, healthcare, business management, etc.

The investigated social media channels were limited to Facebook, Twitter, You-Tube, and Flickr. Research studies using social media data mining for health consumer term usage behavior in a Q&A forum are rarely found in the literature. This study investigates a Q&A forum, analyzes and visualizes the data with SNA and MDS.

Methodology

Research data in this study come from a question and answer (Q&A) site: Yahoo! Answers. Using the search term of diabetes and searching under the category of 'health' on the website of answers.yahoo.com, 2604 records were collected from 08/10/2011 to 11/10/2011. Records not related to diabetes were deleted. As a result, 2565 records were reserved. Each record consisted of one question and several corresponding answers about diabetes.

Term extraction software was used to grab and extract keywords in the records. The total number of words in all records was 1,043,158. A stop words list was introduced into the software to filter the meaningless words. The list contained prepositions, conjunctions, auxiliary terms, articles, numerals, interjections and other function words. Finally, 20,000 unique words were collected from 1,043,158 total words.

A term validation process was executed to deal with synonyms like 'man, men and male' and different forms of the verbs like 'absorb, absorbs, absorbed, absorbing', etc. In the validation process, all the forms of verbs were changed to their regular form, and all the forms of nouns were converted to their original form. Words with no relationship in meaning to diabetes were also deleted.

In a previous study (Zhang and Zhao 2013) a diabetes-oriented schema was produced. The categories (Cause & Pathophysiology, Sign & Symptom, Diagnosis & Test, Organ & Body Part, Complication & Related Disease, Medication, Treatment, Education & Info Resource, Affect, Social & Culture, Lifestyle, and Nutrient) from the schema were identified. These categories were used in this study. The identified categories were related to 2565 records. Each category to be analyzed contained a certain amount of words and their frequency in 2565 records. These words were presented in a high dimensional vector space in which dimensionality was determined by the number of unique words from the identified categories.

MDS works very well in mapping and projecting the relationships of objects in a high dimensional record space onto a two-dimensional or three-dimensional space. People can observe proximity relationships among investigated objects intuitively in a low dimensional MDS display space leading to a better understanding of individual or group differences of the investigated objects (Zhang 2008). MDS was conducted at a term level which enabled users to observe semantic relationships among terms within two identified categories. The software used for MDS analysis was SPSS (Version 20).

In this study, a cross categories mechanism was designed to discover underlying pattern and relationship between categories. Categories of "Complication & Related Disease", "Medication", and "Sign & Symptom" from the schema were selected for analysis. In order to explore the inner connection between pairs of categories ("Complication & Related Disease" and "Medication", "Complication & Related Disease" and "Sign & Symptom"), words from the involved categories were first integrated and combined since the analysis was conducted at the term level.

Input data for MDS analysis are a proximity (similarity or dissimilarity) matrix of investigated objects in a high dimensional space. Its output is a spatial object configuration in a low dimension space where users may perceive and analyze the relationships among the displayed objects (Zhang 2008).

The initial step was to establish a raw term-record matrix where the columns of the matrix were Q&A records extracted from the Q&A forum and the row were terms or words extracted from records. Each category, in fact, corresponded to a term-record matrix. After two related categories were identified, the two corresponding term-record matrices were built, and then these two matrices were integrated and combined into one term-record matrix.

Due to the combination, the matrix had to be revised and adjusted in the following manner. If terms didn't appear in the same records, they were not grouped together in the MDS space. The columns where the summation was equal to 0 in an individual category were removed from the new combined term-record matrix. After this step, the number of the columns in the matrix decreased. In addition, some low frequency words were removed in the matrix because they made little contribution to the later term analysis. After two removal steps, a new word-word proximity matrix was generated based on a similarity measure.

Equation (1) is the converting method used to generate a word-record matrix where a_i is the frequency of word a in the record x and b_i is the frequency of word b in the record y.

Visual Data Mining in a Q&A Based Social Media Website

$$Proximity(x, y) = \frac{1}{d_{AB}} = \frac{1}{c\sqrt[2]{\sum_{i=1}^{n}(a_i - b_i)^2}} \tag{1}$$

After the converting procedure, a final word-word proximity matrix is generated as Eq. (2).

$$P = \begin{pmatrix} b_{11} & .. & .. & b_{1k} \\ b_{21} & .. & .. & b_{2k} \\ ... & ... & ... & ... \\ b_{k1} & .. & .. & b_{kk} \end{pmatrix} \tag{2}$$

The proximity matrix P is a $k \times k$ symmetric matrix. It serves as input data for the MDS analysis. Here k is the number of the valid words in the two categories and n is the number of the valid records in the categories.

In the process of mapping the relationships in high dimensional space onto a low dimensional space, information loss and disparity is inevitable and must be controlled in a tolerable range. Therefore, an evaluation criterion was used to assess the reliability and effectiveness of projecting by MDS. The quality of the projection can be measured by the stress value (S), which is defined in Eq. (3). The smaller a stress S is, the better the relationships among the objects in the low dimensional space reflect the relationships among the objects in the high dimensional space and vice versa (Zhang and Zhao 2013).

$$S = \left(\frac{\sum_{i=1}^{n}\sum_{j=1}^{n}\left(f(T_i,T_j) - D(T_i,T_j)\right)^2}{\sum_{i=1}^{n}\sum_{j=1}^{n}\left(D(T_i,T_j)\right)^2} \right)^{1/2} \tag{3}$$

In Equation (3) n denotes the number of all terms involved; $D(T_i, T_j)$ indicates the Euclidean distance between two terms T_i and T_j in the low dimensional space; and $f(T_i, T_j)$ is the similarity between terms T_i and T_j in the high dimensional space where subscripts i and j are two indexes for T_i and T_j, respectively. Only if the results were eligible in terms of S stress, were they accepted.

In the final MDS space, related words are close to each other. The MDS space can be rotated and zoomed to find an optimal viewing angle. In this way MDS interacts with users to fit users' current interests. After several rounds of adjustment, the MDS analysis resulted in a low dimensional space where the projected terms were displayed and observed; relevant terms were clustered and specified; and term relationships within a cluster were discovered and examined.

Several steps were taken to conduct SNA in this study using the data generated by Eq. (2). The first step was to convert raw data into '##h' files by Ucinet 6 software and use these '##h' files as an input dataset in the visual software of NetDraw. The second step was to generate the draft of a word network and use the thickness of a line to represent the strength of connections between two words which were represented by the value of word-word proximity based on Eq. (2). The third step was to remove the less important relationships and corresponding lines from the draft networks. If the value of word-word proximity was less than 0.3 in Equation (2), its related lines and nodes in draft networks were deleted. The final step relayed out the network using the spring embedding algorithm and deleted isolated nodes. In the final words network, words with strong connections were reserved.

Results and Discussion

The visual data mining on texts harvested from Yahoo!Answers was done at a term level. MDS and SNA visualization data mining techniques were employed to process words from the category of "Complications and Related Disease" with words from "Medication" and "Sign & Symptom" respectively in order to explore the semantic relationship among terms and to discover potential knowledge and patterns behind the relationship among terms. The category of "Complications and Related Disease" contained 91 words, the category of "Medication" contained 74 words, and the category of "Sign & Symptom" contained 95 words, initially.

'Complication & Related Disease' and 'Medication'

In the combined category, the Cosine similarity measure was used to create the term-term proximity matrix. In the MDS analysis, the Minkowski distance measure was used and the Minkowski power was equal to 1, the resultant stress value was 0.01959, and the corresponding RSQ was equal to 0.99880. In Fig. 1, a term followed by a "#" sign indicates it was from the "Medication" category while a term followed by no "#" sign means that it was from the "Complication & Related Disease" category.

In Fig. 1, three big clusters emerged. Cluster 1 included antidepressant medicines (citalopram, Effexor, fluoxetine, and abapent in) and medications for type II diabetes (glucophage, glucovance, and onglyza). Cluster 1 also included complications and related diseases (acanthosis, anaemia, cataracts, hives, infertility, ketosis, and polyphagia). Cluster 2 did not have any salient patterns. Cluster 3 covered a majority of words from the two categories. Importantly, as shown in Fig. 1, the "Complication and Related Disease" category and "Medication" category do not have many internal connections under the topic of diabetes in the Yahoo! Answers site. Many unrelated words mingled and some patterns were obscured in the chaotic word clusters.

Figure 2 is the words network of the categories "Complication & Related Disease" and "Medication". Significant combinations of words were found, including

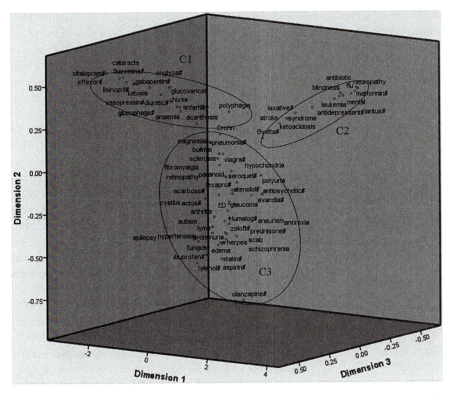

Fig. 1 The MDS display of categories of "Complication & Related Disease" and "Medication"

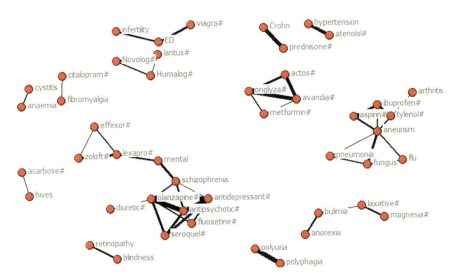

Fig. 2 The words network of categories "Complication & Related Disease" and "Medication"

hives from "Complication & Related Disease" and acarbose from "Medication"; fibromyalgia from "Complication & Related Disease" and citalopram from "Medication"; ED, infertility from "Complication & Related Disease" and Viagra from "Medication"; Crohn from "Complication & Related Disease" and prednisone from "Medication"; hypertension from "Complication & Related Disease" and atenolol from "Medication"; and anorexia, bulimia from "Complication & Related Disease" and laxative, magnesia from "Medication".

To be specific, the first combination of "hives" and "acarbose" brought to our attention that acarbose, as an anti-diabetic drug used to treat type 2 diabetes mellitus and prediabetes, might cause a side effect of hives. This is one of the main findings we got by mining a social Q&A site under the topic of diabetes.

Inspection of the combination of "fibromyalgia" and "citalopram" led us to notice the relationship between fibromyalgia syndrome (FMS) and depressive syndromes since the citalopram is an antidepressant. This is confirmed in a study claiming that emotional depression is common earlier in life and/or at onset of the FMS (Anderberg et al. 2000). Revisiting the questions and answers in the original records, it was found that when diabetics suffered from FMS, citalopram was mentioned in the answers a few times.

What need further discussion are the two relatively large sub-networks in Fig. 2. One noticeable sub-network was comprised of flu, fungus, aneurism, pneumonia, and arthritis from "Complication & Related Disease" and aspirin, ibuprofen, Tylenol from "Medication". The other remarkable sub-network contained mental, schizophrenia from "Complication & Related Disease" and antidepressant, antipsychotic, Effexor, fluoxetine, Lexapro, olanzapine, Seroquel, Zoloft from "Medication". These drugs are usually used to treat depression or psychosis. It is worth mentioning that diuretic has a connection with olanzapine and previous studies showed that olanzapine could cause a side effect of urinary retention which is an indication of a diuretic (Deshauer et al. 2006). Furthermore, olanzapine may precipitate or unmask diabetes in susceptible patients (Koller and Doraiswamy 2002). Other antidepressants may also increase risk of developing diabetes (Rubin et al. 2008).

Some discoveries in this research have verified other user-generated content of social Q&A sites. These include the connection of Viagra, a prescription drug for the treatment of erectile dysfunction (ED); prednisone used to treat Crohn's disease; and atenolol currently recommended only in special circumstances as complementary medication in hypertension (Wikipedia contributors 2013).

'Complication & Related Disease' and 'Sign & Symptom'

In the combined category, the Cosine similarity measure was used to create the term-term proximity matrix. In the MDS analysis, the Minkowski distance measure was used and the Minkowski power was equal to 1. The resultant stress value was 0.16458 and the corresponding RSQ was equal to 0.90483. In Fig. 3, a term followed by a "#" sign indicates it was from the "Sign & Symptom" category while a

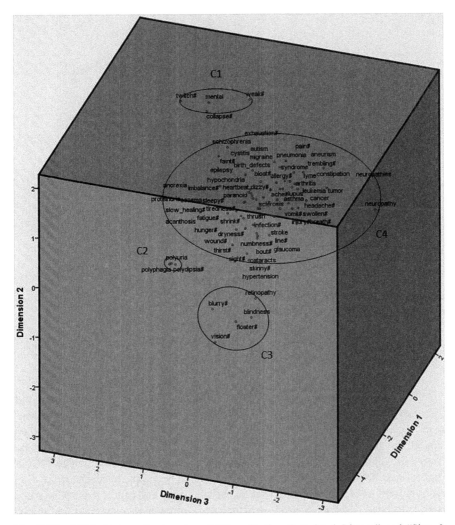

Fig. 3 The MDS display of categories of "Complication & Related Disease" and "Sign & Symptom"

term followed by no "#" sign means that it was from the "Complication & Related Disease" category.

In Fig. 3, four meaningful clusters were identified. In Cluster 1, mental, twitch, collapse, and weak were grouped together. Cluster 2 indicated the signs of polydipsia which are related to diseases of polyphagia and polyuria. In Cluster 3 blindness and retinopathy from "Complication and Related Disease" category were connected to blurry, vision, and floater from "Sign & Symptom" category. With the exception of these three clusters, many words from the two categories gathered chaotically in the Cluster 4 and it was hard to find any distinct patterns.

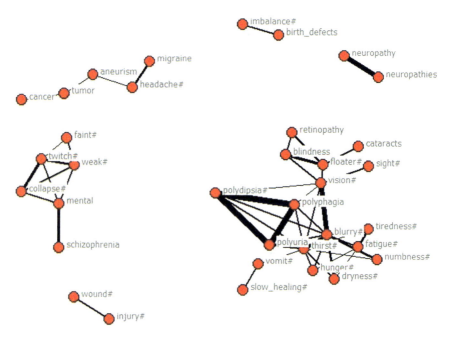

Fig. 4 The words network from categories of "Complication & Related Disease" and "Sign & Symptom"

Visual displays were constructed using SNA words network to reveal more hidden patterns in the relationship of categories "Complication & Related Disease" and "Sign & Symptom". In Fig. 4, not only the patterns revealed using MDS were found, but also other novel and important connections. Firstly, a connection between imbalance (from the "Sign & Symptom" category) and birth defects ("Complication & Related Disease" category) was found. Secondly, headache from "Sign & Symptom" was related to migraine, aneurism, tumor and cancer from "Complication & Related Disease". Thirdly, schizophrenia joined into a words group found in Cluster 1 of the MDS visualization (Fig. 3).

Moreover, cataracts from "Complication & Related Disease" and sight from "Sign & Symptom" were grouped into a word set which emerged in Cluster 3 of the MDS visualization (Fig. 3). That is because they are all related to eyes. It can also be observed that all three complications (blindness, retinopathy and cataracts) had stronger connections (thicker lines) to floater than other words from the "Sign & Symptom" category. Furthermore, lines among polydipsia, polyphagia and polyuria are the thickest in the whole network, which implied their relatedness is the strongest over all the other words. All words related to eyes from both categories were connected to polydipsia, polyphagia and polyuria. Signs such as hunger, thirst, tiredness, numbness, fatigue, dryness, vomit, slow healing were connected because they are the most typical symptoms of diabetes and tend to be listed together by users in a Q&A site.

Conclusion

Social media makes up a large percentage of the content available on the Internet (White et al. 2012). Users from different backgrounds, different domains and with different requirements collaborate to construct the knowledge treasure together (Chai et al. 2009). Precisely for this reason, researchers are able to mine massive data. Ease of access to such wide user-generated databases and their openness of the contents in social media sites create unprecedented opportunities for researchers to aggregate consumer-think for better understanding of health consumers and how they use the content they generate.

In this study, the visualization data mining methods of Multi-dimensional Scaling and Social Network Analysis were employed to conduct consumer health informatics research. Using Yahoo!Answers, data were extracted from the topic of diabetes and relationships between the category of "Complication and Related Disease" and other related categories were explored.

A variety of knowledge and patterns were discovered such as "acarbose might cause a side effect of hives", "emotional depression is at onset of fibromyalgia syndrome", "antidepressant may increase the risk of developing diabetes", "there is a connection between imbalance and birth defects", etc. Some of the discoveries via mining consumer generated content on social Q&A site corroborated previous findings of medical research studies (Anderberg et al. 2000; Deshauer et al. 2006; Koller and Doraiswamy 2002; Rubin et al. 2008; Wikipedia contributors 2013) and enhanced people's understanding of these phenomena.

Future research directions on this topic include, but are not limited to: applying these visual data mining methods and technologies to reveal more patterns in other topics of interest such as depression, arthritis, asthma, etc.; employing other visual data mining methods to explore underlying knowledge about diabetes from the Q&A based social media; and exploring other social media channels with visual data mining methods.

Open Access This chapter is distributed under the terms of the Creative Commons Attribution Noncommercial License, which permits any noncommercial use, distribution, and reproduction in any medium, provided the original author(s) and source are credited.

References

Akay A, Dragomir A, Erlandsson BE (2013) A novel data-mining approach leveraging social media to monitor and respond to outcomes of diabetes drugs and treatment. IEEE Point-of-Care Healthcare Technologies (PHT), pp 264–266

Alexa (2013) The top ranked sites in references category. http://www.alexa.com/topsites/category/Top/Reference. Accessed 24 June 2013

Anderberg UM, Marteinsdottir I, Knorring L (2000) Citalopram in patients with fibromyalgia-a randomized, double-blind, placebo-controlled study. Eur J Pain 4(1):27–35

Atzmueller M (2012) Mining social media: key players, sentiments, and communities. Wiley Interdiscip Rev Data Min Knowl Discov 2(5):411–419

Bian J, Topaloglu U, Yu F (2012) Towards large-scale Twitter mining for drug-related adverse events. Proceedings of the 2012 International Workshop on Smart Health and Wellbeing. Maui, Hawaii, pp 25–32

Chai K, Potdar V, Dillon T (2009) Content quality assessment related frameworks for social media. In Computational Science and Its Applications–ICCSA 2009. Springer, Berlin, pp 791–805

Comar PM, Tan PN, Jain AK (2012) A framework for joint community detection across multiple related networks. Neurocomputing 76(1SI):93–104

Culotta A (2010) Towards detecting influenza epidemics by analyzing Twitter messages. 1st Workshop on Social Media Analytics (SOMA 2010). Washington DC, pp 115–122

Deshauer D, Erwin L, Karagianis J (2006) Case report: edema related to olanzapine therapy. Can Fam Physician 52(5):620

Evans BM, Kairam S, Pirolli P (2009) Do your friends make you smarter?: an analysis of social strategies in online information seeking. Inf Process Manag 46(6):679–692

Ferreira DR, Alves C (2012) Discovering user communities in large event logs. In business process management workshops. Springer, Berlin, pp 123–134

Gazan R (2011) Social QA. J Am Soc Inf Sci Technol 62(12):2301–2312

Guy S, Ratzki-Leewing A, Bahati R, Gwadry-Sridhar F (2012) Social media: a systematic review to understand the evidence and application in infodemiology. Electronic healthcare. Springer, Berlin, pp 1–8

Harper F, Raban D, Rafaeli S, Konstan J (2008) Predictors of answer quality in online QA sites. Proceedings of the 26th Annual SIGCHI Conference on Human Factors in Computing Systems. ACM, New York, pp 865–874

Hashimoto T, Kuboyama T, Chakraborty B, Shirota Y (2012) Discovering emerging topic about the East Japan Great Earthquake in video sharing website. In TENCON 2012–2012 IEEE Region 10 Conference. IEEE, pp 1–6

He W, Zha SH, Li L (2013) Social media competitive analysis and text mining: a case study in the pizza industry. Int J Inf Manag 33(3): 464–472

Hill S, Ready-Campbell N (2011) Expert stock picker: the wisdom of (experts in) crowds. Int J Electron Commer 15(3):73–101

Kaplan AM, Haenlein M (2010) Users of the world, unite! The challenges and opportunities of social media. Bus Horiz 53(1):59–68

Kennedy H (2012) Perspectives on sentiment analysis. J Broadcast Electron Media 56(4):435–450

Kerpen D (2013) Channels. Social media marketing. http://www.smmmagazine.com/channels/. Accessed 30 Aug 2013

Kim JS, Yang MH, Hwang YJ, Jeon SH, Kim KY, Jung IS et al (2012) Customer Preference Analysis Based on SNS Data. Second International Conference on cloud and Green Computing/Second International Conference on Social Computing and its Applications (CGC/SCA 2012). IEEE, pp 609–613

Kim S, Oh S (2009) Users' relevance criteria for evaluating answers in a social QA site. J Am Soc Inf Sci Technol 60:716–727

Kim S, Oh S, Oh J (2008) Evaluating health answers in a social QA site. Proceedings of the American Society for Information Science and Technology (ASIST'08). Columbus, Ohio: Information Today, pp 1–6

Koller EA, Doraiswamy PM (2002) Olanzapine–associated diabetes mellitus. Pharmacother J Hum Pharmacol Drug Ther 22(7):841–852

Lee CH (2012) Unsupervised and supervised learning to evaluate event relatedness based on content mining from social-media streams. Expert Syst Appl 39(18):13338–13356

Liu L, Zhu F, Zhang L, Yang S (2012) A probabilistic graphical model for topic and preference discovery on social media. Neurocomputing 95:78–88

Lobzhanidze A, Zeng W, Gentry P, Taylor A (2013) Mainstream media vs. social media for trending topic prediction-an experimental study. Consumer Communications and Networking Conference (CCNC), 2013 IEEE. IEEE, pp 729–732

Majid A, Chen L, Chen GC, Mirza HT, Hussain I, Woodward J (2013) A context-aware personalized travel recommendation system based on geotagged social media data mining. Int J Geogr Inf Sci 27(4):662–684

Robertson G, Card SK, Mackinlay JD (1989) The cognitive coprocessor architecture for interactive user interfaces. Proceedings of the Second Annual ACM SIGGRAPH Symposium on User Interface Software and Technology. ACM Press, New York, pp 10–18

Rubin RR, Ma Y, Marrero DG, Peyrot M, Barrett-Connor EL, Kahn SE, Knowler WC (2008) Elevated depression symptoms, antidepressant medicine use, and risk of developing diabetes during the diabetes prevention program. Diabetes Care 31(3):420–426

Rosenbaum H, Shachaf P (2010) A structuration approach to online communities of practice: The case of QA communities. J Am Soc Inf Sci Technol 61(9):1933–1944

Shah C, Oh JS, Oh S (2008) Exploring characteristics and effects of user participation in online social QA sites. First Monday 13(9). http://www.uic.edu/htbin/cgiwrap/bin/ojs/index.php/fm/article/view/2182/2028. Accessed 15 Jan 2012

Wang M, Yang K (2012) Constructing visual tag dictionary by mining community-contributed media corpus. Neurocomputing 95:3–10

Wegrzyn-Wolska K, Bougueroua L (2012) Tweets mining for French Presidential Election. 2012 FOURTH INTERNATIONAL CONFERENCE ON COMPUTATIONAL ASPECTS OF SOCIAL NETWORKS (CASON). IEEE, pp 138–143

White JS, Matthews JN, Stacy JL (2012 May) Coalmine: an experience in building a system for social media analytics. In SPIE Defense, Security, and Sensing. International Society for Optics and Photonics, pp 84080A–84080A

Wikipedia contributors (2013) Atenolol. Wikipedia, The Free Encyclopedia. http://en.wikipedia.org/wiki/Atenolol. Accessed 30 July 2013

Zhang D, Si L, Rego VJ (2012) Sentiment detection with auxiliary data. Inf Retr 15(3–4SI):373–390

Zhang J (2008) Visualization for information retrieval. Springer, Berlin

Zhang J, Wolfram D, Wang P (2009) Analysis of query keywords of sports-related queries using visualization and clustering. J Am Soc Inf Sci Technol 60(8):1550–1571

Zhang J, Wolfram D (2009) Visual analysis of obesity-related query terms on Health Link. Online Information Review, 33(1), 43–57.

Zhang J, Wolfram D, Wang P, Hong Y, Gillis R (2008) Visualization of health-subject analysis based on query term co-occurrences. J Am Soc Inf Sci Technol 59(12):1933–1947

Zhang J, Zhao Y (2013) A user term visualization analysis based on a social question and answer log. Inf Process Manag 49(5):1019–1048

Zhang Y (2010) Contextualizing consumer health information searching: an analysis of questions in a social QA community. Proceedings of the 1st ACM International Health Informatics Symposium. ACM, New York, pp 210–219

Information Seeking Behaviour and Usage on a Multi-media Platform: Case Study Europeana

David Nicholas and David Clark

Abstract The article examines the usage of the Europeana.eu website, a multi-lingual online collection of millions of digitized items from European museums, libraries, archives and multi-media collections. It concentrates on three aspects of use: (1) stickiness and site loyalty; (2) social media referrals; (3) that associated with virtual exhibitions. Three methods for obtaining the data are examined: Google analytics, ClickStream logs and http server logs. The analyses produced by Google Analytics are highlighted in the article.

Keywords Information seeking · Google analytics · Log analysis · Multimedia website · Europeana

---

David Nicholas is a Director and founder of the CIBER research group (http://ciber-research. eu). The group is perhaps best known for monitoring behaviours in the virtual space, especially in regard to the virtual scholar and the Google Generation, which has been featured widely in the media, including on BBC TV and Australian TV (ABC). David is also a professor at the College of Communication and Information Studies, University of Tennessee and at the iSchool at Northumbria University. Previously David was Head of the Department of Information Studies at University College London for seven years (2004–2011) and previous to that was Head of the Department of Information Science at City University for a similar period of time. Email:Dave. Nicholas@ciber-research.eu.

David Clark has forty years experience of data processing and information management in publishing and related industries. He returned to full-time education in 1995 to take a masters degree in knowledge engineering. He has a PhD in Computer Science, from the University of Warwick, where he taught and researched from 1997–2001. He then moved to University College London, leaving in 2011 to form CIBER Research Ltd. He is a Director of the CIBER Research Ltd.

D. Nicholas (✉)
College of Communication and Information Studies, University of Tennessee, Knoxville, USA
e-mail: Dave.Nicholas@ciber-research.eu

D. Clark · D. Nicholas
CIBER Research Ltd., Newbury, UK
e-mail: David.Clark@ciber-research.eu

C. Chen, R. Larsen (eds.), *Library and Information Sciences,*
DOI 10.1007/978-3-642-54812-3_6, © The Author(s) 2014

Background

Transactional log studies are becoming more and more popular ways of evaluating websites (Davis 2004; Davis and Solla 2003). In particular, Http server logs and clickstream logs have proven to be very effective ways of analysing behavior on textual websites (Nicholas et al. 2006).The primary goal of many log or usage data studies is to find out about use rather than users. In terms of usage studies, previous log studies have led to different conclusions about the success or otherwise of the Big Deal and consortium subscriptions to journals. Davis (Davis 2002) challenged the composition of geographic based consortia. He recommended libraries create consortia based on homogeneous membership. On the other hand, Gargiulo (2003) analysed logs of an Italian consortium and strongly recommended Big Deal subscriptions. Essentially one of the limitations of basic log analysis is the fact that there is little possibility to link use data with user data, hence a vague and general picture of users' information seeking behaviour is obtained. This technical restriction makes it difficult to use the demographic data of users for finding out about differences in information seeking activities of users in regard to different tasks, statuses, genders and so on. In this paper, Google analytics data will be investigated to explore new ways of evaluating behavior on the web.

Europeana, launched in 2008 as a prototype and operating as a full service since 2010, is a gateway, portal or search engine to the digital resources of Europe's museums, art galleries, libraries, archives and audio-visual collections (Fig. 1). Europeana is regarded as trusted (curated) source connecting users directly to authentic and curated material. It provides multilingual access to 26 million European cultural objects in 2200 institutions from 34 countries. Books and manuscripts, photos and paintings, television and film, sculpture and crafts, diaries and maps, sheet music and recordings, they're all there. Europeana claim that there is no longer the need to travel the continent, either physically or virtually. If you find what you like you can download it, print it, use it, save it, or share it[1].

While Europeana is essentially a portal it also has aspirations well beyond that; it believes it can help stimulate the European digital economy; it also mounts on-line exhibitions and takes part in crowd sourcing experiments (World War 1 is currently the subject of such an experiment). Europeana is also working with other digital channels to distribute their content, most notably Google, Wikipedia and Facebook.

It is a site that currently attracts around five million visitors and is used heavily by humanities scholars, heritage professionals and even tourists. CIBER have been analysing usage of Europeana since 2009 and have now amassed a three-year long-series of data to evaluate Europeana's growth, changes and innovations. As a consequence we have assembled a large evidence base showing how a whole range of people use cultural collections and artefacts, in a virtual environment. Thus we use logging as the basis of insight and prediction about the purpose and motive of the millions who use Europeana.

---

[1] http://www.europeana.eu/

Information Seeking Behaviour and Usage on a Multi-media Platform

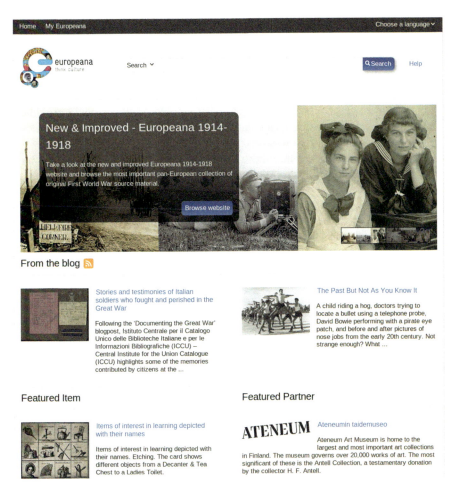

Fig. 1 Europeana home page

Aims and Objectives

The study reported here features our latest research which focuses on three types of digital behavior prevailing in Europeana which we regard to be particularly significant and strategic forms of digital behaviour not only for Europeana, but for all information providers on the Web. These are:

1. **Stickiness and user loyalty**. *Stickiness* is anything about a Web *site* that encourages a visitor to stay longer (engagement) and visit more often (returnees). All information providers are interested in what constitutes stickiness and how they can make their sites stickier.
2. **Social media referral.** Volume and characteristics of the traffic coming from Facebook, twitter and the like, which could potentially drive a lot of traffic to Europeana and encourage much re-use of Europeana content.

3. **Virtual exhibition usage**. Virtual exhibitions are a recent innovation in which Europeana sets much store. Clearly these exhibitions provide a lot of added value for a site which essentially functions as a search engine. Exhibitions could capture the interest of the digital information consumer and armchair tourist. They could 'speak' to a lot of people.

A prime objective of the study is to see what Google Analytics could provide in regard to robust and precise usage data and how it compared with our traditional usage sources—http server logs and ClickStream logs.

While textual websites, like those of scholarly publishers and libraries, have been well researched from a digital usage point of view (Julien and Williamson 2010), very few studies of multi-media platforms have been undertaken, and so in the way the paper is quite unique.

Methodology

For CIBER's earlier Europeana work we relied upon server http request logs using CIBER's own 'deep log' methods (Nicholas et al. 2013). However, for the study reported here we wanted also to see what extent, the now ubiquitous, Google Analytics (GA) data could undertake key information seeking analyses more cheaply and effectively. This is important given the fact that Europeana, like many organisations, are relying increasingly heavily on GA for all their usage and marketing needs. While we have utilised GA heavily in this paper as we will learn GA cannot always supply the data required in a convenient form and have thus supplemented it with our own tried and trusted deep log methods. There is great potential to make better use of GA but it requires considerable investment and effort, not only to interpret the output but in experimental design, preparation and configuration of event tracking code, and this is generally not undertaken by institutions and analysts.

In addition, to the http logs and GA data, we also had access to a series of Click-Streamer logs which had become recently available. However, we only had access to the ClickStreamer series of Portal logs from June to December 2012 (the minimal time-scale necessary for a robust analysis given the seasonal/diverse nature of usage data). As a result we have sometimes used the old series of raw http-request logs for a broader overview and perspective.

Thus, to provide the best and most comprehensive analysis of Europeana usage we have used a variety of data sources. And it is worth pointing out their various strengths and weaknesses. There are, in essence, three points at which we can take the pulse of a website. On receipt of a request by the server; by tapping into the internal process of the site's content management system (CMS); by causing the browser to send an acknowledgement when content is received. The first of these, monitoring incoming traffic, has been used since the web's inception. It relies on http server request log files originally intended for server management and software maintenance. Not being intended for market research purposes, means the record is not always in the most convenient form. On the other hand it may hold informa-

Information Seeking Behaviour and Usage on a Multi-media Platform   61

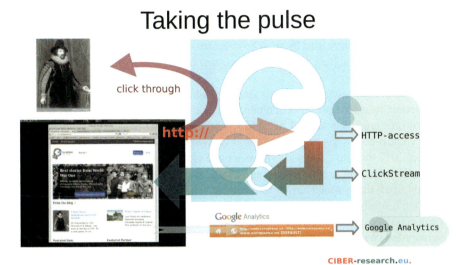

Fig. 2 Taking the pulse of a website using logs

tion that would not otherwise be collected because it did not seem relevant at the relevant at the time.

Figure 2 outlines the web-server process and the points at which usage can be measured. For a very simple website with no CMS the URL requested (e.g. a link in the clickstream) maps more or less directly to a web-page file, which is despatched by the server back to the client (browser). In this case the traditional server log is in effect also the CMS log. But today, CMS is the norm and the request no longer maps direct to a file but is interpreted by the CMS. As a result records are retrieved from a database and a web page constructed on demand. The cost of this flexibility and complexity is that the incoming request is no longer a straightforward and reliable indication of what was served in response. Interpretation of request logs becomes a matter of 'reverse engineering' the programming of the CMS. In such cases logging from within the CMS becomes attractive. For some purposes this is obvious and inherent to the application area: an online shop for example will almost certainly be linked to stock control, and accounting records. These can be considered specialised varieties of 'log file'; they can be used for analysis in similar ways to the server log. Or, a specific form of log may be kept for market research and data mining. For any special logging the problem is to specify in advance what needs recording.

The difficulty of web-server based logging, wherever the monitoring point, is that it does not record what happens at the user end. A web-page is served but there is no record of its receipt. The solution is to insert scripting into the web-page so that on receipt a secondary request is despatched to report back to a logging system. This is the method employed by Google Analytics and others similar solutions such as the open source Piwik. This can, like CMS logging, resolve the 'reverse engineering' problem, but the task of deciding what to track and of deploying the necessary web tracker 'events' to best effect remains. It also needs to be noted that this approach depends on the end-user accepting and not deleting the tracking cookies and scripts. Our research suggests that for this reason significant traffic, perhaps 10–15%, may be untracked by such browser based methods. This could make a big impact on some analyses, especially those regarding relatively lowly used activities and behaviours.

Taking measurements at various stages of what should, in principle, be a single transaction, raises the problem of reconciling the various accounts. Even if the numbers do not agree we should be able to account for differences. The agreement between http-access log and ClickStream is acceptable: over the period June to November 2012 the http-access log shows a page view count higher by 1%. However, as we shall learn in greater detail, agreement between either of these sources and Google Analytics is much harder to establish.

Google Analytics depends on JavaScript being active on the client browser and the acceptance of the Google cookies. Without JavaScript the logging data will not be recorded. Without the cookies it is not possible to identify returning visitors, nor gather reliable information about the sequence and timing of page views. Based on the six-month ClickStream series between 15–30% of visits have a Google cookie set when requesting the landing page, this implies a previous visit to Europeana and retained cookies. For visits comprising more than a single page, the GA cookies are present in 85–90% of page views, thus we think it is highly probable that the remaining 10–15% (possibly one in six visits) have blocked cookies and possibly JavaScript and would not therefore be tracked by Google Analytics.

Unfortunately this estimate of 10–15% untracked visits by Google Analytics does not account for the massive gap between the page views reported by GA and those from the Europeana logs which is 26% in the period June-December 2012. In only one month (September) is the difference (16%) low enough to be plausibly attributable to user blocking of GA. For June the figure is 54%: some further explanation is required.

In the period January–May 2011 a much greater mismatch of page view counts between Google Analytics and the http-access log was observed: the uncorrected figure exceeding 250%. In that case we introduced the concept of an outlier: a series of page requests from a single IP address, often over many days, far too numerous to be the efforts of a single user. Thus the 'visitor' displays all the characteristics of an automated agent or robot bar the user-agent identifier. It could be a cloaked robot. Significantly, such cases tend to go unrecorded by Google Analytics as automated agents retrieve web content but do not run JavaScript. In the early months of 2011 identifying less than a dozen such agents was sufficient to bring the logs and GA into near-enough agreement. A similar process can be applied to the 2012 ClickStream series. For example in August 2012 8.2% of all page-views originated from a single IP address located in Beijing. China has a large population, they may have a considerable interest in European culture, the single IP address could be a proxy for many individual users; on the other hand such heavy and sustained use does not display the irregular pattern of use expected of normal users. If an outlier correction is applied then the difference between GA and the ClickStream data can be coerced into an acceptable error band.

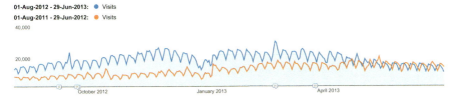

Fig. 3 Visits: August 2011–January 2013 compared to the same time the previous year. (Source: GA)

In sum: Google Analytics' reliance on cookies and scripting is effective in suppressing the effect of cloaked robots and other automated agents that would distort the profile of a normal sentient user; but the same feature will also miss genuine users who have blocked cookies and JavaScript.

Results

Stickiness and Loyalty

Stickiness has traditionally been viewed as a measure of engagement, success, satisfaction and loyalty. If someone spends a long time on a visit or repeatedly visits, then the site might be regarded as 'sticky' and that could be considered a good thing. This is especially the case where the site is not engaged in direct selling; if the value of the site cannot be measured by the revenue it generates then perhaps the value may be measured by the users it detains and retains. In the context of Europeana, however, we need to tread more carefully as it is more of a gateway, portal or search engine than a destination site, and it could be argued that Europeana's main task is to pass on visitors to the original version of the digital object at a provider site, at a healthy rate of knots.

First, let us provide the necessary general usage data as a context to the stickiness investigation. How is overall usage going over time and what patterns can we see? Comparing the more regular and settled periods: autumn 2011 (Aug–Jan) with autumn 2012 (Aug–Jan) (Fig. 3) a clear picture emerges with visitor numbers growing healthily by 120%. The numbers have been growing steadily since July 2012, but the gain 2012 over 2011 was most marked in November. The peak of activity on weekdays compared to weekends is greater, and there is a more pronounced fall-off in activity toward the year-end. The rate of growth has increased compared to a year before, so it appears to be accelerating.

Figure 4 charts the daily visitor count 2010–2013. Note the seasonal pattern which follows the rhythms of the school and academic calendar, the drop each weekend and holiday, and—despite perturbation—the steady spiral of growth.

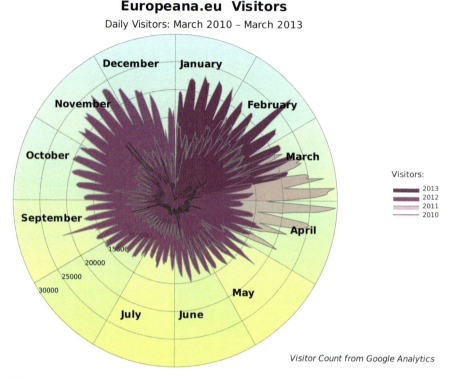

Fig. 4 Europeana daily visits 2010–2013

Returning Visitors

Stickiness has most often been associated with site loyalty and the propensity of people to revisit. Returnees, unlike dwell time, are definitely a quality metric. We have not been able to undertake this analysis before on Europeana because of an absence of cookies in the raw logs (the surest method for identifying revisits). These cookies are available in the 'ClickStream' series, but only from June 2012, so we are really limited to GA data. As mentioned earlier cookie-based visitor identification is not 100 % reliable: cookies may be deleted; the same person may access the site from more than one browser. It is therefore probable that there is a systemic overstatement of 'New' and 'Unique Visitors' and a corresponding under recording of returning visits. But we do not know the extent of this and given the relative importance of this metric, far more meaningful than a Facebook 'like', for instance, Europeana hopes to do more research to establish its real significance, by triangulating the data with demographic, survey or qualitative data.

Only one in four visitors return to Europeana, as compared to two out of five for a typical publisher website. This says something about dependency. Within that 25 %, 10 % return only once, 4 % make three visits, 2 % four. Nine per cent of visi-

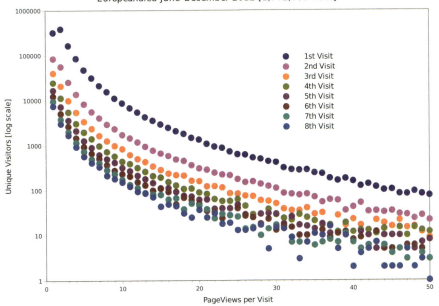

Fig. 5 Europeana: return visits. (Source: GA)

tors returned five times or more. GA may understate the return rate a little but the distribution follows is a typical 'power law' (Fig. 5). This suggests that Europeana's core audience, defined as those people visiting five times of more, is about one-tenth the size of its visitor numbers—about 500,000.

When looking at returning visitors it is well to remember that most visits are very fleeting; even when bouncers (one visit, on view) are ignored many returning visits are measured in seconds rather than days. So strong is this phenomenon that it is difficult to convey on a single chart. The following three charts (Figs. 6–8) are derived from a single dataset, a sample of 600,000 visits made between June and December 2012. These are visits selected because the Google cookies were present and contained timing data for a previous visit. The Google cookie expires 2 years after the last visit so first we look at a timescale of 24 months. In many cases the cookie will have been deleted earlier so the evidence of long-term use of Europeana will be understated. Nonetheless we do see evidence of users who first used Europeana over two years ago, and even a few who have recorded no other visit in the intervening period. But these are counted in single figures compared to the thousands who return within a month (Fig. 6).

When we look even closer (Fig. 8), at those visitors who return within three days rather than months an interesting pattern can be seen. Regular users appear to have a daily routine; there is a distinct series of peaks in the graph at 24, 48, and 72 h. In fact, equipped with this insight, we can turn to a daily plot (Fig. 8) and see the same

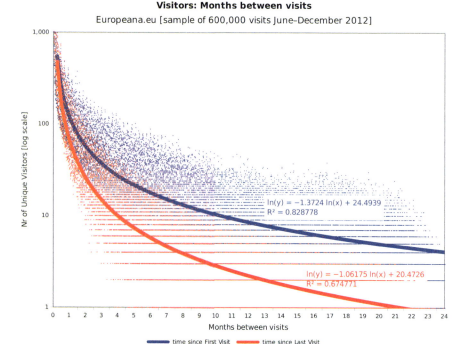

Fig. 6 Europeana: months between visits. (Source: GA)

daily routine persists through a whole month. It is also possible to see traces of a weekly cycle: the daily peak is a little higher at 7, 14, 21 and 28 days.

One explanation for this phenomenon is that a significant part of Europeana use takes place within institutions using browsers set up in kiosk mode. However, even when the data is reprocessed with a filter to remove the most obvious heavy institutions referrals the daily pattern persists.

Engagement

We can calculate levels of engagement by considering both: (a) duration of a visit; (b) numbers pages viewed during a visit. The most recent data shows that 60 % of visits are very short (<10 s); and less than 2 % are recorded by GA as exceeding 30 min (the normal cookie timeout for a visit). Most visits are over in the blink of an eye. This is probably what we would expect of a discovery site rather than a destination site, where the times are much higher. In terms of page views 58 % looked at just one page, less than 5 % view more than 16 pages. Of course this comes with short visits. The site's character is of course changing with the introduction of virtual exhibitions and when we come to the virtual exhibition section we can see people dwelling longer and examining more pages.

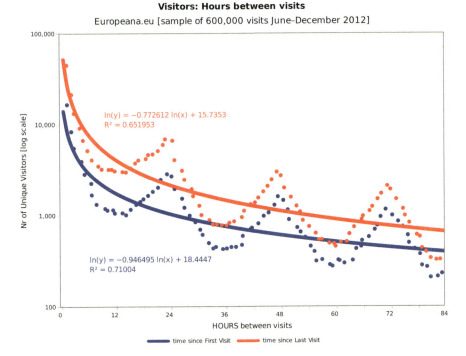

Fig. 7 Hours between visits. (Source: GA)

When looking at figures for duration of visit it is important to note the highly skewed distribution: most visits are very short, a table with ranges of values can be misleading, as is any 'average' figure. Table 1 and Fig. 9 and show visit times for December 2012. The average visit duration is 2 min and 19 s, it varies little depending on what time span is analysed, whereas the chart reveals the full picture: there is much larger range, a few visits are very much longer, but most are extremely short. In December 2012 58% of visits were timed at less than 10 s; only 10% of visits fall broadly (1–3 min) into the 'average' category band.

The story on 'engagement' is an interesting one: usage (page views) has not kept pace with overall growth rates, having grown just over 60% from Autumn to Autumn and with a huge fall (nearly 30%) being recorded in the number of pages viewed per visit (was previously 5.4 and now 3.8) and a smaller, but still large fall (nearly 17%) in the duration of visits. 'Average' is a very poor measure of visit duration so not much can be read into a decline in this figure from 2:46 s, to 2:18 s. Especially as the Bounce Rate has fallen (from 54 to 50%), and we might have expected this to go up in the circumstances. So, it is probable that 'stickiness' has increased (fewer bouncers), but is partly masked by a corresponding reduction in the number of 'unreal users' consuming many pages in long sessions.

These 'unreal users' are not search-engine spiders which are already excluded from the analysis. Nor do we mean 'outliers' which are cases where we have come

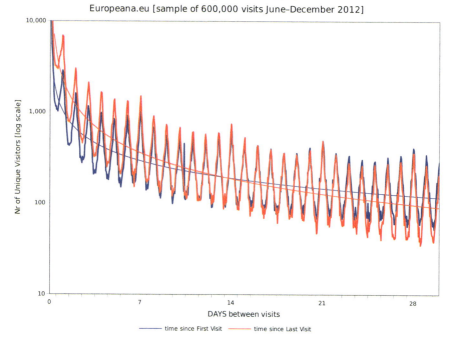

Fig. 8 Days between visits. (Source: GA)

Table 1 Duration of visits, December 2012. (Source: GA)

Visit duration (s)	Visits
0–10	311,193
11–30	57,548
31–60	39,689
61–180	52,233
181–600	39,245
601–1800	23,132
1801+	7,707

to a firm conclusion that the activity is that of a cloaked bot. Once we have discounted these we are still left with patterns of activity that are implausible, such as sessions that never time out or appear to view an unreasonable pages etc. In some cases that can be explained by kiosk applications in libraries, API usage, or by developer testing. Essentially 'unreal users' are that portion of the recorded usage which we find 'not proven'. There is insufficient evidence to classify as robot or outlier, but the suspicion remains that it would be unwise to fully trust any inference from this data.

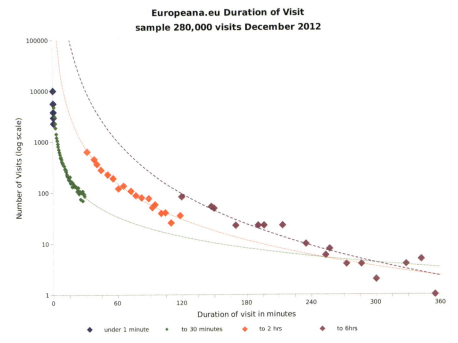

Fig. 9 Europeana: duration of visit. (Source: GA)

Social Media

With so much Europeana (and scholarly publisher) planning (and hopes) resting on social media use for growth and re-use it is worth first pointing out that there are substantial problems in defining 'Social Media', which need to be clarified in order to make a fair and accurate evaluations and comparison of growth rates and contribution to overall traffic.

The Google Analytics 'advanced segment' for social media, as personally defined and used by Europeana, contains 20 sources (referrer domains), some of which have registered insignificant or even no traffic at all during the last six months (October 2012–March 2013) See Table 2. The major sources of social traffic are Facebook, and Wikipedia; there is also significant traffic from WordPress, Blogspot, twitter and, a considerable way behind, Pinterest, the latter being publicised on the Europeana homepage for many weeks during 2013. We shall return to individual performance later in this section, here we shall confine ourselves to the problems of definition.

An interesting definitional case is Twitter. The Twitter traffic is identified by "include Source containing 't.co'". Patently, this is too loose a definition as it will not only pick up 't.co', but any domain containing that sequence of characters e.g. search.bt.com. The result is that that the number of visits captured by this method is at 9,993 (for the most recent six months) four times greater than the actual number of visits from t.co (Twitter). The true total of social sources (40,791) is inflated

Table 2 Social segment definition (GA)

Social	Page views
facebook.com	16928
tweet	0
LinkedIn	361
YouTube	42
reddit	167
digg	14
delicious	83
stumbleupon	0
Flickr	222
MySpace	0
hootsuite	28
retronaut	167
Wikipedia	10882
bit.ly	0
tinyurl	0
t.co	9993
wp.me	0
blogspot	4044
wordpress	4253
Pinterest	1265
sum	48449
intersect	44085
Oct-Mar	3473308

by 19% (48,449).The overall effect on the visit count for the social segment is to some extent mitigated by the fortunate chance that the loose 't.co' rule will pick up blogspot.com which is already included by its own rule. The problem can be fixed by replacing the rule "include Source containing 't.co'" with "include Source Exactly matching 't.co'" or with "include Source Matching RegEx ^t\.co".

Blogs pose definitional problems too (Table 3). The social segment includes blogs but only those from WordPress and Blogger. There are many other blogs hosted elsewhere that are not included. On the other hand treating all referrals originating from a WordPress or Blogger domain may be too broad a definition of a blog. WordPress in particular is a popular hosting platform for photographers' and artists' galleries. No method of classification will be entirely satisfactory but on balance we think the 'social' classification should be broadened to include any domain containing the subdomain 'blog.' or 'blogs.', but excluding blog.europeana.eu. The result is that another 1,085 visits can be added to the social segment.

Google Analytics provides under "Traffic Sources" a "Social" analysis. Looking at the "Network Referrals" section of this report it is clear that the GA definition of 'social' is again far broader than either Europeana's own 'Advanced Segment' definition or the corrected and extended version used by CIBER. How many networks are included depends on the period of the report: for March-April 2013 it includes 48, Jan–May 2012/2013 includes 78 etc. The definition is as long as a piece of string and makes social network behaviour very difficult to delineate.

Information Seeking Behaviour and Usage on a Multi-media Platform 71

Table 3 Social segment blogs (selection only). (Source: GA)

	Oct 1, 2011–Mar 31, 2012	Oct 1, 2012–Mar 31, 2013
agioritikesmnimes.pblogs.gr	64	0
bazoga.over-blog.com	43	0
bgpw.blog.pl	21	21
blog.bnf.fr	21	21
blog.crdp-versailles.fr	43	0
blog.daum.net	21	43
blog.euscreen.eu	0	64
blogs.ec.europa.eu	21	21
blogs.helsinki.fi	21	0
blog.sina.com.cn	0	64
blogs.law.harvard.edu	64	0
blog.slub-dresden.de	21	0
blogs.sch.gr	43	43
boqo.over-blog.com	21	0
cblog.culture.fr	43	0
christypato.blog.br	21	0
deal.blog.kazeo.com	0	128
deal.blog.mongenie.com	213	0
digiblog.hu	21	0
enfinlivre.blog.lemonde.fr	43	0
estudamais8.blogs.sapo.pt	21	0
eueublog.wordpress.com	0	64
fablog.iransalamat.com	43	0
formacion.universiablogs.net	43	0
googleblog.blogspot.com	21	0
kluwercopyrightblog.com	21	0
konzervativci.blog.com.mk	21	0
leblog-ffg.over-blog.org	43	21
libblog.ucy.ac.cy	21	0
pisani.blog.lemonde.fr	43	43
sog.blog.so-net.ne.jp	0	21
somewhereinblog.net	43	43

To conclude there are three 'social' definitions at work here: Google's, Europeana's social segment and CIBER's own expanded version based on a corrected version of the Europeana social segment and used for the following analyses.

Size and Growth in Traffic

To place social media referrals in context it is worth first looking at all referrals. Seventy per cent of the 4.5 M visits to Europeana in the past year (2012) were search referrals, nearly all (97%) from Google. By contrast, runner-up Bing accounts for just 0.5%. Eighteen per cent of visits originate as links from other sites,

11% are direct—typed-in or bookmarked—and campaigns (newsletters etc.) contribute a little over 1%.

Google Analytics was not reporting social referral before Oct 2011, so there is a limited time series, which we can to some extent enhance with log data. The limited data we have show that there was a slight peak in social referrals around the time of a new portal launch in October 2011 (thanks to associated publicity one presumes), but after that it settles down to around 1,000 per week; since August 2012 there has been some irregular growth and the base-rate is now nearing 1500 per week. Between Oct–March 2011/2012 and 2012/2013 the overall year-on-year general visitor growth is 90%. However if we look at the 'social segment' the visitor growth is 34%. Exclude blogs and visitor growth falls to 25%. Looking at blogs alone [the visitor growth rate is 58%. The social element is a little more significant on the exhibitions site and predictably significant for blog.europeana.

In April 2013 Social Referrals only accounted for one per cent of all visits to the site, a bare 0.02% higher than a year previous. It could be that Europeana's social media activity takes place solely within the context of these sites and entirely bypasses Europeana.eu. In such a context we cannot refute claims for the efficacy of 'social media', nor can we support them. In the context of the Europeana.eu website however social referral is not at present significant and is not growing above the trend for the site as a whole. So the action has to be happening elsewhere, on the social media sites themselves.

Individual Social Media

The dominant social media network is Facebook with nearly 30,000 referrals in the year since the new portal launch (Oct 2011). The 'average visit duration' of these Facebook sourced visitors is, according to Google Analytics just over 3 min. Although 'average' is a poor single metric to use in this context—the distribution being log-normal—the duration is slightly higher than the 2.5 min average for all visitors. So more dwell time for social media users, but not really sufficient to build a strong case for more committed users, and anyway see our earlier comments about the problems of using dwell time in isolation as a metric.

Facebook was followed by WordPress in popularity, nearly 9000 referrals, Blogger (over 4200), Twitter (nearly 3300) and Netvibes (just over 2000).

When we consider and compare only the relatively stable Autumn months (Sept–Dec, 2011 and 2012) the overall doubling of traffic on the site is not matched by a corresponding growth in social referrals year on year: Facebook (nearly 10000 referrals, 2012) and Twitter (1650 referrals) traffic in particular shows only a 12% increase in visits. Only WordPress, with only a third of the Facebook traffic (3037 referrals in 2012; 162% year-on-year growth) has kept pace with the overall pace of the site. However, Twitter is an interesting case because while there is little growth in referrals, dwell time has in fact doubled. The average for Twitter was 2.5 min in autumn 2011, 5 min in 2012. Pinterest, Europeana's latest social media venture, a content sharing service that allows members to "pin" images videos and other objects to their pin board, currently featured on the Europeana homepage (and so attracting considerable publicity), surprisingly perhaps comes in at 6th in the social media ranking, with a light traffic flow (681 visits Sep–Dec 2012). The high number of page views per visit from Pinterest (average 12) and very long dwell time (12 min) suggest 'unreal user' activity, something odd is happening here. We suspect, as this feature on the home page is quite recent, that this may be internal development or testing activity. This should be checked, otherwise a false impression might be provided.

We can contrast the traffic flow for the site as a whole with the flow of social media visits using Google Analytics. For the site as a whole most inbound traffic goes direct to a record (about half of all non-search engine referrals) and twelve per cent to 'search'. Interestingly, for social referrals half the inbound traffic goes to the homepage and around seventeen per cent to 'search'. An informal analysis of 'trackbacks' provided by Google Analytics suggests that much of the social traffic may be by people involved in development or research in digital humanities and related fields, not a very representative group: insiders. During the period, 30 Dec 2012–29 Jan 2013, when there were 6,628 social referrals, blog.europeana.eu had 8,000 visitors. It is probable the blog users are already familiar with Europeana in which case it is probably not bringing in many new users.

'My Europeana', a personal/customised facility, may also be considered to belong in the 'social' category. Between June and December 2012 a total of 1400 users were recorded as having logged in with a userid, less than 300 even in the busiest month of November. Though a few users appear to login and view many hundreds of pages in a month there is little evidence of regular and sustained use of 'My Europeana', less than 50, a tiny amount, have used the feature for three or more months in seven. The majority appear in the record one month only during which they view less than forty pages. Overall logged-in users account for one-half per cent of all page views.

Social media, then, is not driving Europeana growth, and unlikely to do from the evidence we have to hand. The example of Pinterest is illustrative. Consider the featuring of a link to Pinterest on the Europeana homepage: this would appear to be of net benefit to Pinterest. Europeana has over 2,000 'followers' on Pinterest and over 600 'pins', but referrals back to Europeana during the last four months of 2012 amount to 680. The big question is what, in the context of Europeana, is social media for? Should we expect it to drive traffic to Europeana, or is Europeana the glue layer that enables Pinterest to be a showcase for Europeana's provider institutions? There is scope for a more comprehensive research programme in this area, linking together the traffic analysis of the Europeana web-presence (including blog, exhibitions, API) with similar data drawn from Europeana's providers.

Of course, all these social media initiatives are insignificant compared to 'the bread and butter' search engine referral; and not just via Google: pionier.net.pl the Polish aggregator site brought in 37,000 (5%) referrals, compared to facebook.com 29,000 (<4%), with all its millions of members. A study by Europeana (http://pro.europeana.eu/pro-blog/-/blogs/1660413) shows that API use by the Polish partners is proving very successful in sending traffic to Europeana.

Most of the social media (narrowly defined) traffic appears to flow into the home page rather than to specific items. This is in marked contrast to referrals from blogs which are more often to a specific page.

Country Analysis

First a note of caution: determining the user's location is only approximate and, particularly when looking at the standard Google Analytics report, language choice and country are not the same: 'Language: en-us' is not the same as 'Country/Territory: United States'. The language indication is merely the default setting of the browser and cannot be relied upon. Location, which is based on IP address allocation, can also cross borders.

Taking this into account it is still somewhat surprising to find that the most active country for social media traffic to Europeana.eu is Spain. In the most recent six-months Spain accounts for 8.8% of social media traffic as defined by Europeana's own Social Media advanced segment, the USA is second (7.1%). Taking into account the much larger population of the USA and the mature state of social media uptake there this is unexpected. However, as we have already observed Social Media accounts only for 1 per cent of visits and visitors, so the statistics are likely to be unstable and be perturbed by factors which can be difficult to identify.

Social Actions and Social Media

In order to find out whether users coming from social media are more likely to share (thought to be a positive by information providers) you first have to define 'likely to share'. The clickstream logs show negligible use of the 'SAVE_SOCIAL_TAG' action. For the period June–December 2012 (the only period for which we have clickstream logs) the action occurred 189 times. Set against 9.6 million accesses to object pages (FULL_RESULT_HTML) and 4.8 million presentations of search results (BRIEF_RESULT:search), and 1.6 views of the homepage (INDEXPAGE) it is clear that not much sharing goes on; so insignificant that we need to look for another definition of 'social media sharing'.

If we turn to the Google Analytics equivalent, 'Social Plugins', the numbers are still low, but better: September 2012–March 2013, 3,945 'Unique Social Actions'. Set against the 3.4 million visits in that period a social sharing action occurs at a rate of one per 866 visits (0.12%). When that report is restricted using Europeana's own 'Social Media advanced segment' the number is reduced to 291 'Unique Social Actions'. There is indeed a greater propensity to share by visitors coming from social media: a rate of one per 146 visits (0.68%). But the actual numbers are very small, in fact of the 142 Social sharing sources used by all visitors only three—Facebook, Google+, and Twitter—appear when the report is restricted to 'social segment' referrals. One reason for this may be that the 'advanced segment' has been defined too narrowly—inputs should match outputs; all the social sites recorded by Google

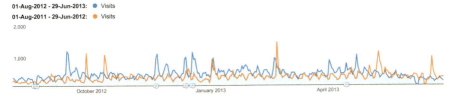

Fig. 10 Exhibitions: visits. (Source: GA)

Analytics as 'social sources' should be included in the segment. The alternative is to restrict the Social Plugins report to match the advanced segment. In that case the 'all users' figure declines to one in 1,104 (0.09%) [the Social segment is, of course, unchanged at 0.68%]. So, users coming from social media are more likely to share. However there might be a strong element of auto-correlation here, a tautology: social media users share because that is what social media is about.

Virtual Exhibitions

Exhibitions were only just featuring towards the end of or Europeana Connect work in 2011 so CIBER came to this topic fresh and very interested in looking at the impact it has had. It looked like a break-through in Europeana thinking and here surely is something that could capture the interest of the digital information consumer and armchair tourist, strategic markets for Europeana. It could 'speak' to a lot of people. Certainly so as the homepage seems to have become increasingly a promotional tool and virtual exhibitions are clearly thought to have a major role here, in promoting, highlighting and sampling Europeana; there is a prominent carousel from which you can choose an exhibition to visit.

The amount of space allocated to comment and feedback on exhibits suggests a degree of interactivity is expected; furthermore exhibitions are by their nature places to view and browse and therefore we should expect that people spend greater amounts of time here than elsewhere on the Europeana site. Dwell time is a more meaningful a metric here.

We have to rely solely on GA for this evaluation (Fig. 10) as we do not have raw log files for the 'exhibitions' site. Sept–Dec, 2011 and 2012 data shows that there has been a 50% increase in visitors, and 'pages per visit' has increased from 7 to 12 pages, the bounce rate is very low (0%) compared to the main site, so people appear to be dwelling; and we might have, at long last, that much sort after stickiness. About 10% of exhibition visitors appear to be using a mobile (tablet) platform, which is also relatively high.

The most recent figures (Tables 4 and 5) show that the overall number of exhibition visits (less than 50,000 Sept–Dec 2012) is still relatively low relative compared to the visits to the main site (1.6 million). That is, just over 3% of all visitors find their way to an exhibition. But that is perhaps an unreasonable comparison; they

Table 4 Exhibitions, Europeana.eu. (Source: GA)

	Sep–Dec 2012	Sep–Dec 2011	(%)
Visits	47,078	30,826	52
Visitors	38,573	26,245	47
Pageviews	550,807	210,396	162
Pages per visit	11.7	6.8	71
Duration of visit	00:02:44	00:02:58	−8
Bounce rate	0%	32%	−99
New Visits	80%	83%	−3

Table 5 Exhibitions, visitors 30 Dec 2012–29 Jan 2013. (Source: GA)

	Visits	Pages/visit	Bounce rate (%)
Royal book collections	2,158	11.4	0.2
1914–1918	1,435	13.1	0.3
European sports	754	11.9	0.0
Total visits	14,078		

are, after all, a relatively novel feature and fifty-thousand visits are significant when placed in contrast to the traffic flows associated with social media.

Thirty-per-cent of visits to exhibitions come from the carousel on the main site homepage (11,881 visits), so homepage promotion appears to be successful. In fact nothing else is really very successful (e.g. newsletters). In contrast to the main site Search traffic is far less significant (less than a quarter) as a source of visitors. Whilst referral traffic tends to be directed to the main page, direct traffic lands on specific exhibitions, notably '1914–1918' with 6,540 visits (13% of total) September–December 2012. There is a strong flow from one exhibit (record) to another which suggests visitors are following the exhibition sequence. In conclusion: exhibitions are sticky and successful but interest (as is the nature of the exhibition trade) is volatile.

Conclusions

For the very first time CIBER has been able to evaluate Europeana usage by all the available quantitative methodologies: deep log analysis, ClickStreamer logs and Google Analytics. In fact we believe this is the first time the three methodologies have been employed in regard to usage of a single website. We were especially interested to find out whether Google Analytics' popularity is matched by its capabilities and this article produces many useful GA derived analyses. GA proved to be a very useful usage tool, albeit one which sometimes underestimates usage, and also one which needs careful calibration and interpretation to obtain full benefits.

Of course, using multiple sources of data has a downside as it highlights differences and divergences which need to be resolved. Considerable effort has gone into ironing out the resulting confusion caused. If you only have one clock you either trust the time it tells, compensating for known errors, or do without. If you have two clocks that tell different times, you cannot trust either: you know less not more.

Information Seeking Behaviour and Usage on a Multi-media Platform

In respect to the results of the analyses:

a. Stickiness and loyalty levels are lower than found elsewhere, say, in scholarly sites but that might be expected of a search engine (or catalogue) that boasts little of its own content. The loyal users Europeana has are the cultural institutions and their members. It is estimated that Europeana's core audience, defined as those people visiting five times of more, is about one-tenth the size of its visitor numbers—about half a million people. Regular users tend to be routine users. In regard to engagement: most visits are over in the blink of an eye (10 s), with just one page viewed. This is probably what you would expect of a discovery site rather than a destination one. The trend appears to be towards a less engaged user, but this needs further investigation as it might be due to other factors.

b. Social Media: taking Europeana's definition ('social segment') the overall year-on-year visitor growth is 34%, compared to an overall visitor growth for European of 90%. Exclude blogs and visitor growth falls to 25%. Looking at blogs alone the visitor growth rate is 58%. Social media use is a complex area which is bedevilled by problems of identification, definition, novelty and interpretation. Given the importance accredited to it in Europeana planning circles, and the passions typically associated with it, there is a need for a detailed investigation to discover why it has driven relatively low volumes of traffic towards Europeana (around 1% of all traffic), why usage is not growing relatively speaking, whether it is generating more 'quality' traffic from users with a greater propensity to share and what significance can be read into use of Europeana data 'offshore', on sites like Facebook. There is a greater propensity for social media to share, but the activity itself is very uncommon.

c. Virtual exhibitions are an undoubted and a qualified success, which seem highly fit for purpose: for viewing rather than reading. They are popular, sticky, and generate high levels of engagement. They are the elephant in the room.

Open Access This chapter is distributed under the terms of the Creative Commons Attribution Noncommercial License, which permits any noncommercial use, distribution, and reproduction in any medium, provided the original author(s) and source are credited.

References

Davis PM (2002) Patterns in electronic journal usage: challenging the composition of geographic consortia. Coll Res Libr 63(6):484–497

Davis PM (2004) Information-seeking behavior of chemists: a transaction log analysis of referral URLs. J Am Soc Inf Sci Technol 55(4):326–332

Davis PM, Solla LR (2003) An IP-level analysis of usage statistics for electronic journals in chemistry: making inferences about user behavior. J Am Soc Inf Sci Technol 54(11):1062–1068

Gargiulo P (2003) Electronic journals and users: the CIBER experience in Italy. J Ser Community 16(3):293–298

Julien H, Williamson K (2010) Discourse and practice in information literacy and information seeking: gaps and opportunities. Inf Res Int Electro J 15(1):n1

Nicholas D, Clark D, Rowlands I, Jamali HR (2013) Information on the go: a case study of Europeana mobile users. J Am Soc Inf Sci Technol 64(7):1311–1322

Nicholas D, Huntington P, Jamali HR, Watkinson A (2006) The information seeking behaviour of the users of digital scholarly journals. Inf Process Manag 42(5):1345–1365

Exploratory Search: A Critical Analysis of the Theoretical Foundations, System Features, and Research Trends

Tingting Jiang

Abstract Humans are explorers by nature. Almost all searches are exploratory to a certain extent. As a result of the subdivision of the information seeking domain, exploratory search has become a new research focus arousing extensive attention. This chapter introduces the concept of exploratory search and illustrates its basic theoretical foundations, clarifying its complex meaning from the aspects of the problem context and the search process. Four different methods of classifying search results are identified based on a survey of existing exploratory search systems, including hierarchical classification, faceted classification, dynamic clustering, and social classification. Their inherent characteristics and practical applications are reviewed in detail, and the visualization support for presenting the classified search results is explored in addition. The development trends of the exploratory search field are predicted according to the social nature of information seeking.

Keywords Exploratory search · Systems · Users · Classification · Visualization · Social

Introduction

Online information seeking is an indispensable part of our daily lives and work. Explicit information needs, e.g. the needs for weather, flight, and stock information, can be quickly satisfied by powerful Web search engines. This reflects the look-up model that focuses on matching user queries with document surrogates (Bates 1989). Specific queries will lead to accurate search results, and one does not need to make any evaluation or comparison (Marchionini 2006).

Tingting Jiang is currently an associate professor at the School of Information Management, Wuhan University. She received her PhD in Library and Information Science from the University of Pittsburgh. Her current research interests include information seeking behavior, information architecture, information visualization, and Web 2.0. Tingting Jiang can be contacted at: tij@whu. edu.cn.

T. Jiang (✉)
School of Information Management, Wuhan University, Wuhan, China
e-mail: tij@whu.edu.cn

C. Chen, R. Larsen (eds.), *Library and Information Sciences,*
DOI 10.1007/978-3-642-54812-3_7, © The Author(s) 2014

Nevertheless, the lookup model is not applicable to many real-world scenarios. Scientific researchers may want to dig into a new research topic; budget travelers may want to make an affordable travel plan; youngsters may want to learn the secrets of career success; and so on and so forth. The information needs involved in these problems cannot be directly translated into appropriate queries, because people are not familiar with the knowledge domain that is related to the search, they do not know the means of achieving their goals, or the goals are not clear in themselves (Nolan 2008).

In tackling the above problems, as a matter of fact, people have to define their search goals in the first place. The information they obtain at the beginning of the search process may be of poor relevance. However the more information they absorb, the more thoroughly they understand the problem. In this way people get to distinguish between what they already know and what they should know. The gap in between is the information need. With the need taking shape gradually, people will be more and more able to formulate queries and identify relevant items. At this moment, the power of the search system in automatic matching starts to play its role truly. Whether people can find satisfying solutions to the original problem is further dependent upon their skills of extracting valuable information from search results. Here we see the user-dominated non-linear search, known as "exploratory search".

Exploratory search is a special type of information seeking. The 2005 Exploratory Search Interface Workshop was the first milestone in the history of this sub discipline (White et al. 2005). It was followed by a series of influential events, including the 2006 ACM SIGIR Workshop on Evaluating Exploratory Search Systems, the 2007 ACM SIGCHI Workshop on Exploratory Search and HCI, and the 2008 NSF Invitational Workshop on Information Seeking Support Systems. Moreover several academic journals, such as the *Communications of the ACM, the International Journal of Information Processing and Management,* and *Computer*, have published special issues on exploratory search.

Related Work

Classical Theories Related to Exploratory Search

Many researchers from the areas of information retrieval, human-computer interaction, information organization, and information behavior have devoted their attention to exploratory search. Indeed, exploratory search studies can seek theoretical roots in these areas. Below is a brief review of frequently cited related theories from two aspects, i.e. users' internal cognition and external behavior.

Interactive Information Retrieval and Cognitive Information Retrieval

Interactive information retrieval changes the system-centered tradition adopted by early information retrieval research and concentrates more on the user's input and control in the search process. It is closely related to cognitive information retrieval because the main purpose of interaction is to influence the user's cognitive state to make him/her more effective in information searching (Saracevic 1996).

As Ingwersen (1996) stated, all the interactive activities in information retrieval could arouse cognition processes. He created the polyrepresentations of both the information space of information retrieval systems and the cognitive space of users. While the former consists of the system setting and information objects, the latter includes four elements, i.e. work-task/interest domain, current cognitive state, problem space, and information need, which follow the bottom-up order of causality.

Similarly, Saracevic's (1997) stratified model also considers two sides: human and computer. In this model interaction is understood as a sequence of processes occurring at several levels, such as the cognitive, affective, and situational levels on the human side and the engineering, processing, and content levels on the computer side.

Guided by the hypothesis of anomalous states of knowledge (ASK), Belkin (1996) established the episode model in which an information seeking episode was defined as a series of interaction between the user and the information. The type of interaction at a certain time point is determined by the user's goals, intentions, situations, and the interaction is supported by such processes as representation, comparison, presentation, navigation, and visualization, etc.

The interactive feedback model by Spink (1997) resulted from an empirical study exploring how interaction occurred during mediated online searching. The search process may consist of multiple cycles, and multiple interactive feedback loops may be seen in each cycle. The interactive feedback covers the users' judgment regarding content relevance, term relevance, and magnitude as well as their review of tactics and terminologies.

Evolving Search and Information Foraging

Bates (1989) put forward two important arguments in her evolving search theory. First, users' query will keep changing in most real-world searches. Such changes may be not limited to term modifications. As the new information encountered in the search brings in new ideas, users' information needs will evolve. Second, an information need is not met by a single set of best results. Instead, the user will collect some useful information at each stage of the ever-modifying search, and the search goal is achieved by combining all these fragments. So to speak, evolving search follows the "berrypiking" pattern.

The theory of information foraging is more concerned with the evolution of search activities. There is an analogy between humans looking for information and animals looking for food in the nature. The best foragers are able to maximize the rate of valuable information acquired per unit cost. According to Pirolli and Card (1999), the task environment of information foraging presents a "patch" structure. Information is located in patches, and foragers assess the value of a patch in virtue of information scent, the perception of the patch gained from proximal cues.

In order to improve their efficiency in information foraging, people may try to lower the average costs of moving between the patches or increase the benefits of information acquisition in the current patch.

Important Efforts to Define Exploratory Search

Evolving search and information foraging emphasize the influences of environmental changes on users' search directions, whereas interactive information retrieval and cognitive information retrieval believe that users' subjective characteristics and the interaction objects (i.e. system or information) can affect each other given a specific search goal. These theories all play their roles in shaping the understanding of exploratory search by considering users' physical and mental functions in search. More recently, White and Roth (2009, p. 6) provided a more comprehensive definition of the concept that is twofold: exploratory search "can be used to describe an information-seeking problem context that is open-ended, persistent, and multi-faceted; and to describe information seeking processes that are opportunistic, iterative, and multi-tactical."The two aspects are not separable since the resolution of complex or vague information problems will definitely rely on non-linear search processes.

The Problem Context

Humans search because they realize the occurrence of information problems. In order to keep their lives and work running smoothly, they must deal with various tasks everyday, which provides the problem contexts for their search activities (Ingwersen and Järvelin 2005). Byström and Hansen (2005), Kim and Soergel (2005), and Li (2009), etc. have created different task classification frameworks. Tasks can be characterized based on many dimensions, but there are three essential and general ones, i.e. the specificity, volume, and timeliness of task goals (Marchionini 1995).

A highly specific task leads to the search of single facts, and users have the confidence to determine their validity. An unspecific task instead aims to engender interpretations or viewpoints, but users will be less certain about achieving their goals. Volume is reversely related to specificity. While a fact may be of low volume, containing merely a name, a number, or an image, interpretations or viewpoints usually need to be extracted from one or more documents. Timeliness refers to the expected time to acquire an answer. This can be as short as a moment or a few minutes, or as long as hours, days, or even months (Marchionini 1995).

In Marchionini (2006), exploratory tasks were distinguished from lookup tasks. The latter, also the basic kind of search tasks, involve discrete and well-structured information problems. That is, specific and finite search goals are immediately attainable. The former however become increasingly pervasive as both people's needs

Exploratory Search: A Critical Analysis of the Theoretical Foundations ...

and Web resources diversify. The seeking of information induced by ill-structured information problems is usually interwoven with learning or investigation. Searches that support learning or investigation aim to achieve the higher levels in Bloom's taxonomy of educational objectives.

The Search Process

A search process takes place within a particular problem context, and Wilson (1999) divided it into four stages: problem identification, problem definition, problem resolution, and solution statement. The transition from one stage to the next is always accompanied by the remarkable decrease of uncertainty. Uncertainty, a negative cognitive factor commonly seen in information seeking, will give rise to such affections as anxiety and lack of confidence (Kuhlthau 1999). In his communication theories, Shannon said that the more information people received, the lower their uncertainty. But in information science, it was thought that new information might sometimes result in the rebound of uncertainty especially during the earlier stages of the search process (Kalbach 2008).

The uncertainty aroused by exploratory problem context may fluctuate more evidently. Such fluctuation tends to ease as time progresses, with uncertainty decreasing meanwhile. But under some special circumstances, e.g. the search becoming more extensive and/or complex, it is possible that uncertainty will continue to fluctuate or even increase (White and Roth 2009). This can happen during any stage of the search process, and users will have to return to the previous stage so as to lessen the uncertainty again. As a result, an exploratory search process is made up of the four successive stages and the three feedback loops.

User behavior, unlike uncertainty, is the tangible and measurable variable in the search process. Wilson (1997), Choo et al. (2000), and Bates (2002) have investigated various information seeking modes. It is agreed that querying and browsing are the two basic active modes, i.e. users consciously investing time and energy to acquire information. While querying demands humans to recall from memory appropriate words to represent their information needs, browsing utilizes their perceptual abilities to recognize relevant information to their needs from the context (Marchionini 1995). The exploratory search process is characteristic of the alternation and iteration of the two modes (Marchionini 2006).

Theoretical Foundations of Exploratory Search Illustrated

Following the twofold definition of exploratory search, this study created two illustrations especially to ensure an easier and better understanding of the exploratory problem context and the exploratory search process. They will be further interpreted as follows.

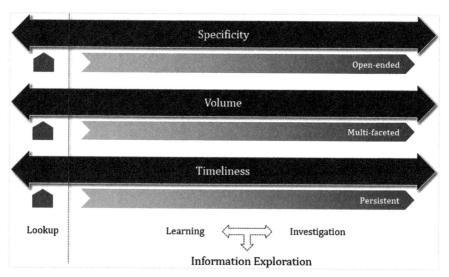

Fig. 1 The exploratory problem context model

Figure 1 represents each of Marchionini's (1995) dimensions of tasks, i.e. unspecificity, volume, and timeliness, with a continuum. With lookup problems being situated at the left ends on all three continua, exploratory problems occupy the remaining ranges. The less structured a problem is, the more cognitive resources users will have to invest, and the more closely the problem will approach the right ends on the continua where the characteristics of "open-ended", "multi-faceted", and "persistent" become the most significant.

Learning and investigation present two different levels of information exploration. Learning search is about accumulating existing knowledge on a certain topic or domain. What users anticipate are interpretive answers that help eliminate the unknown. The large volume of information objects they obtain can include texts, images, audios, and videos, etc. Some of these may verify or complement each other, but some may contradict or oppose each other. Users need to spend extra time viewing, comparing, and judging them therefore. Such internal cognitive processing activities will conduce towards a more solid human knowledge base. Investigative search, furthermore, is about creating new knowledge. Based on the analysis, synthesis, and assessment of the valuable contents extracted from information objects, users are capable of making intelligent decisions, planning, and predictions. This is a more advanced type of cognitive processing activity that usually lasts for a longer time and largely relies on users' current knowledge state to elicit evaluative answers embodying their own viewpoints.

In Fig. 2 a model of exploratory search process is presented. It adopts Wilson's (1999) four stages of the search process and integrates them with the behavioral characteristics of exploratory search. From the preliminary identification to sufficient definition of an information problem, users to a great extent rely on heuristic

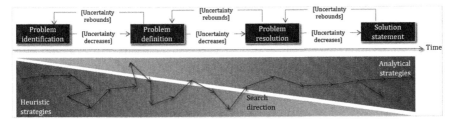

Fig. 2 The exploratory search process model

strategies in which browsing dominates. They navigate to potentially valuable collections of information and locate relevant concepts in the content via rapid scanning. It is important that they relate the concepts to one another to further clarify the core information need. When seeking answers to the problem, users instead adopt more frequently analytical strategies in which querying dominates. They decompose the information need into several parts that are more manageable and translate those parts into parallel or sequential queries. With the feedback from search systems users will gain a better understanding of the relevant concepts, which enables them to formulate more accurate queries and obtain more satisfying answers.

It should be noted that tentative querying before browsing is a component of heuristic strategies and targeted browsing after querying is a component of analytical strategies. Browsing is driven by external information, which gives users the opportunity to encounter new concepts of interest. The encountering will conduce to the generation of new needs and guide their searches to new directions. Internally driven querying seldom brings about an obvious change of the search direction. Nevertheless if a query returns no result, a new problem may be discovered. As a whole, users will proceed along an unpredictable non-linear path during the exploratory search process.

A Survey of Exploratory Search Systems

Thanks to the increasingly solid theoretical foundations, various exploratory search systems have been built to provide new technological capabilities and interface paradigms that facilitate the user-system interaction to improve the efficiency of querying and browsing (White et al. 2008). The support for query formulation and reformulation, in fact, is also very common in general search systems, such as query suggestion and expansion tools (Croft et al. 2010). However the support for search result browsing is exclusive in exploratory search systems. Existing systems have been trying to enhance users' abilities to understand and control massive result collections through information classification and visualization (White and Roth 2009).

Information Classification for Exploratory Search

As we know, mainstream Web search engines value precision, especially the high relevance of the results on the first search result page. Differently, exploratory search systems pay more attention to recall because the lower-ranking pages may also contain useful information (Marchionini 2006). It is thus necessary to relieve users' browsing burden when they navigate through each page. Exploratory search systems have introduced a variety of methods to classify search results for this purpose. With many results divided into a few groups, users are more able to identify the key information (Jiang and Koshman 2008).

Classification is a process that involves "systematic arrangement of entities based on analysis of the set of individually necessary and jointly sufficient characteristics that defines each class" (Jacob 2004). This study conducted a comprehensive survey on the result classification methods employed by exploratory search systems, including fully functional systems that are/were available to ordinary users as well as prototype systems mentioned in the literature. As indicated by the survey, there are four major ways to decrease the density of the result space, i.e. hierarchical classification, faceted classification, dynamic clustering, and social classification.

Hierarchical Classification

Hierarchical classification refers to a system of fixed non-overlapping classes within a hierarchical enumerative structure to exactly reflect a pre-determined ordering of reality. It results from the top-down division of the information space according to some "logic" (Taylor and Wynar 2004). The parent-child relationships between superordinate and subordinate classes are usually presented in trees. The use of general hierarchical classification systems, e.g. Dewey Decimal Classification and Library of Congress Classification, to arrange library resources can be traced back to the 19th century. Nowadays, Yahoo! Directory and Open Directory Project are the two most widely known hierarchical classification systems for Web resources. They are compiled and maintained by experts and users respectively.

Hierarchical classification has been used to organize search results in several studies. Chen and Dumais (2000) developed an interface where webpages returned by the search engine were assigned into the classes of LookSmart, a Web directory, on the fly with text classification algorithms. They found that users were 50% more efficient at finding information on this category interface than on the list interface. CitiViz was a visual search interface that displayed an overview of the document sets in a digital library based on the ACMComputing Classification System. Its effectiveness exceeded the traditional list in various exploratory tasks (Kampanya et al. 2004). Besides, hierarchical classification can help improve the internal search of websites. For instance, the website of UC Berkeley once introduced the Cha-Cha system that showed within-site search results in its own hierarchical sitemap (Chen et al. 1999). Another similar example is the WebTOC system by the HCI Lab at the University of Maryland (Nation 1998).

These are early attempts to create exploratory search systems and they have a common preference for hierarchical classification to enhance search result organization. Provided with a familiar and stable hierarchical classification, users are able to establish their mental models about the whole result space rapidly and to see their positions in the space. On the one hand, their familiarity with the classification system can reduce the difficulties in grasping the system. On the other hand, the stableness of the classification system can lessen their anxiety in the search process. Nevertheless it is not easy to make efficient use of hierarchical classification in result organization. One thing to consider is how to balance the breadth and depth of the hierarchy. Also the problem of polyhierarchy (i.e. an item falling into two different categories at the same time) needs to be addressed (Morville and Rosenfeld 2006).

Faceted Classification

Faceted classification, simply speaking, is composed of several facets and a number of categories under each facet (Tunkelang 2009).The facet corresponds to an attribute of the information collection and the categories contained represent various values of that attribute (Hearst 2006). As early as the 1960s, Ranganathan (1960) introduced the notion "facet" to library and information science. In his Colon Classification Scheme, the five fundamental facets are personality, matter, energy, space, and time. But in most cases facets are created for particular domains, such as the author, language, and year of a book, or the price, brand, and size of a laptop.

Flamenco (Hearst 2006), mSpace (Schraefel et al. 2005), and Relation Browser (Capra and Marchionini 2008) are pioneer studies which applied faceted classification in search. These prototype systems, though different in terms of information type and interface design, all provide a set of small categorical hierarchies instead of one large cover-all topical hierarchy. Users are allowed to browse the hierarchies one by one and select the most appropriate category in each, which enables them to narrow down the search scope gradually. Related user studies showed that faceted classification was easy to understand, and many searchers preferred this approach for it avoided empty results and supported exploration and discovery (Yee et al. 2003).

We can find faceted classification in a wide variety of search environments. On E-commerce platforms, both C2 C (e.g. eBay and Taobao) and B2 C (e.g. Overstock and Bestbuy), faceted search are making full use of products' structured metadata to improve their find ability, producing great business value (Dash et al. 2008). In addition, next-generation library catalogs are now featuring faceted search. Many university libraries, such as those of Duke University, Harvard University, and the University of Pittsburgh, depend on discovery service providers (e.g. Endeca, AquaBrowser, and Summon) to offer faceted browsing experience to their patrons (Yang and Wagner 2010).

By taking multiple conceptual dimensions into consideration, faceted classification better satisfies different users who view the world differently. It is an effective way to cope with the challenges in information organization brought about by compound concepts. And faceted search is in essence a form of exploratory search. After the search results are mapped onto a faceted classification system, users can look into them in a more flexible manner, i.e. examining any number of facets in any order. If combining the labels of all the categories ever selected, one can see a complex Boolean query. This approach favors recognition over recall to alleviate human mental work. Thanks to the logical and predictable structure of faceted classification, faceted search systems will become the prevailing search tools in electronic environments.

Dynamic Clustering

The basic idea of clustering is grouping information items by algorithms so that the items within one group are similar or relevant and different groups are obviously distinct (Manning et al. 2008). Since van Rijsbergen's (1979) Cluster Hypothesis – "closely associated documents tend to be relevant to the same request", more and more researchers in the area of information retrieval deemed clustering the retrieved documents into groups with common subjects a natural alternative to ranking them in a linear list (Croft and Leouski 1996).

Vivisimo Enterprise Search was among the first clustering search systems in practice. It was characteristic of post-retrieval clustering, a three-step process: (1) generating the clustering structure based on the content of the search results; (2) inserting the result items into appropriate categories in the structure; and (3) selecting and preparing the categories to be presented to users (Koshman et al. 2006). Clusty (now Yippy), one of the most influential clustering search engines on the Web, was built upon the technical support of Vivisimo. Other leading systems include iBoogie, PolyMeta, and Carrot2, etc., but some early systems, such as Grokker, KartOO, WebClust, and Mooter, have been shut down for various reasons. These systems mostly perform clustering on the top search results and their clustering structures can be single-level or multi-level (Jiang and Koshman 2008).

The usability of a clustering structure is largely determined by the quality of category label. Carpineto et al. (2009) divided clustering algorithms according to their category description methods into three types, i.e. data-centric, description-aware, and description-centric. Clustering search engines often adopt the description-centric algorithms. They emphasize that the descriptions of category labels should be simple and clear and that undescribable categories should be removed for being of little value to users. In general, clustering search engines will also support metasearch. More specifically, they obtain and aggregate search results from Google, Bing, and other Web search engines via API and instead focus on the clustering work. Metasaearch compensates for the limited scope of a single search engine index, which helps users achieve the comprehensive examination of search results on a uniform interface (Morville and Callender 2010).

Clustering technologies are of great significance to exploratory search. The best of clustering is that the classification structure is automatically generated for the current situation. Dynamic classification gets rid of the complexity and cost of building and maintaining a fixed scheme. In addition to providing users a convenient way to view the results under specific topics, clustering solves the problem of polysemy. The results are differentiated according to their meanings, facilitating users to make selective browsing. Furthermore, clustering gathers the related results that originally scatter on different search result pages. With all the important topics surfacing at once, users can review the whole result space in a more systematic manner.

Social Classification

Social classification, also known as folksonomy, is made up of people-contributed free tags and takes the form of a flat and loose namespace (Kroski 2005). This type of classification is firstly seen in social tagging systems where users assign tags to resources for the purpose of self-organization (Smith 2007). Depending on the tagging privilege, it can be narrow or broad (Golder and Huberman 2006). Flickr, Vimeo, Reddit, and LiveJournal etc. are representative social tagging systems featuring narrow folksonomies, while BibSonomy, Folkd, LibraryThing, and Douban etc. broad folksonomies. In these systems, users tend to explore the resources that have already been tagged by others (Millen and Feinberg 2006). Usually, users who are accustomed to discovering resources by tag are active tag contributors. Since tags express explicit topics, they can increase the directedness of the browsing process as intermediaries (Jiang 2013).

Amazon, a diversified E-commerce platform, has introduced product tagging. When looking for products, customers may conduct tag search, i.e. the query being recognized as a tag. All the products to which the tag has been assigned will be returned, and the suggestions of relevant tags allow users to refine the results further. In Amazon, social classification is independent of the existing hierarchical departments of products. Similarly, the libraries of the University of Pennsylvania and the University of Michigan also have complemented their traditional hierarchical classification of book resources with social classification, engendering the PennTags and Mtagger systems respectively (Pirmann 2012).

As a basic classification method on the Web 2.0 and a supplemental method on the Web 1.0, social classification shows potential in exploratory search for being inexpensive to create and responsive to changes. Tagging is essentially an individual activity because people tag according to their personal understanding and in a distributed manner. However the social aspect of tagging consists in the fact that tags are aggregated by the system. At the micro level, the bibliographic record of each resource is composed of the tags ever attached to it; and at the macro level, all the tags from all the users constitute a classification system. When users tag a resource, they not only facilitate their own future retrieval of the resource, but also create a path for others to find it.

Information Visualization for Exploratory Search

Many exploratory search systems provide visualization tools to aid the presentation of search results after they are classified or grouped. Simply speaking, visualization is showing abstract information with intuitive graphs. There are three elements in Spence's (2007) visualization process model: representation, presentation, and interaction. Visualizations represent data values and relations in various forms, present them in constrained spaces, and allow users to select the required view via interaction. Since interaction is in the control of users, their perception and cognition have a strong impact on the effectiveness of visualizations (Tory and Moller 2004). Human's perceptual system is responsible for importing the representations, and cognitive system adding meaning to them and storing the consequent understanding in memory (Spence 2001).

As Koshman (2006, p. 20) pointed out, "the notion of visualization supporting exploratory search can be an extremely powerful model that applies the high bandwidth of human perceptual processing to reduce or mediate uncertainty surrounding initial queries and to see new relationships among the retrieved data set that would not be present in a traditional linear search result listing." It was noticed in the survey of exploratory search systems that each of the above ways of search result classification had aroused some interest in the design and development of corresponding visualizations.

Visualizations for Hierarchical Classification

Given its inherent structural traits, hierarchical classification is often associated with the tree visualization. A representative example is the CitiViz search interface already mentioned (Fox et al. 2006). In addition to an expandable tree list (Fig. 3 left), it introduced a hyperbolic tree (Fig. 3 upper right) and a 2D scatter plot (Fig. 3 middle right). Hyperbolic trees are generated by misshaping the original tree structure. The distortion will enlarge the branches of interest with more details and meanwhile shrink the adjacent branches to occupy less space, supporting the "focus+context" display (Lamping et al. 1995). This hyperbolic tree consists of rectangle nodes and bubbles attached to them. They respectively represent subject categories and the result document sets falling into the categories. A single click on a node will bring it from context to focus smoothly. The size of each bubble is proportional to the quantity of documents in it. When a bubble is selected, the documents contained will map onto the scatter plot where the x-axis is rank and the y-axis date. The towers on the scatterplot stand for individual documents with the layer colors indicating the subject categories which the documents belong to. CitiViz color-coded the topical categories and used the coding system to connect three different visualization views. It not only catered to different users' perceptual habits but also reinforced their understanding with multiple levels of details.

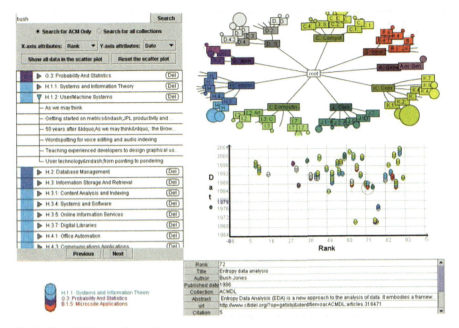

Fig. 3 The CitiViz search interface

Also worth mentioning is ResultMap designed by Clarkson et al. (2009), a search tool based on the treemap visualization. Treemaps transform tree structures into recursively nested rectangle zones, making good use of space. Each rectangle is filled with smaller rectangles, indicating the parent-child relationships. The area of a rectangle is often in proportion to the value of a particular attribute describing the dataset (Shneiderman and Wattenberg 2001). As shown in Fig. 4, Result Map demonstrated all the documents in a knowledge repository on a treemap according to their hierarchical relationships and ensured a stable expression of the entire information space. The result documents returned by each query will be highlighted on the treemap and the colors suggested their types so that users can access the details of the documents. The treemap appears on every search result page, right beside the result list. In particular, mouse hover on a certain rectangle will change the display of related results in the list and vice versa. The interaction between the visual and textual presentations is therefore made possible.

Visualizations for Faceted Classification

Most faceted search systems, strictly speaking, are actually text-based. For example, Flamenco just distinguished the facets with colors. It is perhaps because the textual interfaces are already easy to understand and use, not much energy

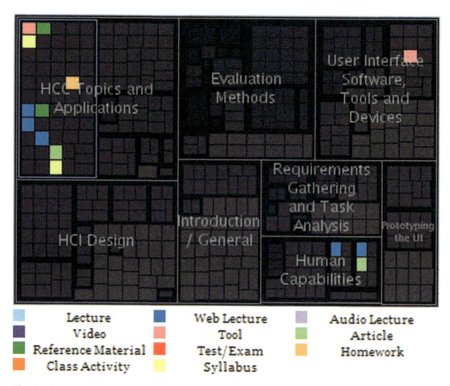

Fig. 4 The result maptreemap visualization

has been devoted to developing visualizations for faceted classification. The most remarkable attempt so far should be FacetMap by Smith et al. (2006). This purely graphic system employed round-cornered rectangles and ovals to represent facets and their categories respectively, as seen in Fig. 5a. More frequently used facets will appear larger on the screen with more categories exposed, but all the ovals are of the same size with the exact numbers of items contained provided under the category labels. Users can easily drill down to the information items at the lowest level by selecting relevant facets, categories, and sub-categories along the way (Fig. 5b). In fact FacetMap realized the "overview+detail" display that was different from distortion. When a facet is enlarged to show more details through semantic zooming, other facets are excluded from the limited screen. Users may lose the control of interaction and even feel disoriented (Heo and Hirtle 2001).

Visualizations for Dynamic Clustering

Unlikely, visualizations are a common component of clustering search systems. Although text-based tree lists are widely used, visualizations are able to reveal

Exploratory Search: A Critical Analysis of the Theoretical Foundations ... 93

Fig. 5 The FacetMap visualization for faceted search. (**a**) The overview. (**b**) A low-level view

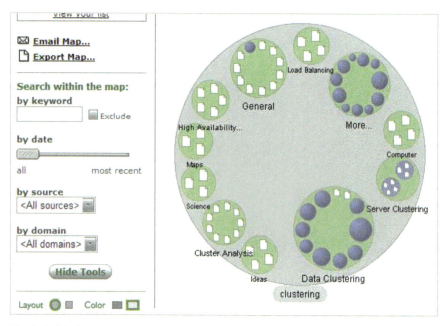

Fig. 6 Grokker's map view

the relationships between clusters and items more efficiently for possessing richer spatial attributes. The abovementioned Grokker, KartOO, and Carrot2 have developed interactive 2D visualizations that facilitated the examination of search results (Koshman 2006; Kothari 2010). Grokker's map view (Fig. 6) followed the "overview+detail" display to show the nesting of categories (green circles), subcategories (blue circles), and result items (white page icons), and users were supported to move forward or trace back level by level. KartOO positioned result items (yellow document icons) within the same cluster on a cartographic map (Fig. 7). One can see the connections between adjacent items, and the labels in between indicate the subject they share. Carrot2 offers two visualization views, i.e. Circles (Fig. 8a) and Foam Tree (Fig. 8b), which differ in shape. The colored zones representing the clusters are arranged by cluster size.

3D approaches involving real-world metaphors have been proposed to visualize clustered results. Figure 9 shows a prototype visualization module that presents the search results from Carrot2 in a new way (Akhavi et al. 2007). The algorithm traverses the original clustering hierarchy and transforms the clusters into tree branches and result items fruits in a 3D space. Bonnel et al. (2006), innovatively, used the metaphor of cities. Result items are visualized as buildings, with the neighboring districts standing for related topics (Fig. 10). Building height suggests result relevance and building surface is filled with the page snapshot of the result. 3D visualizations, however, were thought to be ineffective because the third dimension could inhibit users and make the interface more confusing (Risden et al. 2000).

Fig. 7 KartOO' cartographic map

What's more, displaying 3D visualizations on 2D devices is in itself problematic (Modjeska 2000).

Visualizations for Social Classification

The tag cloud visualization came into being to address the structural looseness of social classification. It is a text-based visualization method that displays the tags in alphabetical order and indicates their frequencies with font size. Most tag clouds only include the most active tags for they reflect the popular topics people are concerned with recently (Sinclair and Cardew-Hall 2008). One will be redirected to all the resources associated with a specific tag by a simple click on that tag; and sometimes, the click may also lead to the users who have added the tag and/or other co-assigned tags. The insufficiencies of the tag cloud are also obvious, and a major one is that semantically related tags may scatter in the cloud because they are not alphabetically close. The efficiency of a cloud will be greatly influenced when it reaches a certain scale. It is difficult for users to quickly identify the most useful ones from tens of thousands of tags (Hearst and Rosner 2008).

Researchers have been improving tag clouds. In Hassan-Montero and Herrero-Solana (2006), insignificant tags (e.g. "toread" and "diy") were removed from the cloud and synonymies were merged to make space for more substantial tags (e.g. "philosophy" and "religion"). After lowering the semantic density, the researchers

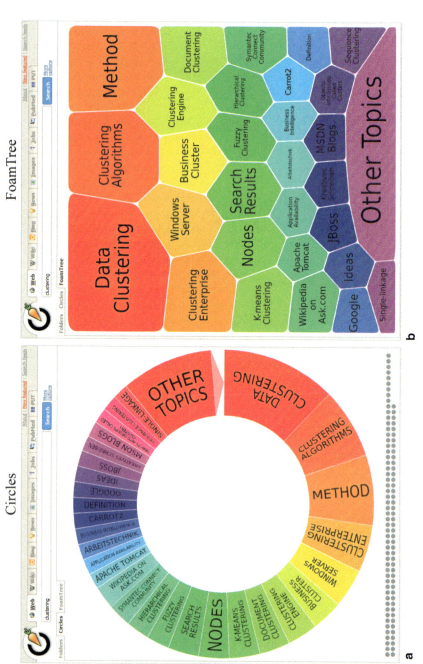

Fig. 8 Carrot2's visualization views. (**a**) Circles. (**b**) FoamTree

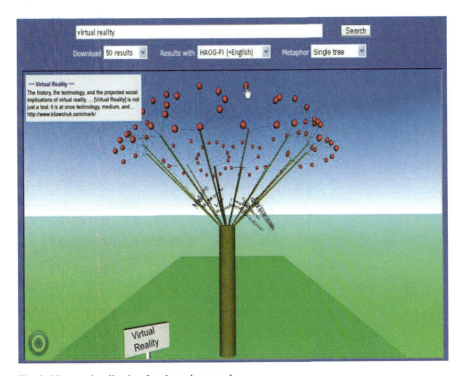

Fig. 9 3D tree visualization for clustering search

changed the layout of the tag cloud with clustering algorithms: frequently co-occurrent tags appear on the same row (Fig. 11). This is conducive to topic differentiation and knowledge discovery. Chen et al. (2010) created the TagClusters visualization, a tag cloud variation based on tag clustering. In this brand new view (Fig. 12), tags are no longer displayed in rows; instead, their relative positions are determined by co-occurrence. Semantically related tags determined by text analysis will form a tag group as represented with the translucent pink zone. The name of a group, i.e. the purple uppercase label, is in proportion to the total frequencies of all the tags in that group. A tag group may further contain sub-groups, and different sub-groups can overlap. This view facilitates users to understand the affiliations and associations between tags.

The Future of Exploratory Search

There is no denying that the technological development in information classification and visualization is an impetus to exploratory search systems. A handful of researchers however have recognized that the future of exploratory search lied in

HOME
< BACK
NEXT >
CityViewer
Query
orange
SEARCH
Specific actions
none
Descriptive words
100
http://www.orange-entreprises.com/
http://www.orangecaraibe.com/
http://orangefilmcourt.orange.fr/

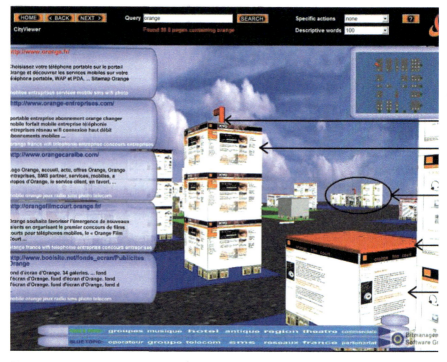

Fig. 10 3D city visualization for clustering search

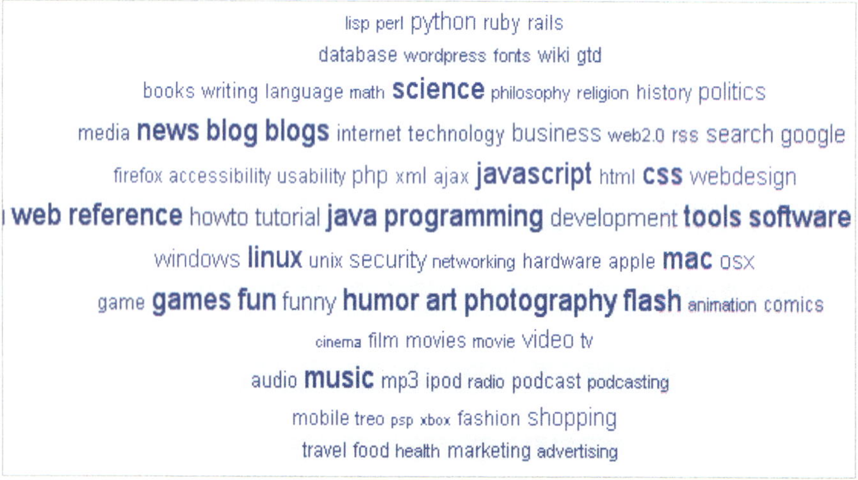

lisp perl python ruby rails
database wordpress fonts wiki gtd
books writing language math science philosophy religion history politics
media news blog blogs internet technology business web2.0 rss search google
firefox accessibility usability php xml ajax javascript html css webdesign
web reference howto tutorial java programming development tools software
windows linux unix security networking hardware apple mac osx
game games fun funny humor art photography flash animation comics
cinema film movies movie video tv
audio music mp3 ipod radio podcast podcasting
mobile treo psp xbox fashion shopping
travel food health marketing advertising

Fig. 11 A clustering-based tag cloud

Fig. 12 TagClusters

the vast social space. Evans and Chi (2008) found based on a survey of 150 participants that interpersonal communication played an indispensable role throughout the entire search process, including the pre-search problem statement, information collecting and selecting, and post-search result sharing. In Kammerer et al. (2009), tag data from a social bookmarking site was added to search results and user feedback was used to further improve the relevance of result listings. The experiment suggested that exploration of new knowledge in ill-structured domains could be effectively supported in this way.

Social interaction, both explicit and implicit, will become a core component of exploratory search in the near future. People are not separated from one another during information seeking. They may acquire information from others out of various reasons, and such tendency can be very strong (Chi 2009). Morville and Rosenfeld (2006) also deemed seeking help from others an information seeking mode as important as querying and browsing. In existing exploratory search systems, nevertheless, users are still independent searchers in the traditional sense even though their exploration activities have become more effective with system-offered informational clues.

In the Web 2.0 era, the growth of social software has brought about wider and more frequent communication and sharing of information. People's everyday information seeking is inevitably mixed with their social interaction, which will create new possibilities for exploratory search systems. One the one hand, human-to-human conversations are beneficial to lowering vocabulary barriers. Querying in more natural ways will reduce users' cognitive loads. On the other hand, the "collective intelligence" of many individuals can produce social clues. In other words, new comers may follow the trails of actions left by previous users to identify appropriate browsing paths already taken by the majority. Svensson (1998) distinguished these two types of social interaction as direct and indirect social navigation.

Navigation is searching without a clear goal, and social navigation is navigation guided by human beings (Svensson 2002). Direct social navigation means that navigators seek personalized advice from others through two-way communication. In this way they may not only find the answers to such basic questions as "where am I", but also stand a chance of clarifying their goals and choosing a correct path towards the destination. Indirect social navigation, in contrast, features one-way communication in which advice givers provide guidance to navigators unintentionally. This takes the form of "cumulative information", a dynamic concept. People entering and occupying the information space break its original design and influence its growth, just like that the regularly walked track in the forest becomes a road (Svensson 1998).

In the early days social navigation support systems were mostly history-enriched environments on the basis of indirect social navigation. The rise of social software since 2005 provides a promising setting of research. Millen and Feinberg (2006) found in a study on the social bookmarking service dogear that viewing others' bookmark collections and clicking on tags to view the associated bookmarks were the commonest forms of social navigation. Vosinakis and Papadakis (2011) integrated spatial, semantic, and social navigation in the 3D environments of virtual worlds. The prototype framework they proposed included thematic discussions, user trails and tags, semantic filters, linked data and other features. Shami (2011) designed a social file sharing system, Cattail. It supported social navigation through a recent events stream and downloading history sharing. System evaluation results implied that Cattail could help users discover more relevant people and content.

In summary, the existing research on exploratory search has been focusing on individual users' search activities, ignoring the significance of social support to information exploration. There is a natural trend that social navigation research merges into this area. We may gain a great deal of enlightenment from the findings on both direct and indirect social navigation. The boom of social software, at the same time, increases the feasibility of realizing social interaction in exploratory search. Others' advice or activities usually have a strong impact on people's informational decisions. The interest in social interaction will diversify future research on exploratory search.

Open Access This chapter is distributed under the terms of the Creative Commons Attribution Noncommercial License, which permits any noncommercial use, distribution, and reproduction in any medium, provided the original author(s) and source are credited.

References

Akhavi MS, Rahmati M, Amini NN (August 2007). 3d visualization of hierarchical clustered web search results. In Computer Graphics, Imaging and Visualisation, 2007. CGIV'07. IEEE. pp 441–446

Bates MJ (1989) The design of browsing and berrypicking techniques for the online search interface. Online Inf Rev 13(5):407–424

Bates MJ (2002) Toward an integrated model of information seeking and searching. New Rev Inf Behav Res 3:1–15

Belkin NJ (1996) Intelligent information retrieval: whose intelligence. ISI 96:25–31

Bonnel N, Lemaire V, Alexandre CH, Morin A (2006, February) Effective organization and visualization of web search results. In IASTED International Conference on Internet and Multimedia Systems and Applications (EuroIMSA'06). pp 209–216

Byström K, Hansen P (2005) Conceptual framework for tasks in information studies. J Am Soc Inf Sci Technol 56(10):1050–1061

Capra RG, Marchionini G (2008, June) The relation browser tool for faceted exploratory search. In Proceedings of the 8th ACM/IEEE-CS joint conference on Digital libraries. ACM. pp 420–420

Carpineto C, Osiński S, Romano G, Weiss D (2009) A survey of web clustering engines. ACM Comput Surv (CSUR) 41(3):17

Chen H, Dumais S (2000, April) Bringing order to the web: automatically categorizing search results. In Proceedings of the SIGCHI conference on Human factors in computing systems. ACM. pp 145–152

Chen M, Hearst M, Hong J, Lin J (1999) Cha-Cha: a system for organizing intranet search results. In Proceedings of the 2nd USENIX Symposium on Internet Technologies and Systems pp 1–14

Chen YX, Santamaría R, Butz A, Therón R (2010) TagClusters: Enhancing semantic understanding of collaborative tags. Int J Creat Interfaces Comput Graph (IJCICG) 1(2):15–28

Chi EH (2009) Information seeking can be social. Computer 42(3):42–46

Choo CW, Detlor B, Turnbull D (2000) Information seeking on the web: an integrated model of browsing and searching. First Monday 5(2)

Clarkson E, Desai K, Foley J (2009) Resultmaps: visualization for search interfaces. Vis Compu Graph IEEE Trans 15(6):1057–1064

Croft WB, Leouski AV (1996) An evaluation of techniques for clustering search results. Computer Science Department Faculty Publication Series, 36

Croft WB, Metzler D, Strohman T (2010) Search engines: information retrieval in practice. Reading, Addison-Wesley, p 283

Dash D, Rao J, Megiddo N, Ailamaki A, Lohman G (2008, October) Dynamic faceted search for discovery-driven analysis. In Proceedings of the 17th ACM conference on Information and knowledge management. ACM. pp 3–12

Evans BM, Chi EH (2008, November) Towards a model of understanding social search. In Proceedings of the 2008 ACM conference on Computer supported cooperative work. ACM. pp 485–494

Fox EA, Neves FD, Yu X, Shen R, Kim S, Fan W (2006) Exploring the computing literature with visualization and stepping stones pathways. Commun ACM 49(4):52–58

Golder SA, Huberman BA (2006) Usage patterns of collaborative tagging systems. J Inf Sci 32(2):198–208

Hassan-Montero Y, Herrero-Solana V (2006, October) Improving tag-clouds as visual information retrieval interfaces. In International Conference on Multidisciplinary Information Sciences and Technologies, pp 25–28

Hearst MA (2006) Clustering versus faceted categories for information exploration. Commun ACM 49(4):59–61

Hearst MA, Rosner D (2008, January) Tag clouds: data analysis tool or social signaller? In Hawaii International Conference on System Sciences, Proceedings of the 41st Annual. IEEE. pp 160–160

Heo M, Hirtle SC (2001) An empirical comparison of visualization tools to assist information retrieval on the Web. J Am Soc Inf Sci Technol 52(8):666–675

Ingwersen P (1996) Cognitive perspectives of information retrieval interaction: elements of a cognitive IR theory. J Doc 52(1):3–50

Ingwersen P, Järvelin K (2005) The turn: integration of information seeking and retrieval in context, vol 18. Springer

Jacob EK (2004) Classification and categorization: a difference that makes a difference. Libr Trends 52(3):515–540

Jiang T (2013) An exploratory study on social library system users' information seeking modes. J Doc 69(1):6–26

Jiang T, Koshman S (2008) Exploratory search in different information architectures. Bull Am Soc Inf Sci Technol 34(6):11–13

Kalbach J (2008) On uncertainty in information architecture. J Inf Archit 1(1):48–56

Kammerer Y, Nairn R, Pirolli P, Chi EH (2009, April) Signpost from the masses: learning effects in an exploratory social tag search browser. In Proceedings of the SIGCHI conference on human factors in computing systems. ACM. pp 625–634

Kampanya N, Shen R, Kim S, North C, Fox EA (2004) CitiViz: a visual user interface to the CITIDEL system. In research and advanced technology for digital libraries. Springer, Berlin, pp 122–133

Kim S, Soergel D (2005) Selecting and measuring task characteristics as independent variables. Proc Am Soc Inf Sci Technol 42(1)

Koshman S (2006) Exploratory search visualization: identifying factors affecting evaluation. EESS 2006, 20

Koshman S (2006) Visualization-based information retrieval on the web. Libr Inf Sci Res 28(2):192–207

Koshman S, Spink A, Jansen BJ (2006) Web searching on the vivisimo search engine. J Am Soc Inf Sci Technol 57(14):1875–1887

Kothari SS (2010) Evaluating the efficacy of clustered visualization in exploratory search tasks. Purdue University, West Lafayette, Indiana

Kroski E (2005) The hive mind: Folksonomies and user-based tagging. Library 2:91–103

Kuhlthau CC (1999) The role of experience in the information search process of an early career information worker: perceptions of uncertainty, complexity construction, and sources. J Am Soc Inf Sci 50(5):399–412

Lamping J, Rao R, Pirolli P (1995, May) A focus+ context technique based on hyperbolic geometry for visualizing large hierarchies. In Proceedings of the SIGCHI conference on Human factors in computing systems. ACM Press/Addison-Wesley Publishing Co., pp 401–408

Li Y (2009) Exploring the relationships between work task and search task in information search. J Am Soc Inf Sci Technol 60(2):275–291

Manning CD, Raghavan P, Schütze H (2008) Introduction to information retrieval, vol 1. Cambridge University Press, Cambridge

Marchionini G (1995) Information seeking in electronic environments. Cambridge University Press, Cambridge

Marchionini G (2006) Exploratory search: from finding to understanding. Commun ACM 49(4):41–46

Millen DR, Feinberg J (2006, June) Using social tagging to improve social navigation. In Workshop on the Social Navigation and Community based Adaptation Technologies

Modjeska DK (2000) Hierarchical data visualization in desktop virtual reality (Doctoral dissertation, University of Toronto)

Morville P, Callender J (2010) Search patterns. O'Reilly

Morville P, Rosenfeld L (2006) Information architecture for the World Wide Web: designing large-scale web sites. O'Reilly Media

Nation DA (1998, April) WebTOC: a tool to visualize and quantify Web sites using a hierarchical table of contents browser. In CHI 98 Cconference Summary on Human Factors in Computing Systems. ACM. pp 185–186

Nolan M (2008) Exploring exploratory search. Bull Am Soc Inf Sci Technol 34(4):38–41

Pirmann C (2012) Tags in the catalogue: insights from a usability study of librarything for libraries. Libr Trends 61(1):234–247

Pirolli P, Card S (1999) Information foraging. Psychol Rev 106(4):643–675

Ranganathan SR (1960) Colon classification: basic classification, 6th edn. Asia Publishing House, New York

Risden K, Czerwinski MP, Munzner T, Cook DB (2000) Initial examination of ease of use for 2D and 3D information visualization of Web content. Int J Hum-Comput Stud 53(5):695–714

Saracevic T (1996) Modeling interaction in information retrieval (IR): a review and proposal. In Proceedings of the ASIS annual meeting, vol 33. pp 3–9

Saracevic T (1997, January) The stratified model of information retrieval interaction: extension and applications. In Proceedings of the ASIS annual meeting, vol 34. pp 313–327

Schraefel MC, Alex D, Smith E, Russel A, Owens A, Harris C, Wilson M (2005) The mSpace classical music explorer: improving access to classical music for real people. In MusicNetwork Open Workshop, Integration of Music in Multimedia Applications

Shami NS, Muller M, Millen D (2011) Browse and discover: social file sharing in the enterprise. In Proceeding of the ACM 2011 Conference on Computer Supported Cooperative Work, pp 295–304

Shneiderman B, Wattenberg M (2001, October) Ordered treemap layouts. In Proceedings of the IEEE Symposium on Information Visualization 2001, vol 73078

Sinclair J, Cardew-Hall M (2008) The folksonomy tag cloud: when is it useful? J Inf Sci 34(1):15–29

Smith G (2007) Tagging: people-powered metadata for the social web, safari. New Riders

Smith G, Czerwinski M, Meyers BR, Robertson G, Tan DS (2006) FacetMap: a scalable search and browse visualization. Vis Comput Graph IEEE Trans 12(5):797–804

Spence R (2001) Information visualization, 1st edn. Addison-Wesley

Spence R (2007) Information visualization: design for interaction, 2nd edn. Prentice Hall

Spink A (1997) Study of interactive feedback during mediated information retrieval. J Am Soc Inf Sci 48(5):382–394

Svensson M (1998) Social navigation, in Dahlback N. Exploring navigation: towards a framework for design and evaluation of navigationin electronic spaces. Swedish Institute of Computer Science, pp 73–88

Svensson M (2002) Defining, designing and evaluating social navigation (Doctoral dissertation, Stockholm University)

Taylor AG, Wynar BS (2004) Wynar's introduction to cataloging and classification. Libraries Unlimited Inc.

Tory M, Moller T (2004) Human factors in visualization research. IEEE Trans Vis Comput Graph 10(1):72–84

Tunkelang D (2009) Faceted search. Synth Lect Inf Concepts Retr Serv 1(1):1–80

van Rijsbergen CJ (1979) Information retrieval. Butterworths, London

Vosinakis S, Papadakis I (2011) Virtual worlds as information spaces: supporting semantic and social navigation in a shared 3D environment. In Proceedings of 3rd International Conference on Games and Virtual Worlds for Serious Applicants, pp. 220–227

White RW, Kules B, Bederson B (2005, December) Exploratory search interfaces: categorization, clustering and beyond: report on the XSI 2005 workshop at the Human-Computer Interaction Laboratory, University of Maryland. In ACM SIGIR Forum, vol 39, No. 2. ACM. pp 52–56

White RW, Marchionini G, Muresan G (2008) Evaluating exploratory search systems: introduction to special topic issue of information processing and management. Inf Proc Manag 44(2):433–436

White RW, Roth RA (2009) Exploratory search: beyond the query-response paradigm. Synth Lect Inf Concept Retr Serv 1(1):1–98

Wilson TD (1997) Information behaviour: an interdisciplinary perspective. Inf Process Manag 33(4):551–572

Wilson TD (1999) Models in information behaviour research. J Doc 55(3):249–270

Yang SQ, Wagner K (2010) Evaluating and comparing discovery tools: how close are we towards next generation catalog? Libr Hi Tech 28(4):690–709

Yee KP, Swearingen K, Li K, Hearst M (2003, April) Faceted metadata for image search and browsing. In Proceedings of the SIGCHI conference on Human factors in computing systems. ACM. pp 401–408

Part IV
Informatics

Scientific Datasets: Informetric Characteristics and Social Utility Metrics for Biodiversity Data Sources

Peter Ingwersen

Abstract The contribution places biodiversity datasets in relation to other central elements of the modern scientific communication system and defines quantitative analyses of metadata of such datasets as belonging to the intersection of Scientometrics and Webometrics. The analyses show that rank distributions of social utility evidence, such as search events and retrieved and viewed dataset records over a given range of datasets follow power law characteristics. A variety of dataset usage index (DUI) metrics is exemplified and illustrated by dataset indicators from three large, medium and small US and Danish dataset providers observed over a one-year period and compared to recent developments. Metrics discussed are of absolute as well as relative nature and include popularity, social attractiveness, and usage and interest impact scores.

Keywords Science communication · Biodiversity datasets · Webometric analysis · Social utility; Altmetrics · Dataset usage · Usage indicators · Rank distributions · Power law

Introduction

Scientific datasets are becoming increasingly vital to understand as a central component of the modern scientific communication process—Fig. 1. Like for academic publications indexed in traditional citation databases, such as the Web of Science, PubMed or SCOPUS, entire datasets do rarely become deleted from the database or archive. Their original records are rarely edited or erased; but datasets, in particular biodiversity datasets, may indeed be updated and grow in number of records over time or be modified or restructured. This characteristic is associated with the

---

Peter Ingwersen, Professor Emeritus, Royal School of Information and Library Science, University of Copenhagen, Denmark. Research areas: Interactive IR evaluation and theory; Webometrics-Scientometrics; Research evaluation. Awarded the Derek de Solla Price Medal, 2005 and the ASIST Research Award, 2003. He has initiated the CoLIS and IIIX conferences and published several highly cited research monographs and journal articles on IR and Scientometrics. Telephone: +45 32 34 15 00; E-mail: clb798@iva.ku.dk

---

P. Ingwersen (✉)
Royal School of Library and Information Science, University of Copenhagen
Birketinget 6, 2300 Copenhagen, DK, Denmark
e-mail: clb798@iva.ku.dk

C. Chen, R. Larsen (eds.), *Library and Information Sciences,*
DOI 10.1007/978-3-642-54812-3_8, © The Author(s) 2014

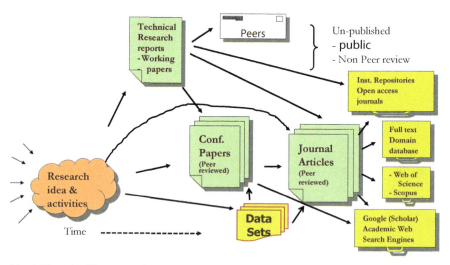

Fig. 1 The scientific communication process. Revised from Ingwersen (2011)

potential for change also observed in many Web-based documents. However, unlike references given in academic publications crediting influence or direct knowledge import from other publications no common standards are available for crediting scientific datasets across the array of disciplines (Green 2009). Thus, none of the aforementioned citation-based systems explicitly take into account scientific datasets as targeted objects for use in academic work.

For biodiversity data a task force was working on this issue in order to generate recommendations for the foundation of a workable citation mechanism (Moritz et al. 2011). In addition, a set of Data Usage Index (DUI) indicators has been developed (Ingwersen and Chavan 2011). The central indicators for the development of a DUI were based on search events and dataset download instances. The DUI is intended also to provide novel insights into how scholars make use of primary biodiversity data in a variety of ways. Similar to scientometric analyses applying rank distributions, time series, impact measures and other calculations based on academic publications (Moed 2005), the social usage of primary biodiversity datasets has led to observations of their statistical characteristics as well as the development of a family of indicators and other derived significant measures. The indicators can be regarded a kind of social utility metrics which, like citations, ratings or recommendations, may be applied as impact measures in research evaluation and form supporting relevance evidence for retrieval purposes (Ingwersen and Järvelin 2005).

Initially, the presentation places the biodiversity dataset indicators within the framework of Informetrics, as a sub-section of scientometric analysis and associated with Webometrics. This is followed by examples of selected rank distribution properties of biodiversity datasets in order to observe if such distributions are similar to those observed for academic journals and articles, i.e. if they follow Bradford-like long-tail distributions. In such power-law-like cases it is expected that information management solutions similar to those used in repository management and libraries can be applied to biodiversity datasets. In addition, one may expect such statistical properties to lead to useful social utility-based research monitoring metrics. A selection of DUI indicators that are useful from this perspective, such as *Usage* and *Interest Impact* scores and relative data usage impact, will be highlighted and exemplified. The presentation ends with a brief discussion of consequences of the biodiversity dataset characteristics from the perspectives of dataset management, retrieval and evaluation.

Biodiversity Datasets in the Informetric Framework

The scientific communication system displayed in Fig. 1 (Ingwersen 2011) contains several key components that may serve as fix points for scientometric indicator developments. Foremost they center on official research output, such as conference proceeding papers and journal articles, but also monographic publications, working papers and research reports are relevant in this respect. Patents (not shown on the Figure) signify additional particular kinds of research output, with own databases and indicator systems. With increased accessibility through the Web institutional repository publications as well as a growing body of scientific datasets of various kinds are available to researchers. In particular, datasets are used and re-used in order to carry out many different kinds of analyses, e.g. meta-analyses; benchmarking; bio topographic studies; genomics analyses, etc. Like for publications, datasets can be analyzed for their properties, for instance, with respect to volume of records, objects or topics they index and describe, and properties of authorship. Biodiversity datasets are interesting, because most are available on the Web often in a standardized database setting, but they require a lot of work to establish and this resource is only indirectly credited in the publications actually relying on biodiversity datasets. Thus the development of the set of DUI indicators analyzed below.

By being accessible on the Web one might argue that biodiversity dataset indicators based on social usage (on the web) belong to Webometrics, alternatively to the range of so-called 'altmetrics' indicators (Kurtz and Bollen 2010), Fig. 2. Webometric analyses imply quantitative studies of the Web, including usage of web-based resources. 'Altmetrics' has recently been proposed as a sub-area of Webometrics fundamentally dealing with the study of usage of social media (on the Web) such as Twitter, Facebook, blogs, and similar social networks. Typically, the actual usage population is fairly unknown in 'altmetric' analyses—as in many but not all webometric research areas—implying that the statistical properties are difficult to assess or control. In biodiversity dataset usage this is also the case: who is behind the searching computer is unknown to the online analyst, but the geographical area from which the search is done is known to the biodiversity dataset server. In addition, some properties are well known: the affiliation of the dataset provider; the size of the dataset in question; the topics and objects covered by the dataset.

It is thus fair to state that Informetric analyses of biodiversity datasets belong to Scientometrics, i.e. quantitative analyses of the science system(s), using Bibliometric methods, such as rank distributions, and intersected with Webometrics since the datasets are available through the Web, Fig. 2. Whether to use the notion

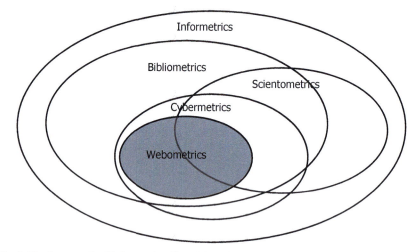

Fig. 2 The framework of Informetrics (from Björneborn and Ingwersen 2004, p. 1217).

of 'altmetrics' or simply webometrics for the analyses made is an open question, which I as instigator of Webometrics as a study area (Thelwall et al. 2005) will let the community to decide.

Biodiversity Dataset Characteristics

The objectives of the proposed DUI were (Ingwersen and Chavan 2011, p. 2) "[to] make the dataset usage visible, providing deserved recognition of their creators, managers, and publishers and to encourage the biodiversity dataset publishers and users to:

- Increase the volume of high quality data discovery, mobilisation and publishing;
- Further use of primary biodiversity data in scientific, conservation, and sustainable resources use purposes; and
- Improve formal citation behaviour regarding datasets in research."

In order to do so understanding of the characteristics of the datasets and their behaviour in the scientific life-cycle is central. Biodiversity datasets are presently accessible online through the Global Biodiversity Information Facility (GBIF) located in Copenhagen, Denmark. The structure and prospects of GBIF is outlined by Chavan and Ingwersen (2009). The GBIF data portal was established in 2001 (http://data.gbif.org.) and holds currently over 400 million records published in more than 10,000 datasets by almost 500 data publishers, with the largest data set containing more than 21 million records. The Data Usage Index (DUI) indicator developments were based on data usage logs of the GBIF data portal. The logs provide general usage data on kinds of access and searches via IP addresses as well as download events of datasets within the control of the GBIF data portal. As a spin-off the usage logs also provides different rank distribution characteristics, which are directly

Scientific Datasets: Informetric Characteristics and Social Utility Metrics ... 111

Table 1 Top-18 distribution of search events and number of records viewed, ranked by Search Events in the Danish Biodiversity Information Facility (DanBIF); (GBIF, December 1–31, 2009). Search density signifies no. of records per search event

Data set	Search events	Rank by no. of rec.	Searched records	Search density
Danish Mycological Society, fungal records database	1149	2	32394	28.2
Botanical Museum, Copenhagen, Mycology Herbarium	1035	3	22242	21.5
Niva Bay species list, Sjalland, Denmark	387	18	2834	7.3
Heilmann-Clausen)	372	6	9145	24.6
DOF	339	1	35758	105.5
Galathea II, Danish Deep Sea Expedition 1950–52	329	7	8912	27.1
Priest Pot species list, Cumbria, Britain	325	15	3520	10.8
Herbarium	249	4	19925	80.0
Western Palearctic migrants in continental Africa	191	5	13655	71.5
Botany registration database by Danish botanists	172	11	5083	29.6
Palaearctic	161	10	5556	34.5
DOF 2001–2006	158	8	8560	54.2
University's Arboretum	152	12	4714	31.0
Marine Benthic Fauna List, Denmark	137	19	2532	18.5
Botanical Museum, Copenhagen, the Lichen Herbarium	133	14	3618	27.2
Botanical Museum, Copenhagen, type specimens	60	30	161	2.7
Danish Ants (Formicidae)	56	13	3952	70.6
Galapagos grasses and sedges	54	29	194	3.6

accessible online for analysts through the GBIF Portal and its datasets—eventually via known dataset providers.

Table 1 demonstrates the top-rankings of a typical distribution of different datasets produced by the same dataset provider (Biodiversity data: Danish Biodiversity Information Facility, DanBIF, GBIF 2010) at a specific time period, i.e. one month, December 2009. During the selected time slot the provider was searched in total 5,704 times and the users looked at 207,622 records from the 36 available datasets, with an average search density of 36.4 records. Out of this volume the GBIF logs inform that 42,923 records were downloaded through 538 download events (average download density = 79.8 records), not shown on Table 1. Like for journal articles distributed over a publishing journal according to citations, the GBIF mobilized dataset records might be distributed over datasets according to usage (downloads) or searching.

Detailed analyses of the GBIF logs reveal that similar to articles vs. journals a Bradford distribution can be observed for searched biodiversity dataset records dispersed over datasets. A Bradford rank distribution of journals is a Gini-index

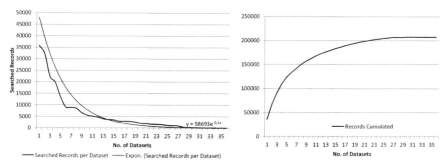

Fig. 3 Rank distribution of 36 datasets in DanBIF according to searched records (GBIF. December 1–31, 2009). Actual distribution (*left*) and cumulated distribution (*right*)

like distribution of the power law form $a;\ an;\ an^2$—where a signifies the number of journals publishing the upper tertile of articles (≈ datasets producing the upper tertile of records, searches or downloads) and n a constant specific for that scientific area (Garfield 1979; Moed 2005). Although the number of datasets in the distribution is quite small (36) we may, with good will, observe an approximation to a Bradford distribution for the searched records: the first tertile (69,207 records) of the total number of records (207,622) is covered by the top-2 1/2 datasets alone (sorted by Record Number = 79,273 records). The next 6 1/2 datasets cover 74,086 records, approximating the second tertile. The remaining 27 datasets cover the last tertile. This approximates to $a = 2.5$ datasets; $a\ n = 2.5 \times 3$ (= 7 1/2 datasets) and $a\ n^2 = 2.5 \times 9$ (= 22 1/2 datasets). A Bradford distribution for a given range of datasets implies that very few datasets (2–3) cover a large portion (> 33%) of the entire volume of records in the area covered by the range of datasets (here defined by the provider), followed by a long tail phenomenon.

In fact, the pattern shown is steeper than suggested by a standard Bradford distribution. More than 2/3 of the searched records in the DanBIF biodiversity collection (142,000 records) were covered by only 7 datasets (20%), Fig. 3, right-hand side. From Table 1 we observe that of the top-10 datasets ranked according to search events (popularity) seven datasets were also those sets with most used records as searched and viewed by peer biodiversity researchers world-wide. The pattern can be monitored over time for consistency, see example Table 2 for the HUA provider. During the monitored month in 2009 the DOF dataset was the most used set according to *Searched Records* but ranked fifth with respect to *Searching Event* frequency, i.e. popularity. In addition the DOF dataset had the highest Search Density (105.5 records per search event).

Figure 4 displays the corresponding rank distribution of search events over the 36 DanBIF datasets during the same time slot, again providing a long tail distribution, but with two datasets standing out as most searched (popular) datasets. Cumulated they constitute 38% of all events taking place during the period (2184 search events of a total of 5704 events), Fig. 4, right-hand side.

Data can be extracted from other elements of the GBIF data portal logs in order to generate rank distributions, e.g. associated with specific species or of frequent

Scientific Datasets: Informetric Characteristics and Social Utility Metrics ... 113

Table 2 Dataset indicator examples. Record No. as per December 31, 2009

Indicator	Formula	OBIS Dec09	DanBIF-09b	HUA-09a	HUA-09b	DK 2009b
Searched Records	$s(u)$	2,092,927	5,682,095	2,299,133	7,328,160	13,010,255
Download Freq.	$d(u)$	555,835	854,761	809,468	717,102	1,571,863
Record Number	$r(u)$	11,140,298	4,995,544	259,077	259,077	4,836,771
Search Events	$S(u)$	42,860	249,214	126,449	198,910	448,124
Download Events	$D(u)$	601	4,486	2,059	1,760	6,246
Dataset Number	$N(u)$	180	38	2	2	40
Datasets used	$n(u)$	171	36	2	2	38
Search Density	$s(u)/S(u)$	48.83	22.80	18.18	36.84	29.03
Download Density	$d(u)/D(u)$	924.85	190.54	393.14	407.44	251.66
Usage Impact	$d(u)/r(u)$	*0.05*	*0.17*	*3.12*	*2.77*	*0.32*
Interest Impact	$s(u)/r(u)$	*0.19*	*1.14*	*8.87*	*28.29*	*2.69*
Usage Ratio	$d(u)/s(u)$	0.27	0.15	0.35	0.10	0.12
Usage Balance	$D(u)/S(u)$	0.014	0.018	0.009	0.009	0.014

The Herbarium of University of Aarhus (HUA), covers two periods: Jan–June (a) and July–Dec. (b), 2009; the Danish Biodiversity Information Facility (DanBIF) July–Dec., 2009 (b); and Ocean Biogeographic Information System (OBIS) analyzed December 1–31, 2009 (GBIF Portal 2010; Ingwersen and Chavan 2011)

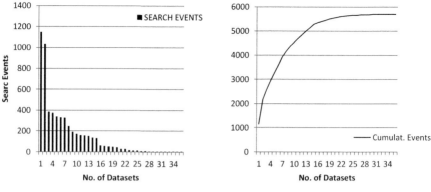

Fig. 4 Rank distribution of search events across the 36 datasets in DanBIF (GBIF; December 1–31, 2009). Actual distribution (*left*) and cumulated distribution (*right*)

```
Herbarium of the University of Aarhus statistics
================================

Event                             Event count    Number of records returned
Usage -occurrence search               15205     266993
Usage -dataset metadata viewed            99          0
Usage -taxon shown                        12          0
Usage -occurrence detail viewed          133        133
Usage -occurrence download              4219     808187
Usage -taxonomy download                   7      22441
```

Fig. 5 Extract of GBIF Event log file downloaded covering February–August 2013. (Biodiversity data: Herbarium Database Aarhus University HAU, GBIF 2013)

visits gaining access into specific dataset providers or datasets, via IP addresses. These latter distributions rank the top players that *import knowledge* in specific areas or from particular providers, datasets or species/taxa. Only the GBIF server staff is able to extract such data whilst the shown distributions are publicly available online. As part of its architecture the GBIF data portal supplies up-to-date lists of datasets as well as of dataset publishers, sorted alphabetically and detailing dataset name, Record Number and an entry to the dataset event log. The lists and structured event logs per dataset and provider can be downloaded easily (Fig. 5) and eventually re-ranked or manipulated statistically offline.

A recent online analysis of the GBIF event log demonstrates that, for instance, the Danish Mycological Society (Row 1, Table 1) at present holds 81,000 records, and during the month December 1–31, 2012 the dataset was searched 250,001 times retrieving and viewing 5,234,732 records with a search density of 20.9 records per event (Biodiversity data: Danish Mycological Society, GBIF 2013). These figures illustrate the dramatic increase of the usage of the GBIF portal over a period of one month during three years, see Table 1 for comparison.

Dataset Usage Index Indicators

In (Ingwersen and Chavan 2011) the range of DUI indicators is defined, exemplified and discussed. They are based on the extracts of data from the GBIF event logs for datasets and are constructed according to common scientometric standards for research evaluation indicators (Moed 2005). Below we point to the most prominent indicators and discuss briefly their potentials, since they are characteristic for biodiversity datasets that are publicly available, searched and downloaded. Table 2 demonstrates 13 of the indicators, exemplified by dataset properties from three different dataset providers: The large network-like US-based Ocean Biogeographic Information System (OBIS) and the two Danish providers DanBIF and Herbarium of University of Aarhus (HUA).

The Number of Datasets produced by a publisher (N(u)) at a given point in time may characterize the publisher into small (N < 10), Medium (10 < N < 100), Large (100 < N < 300) and ultra-large (N > 300). The reason behind this classification is that it is meaningless to compare between providers of quite different sizes. Like for citation impact small (often specialized) universities should not be compared to large universal universities. DanBIF is thus regarded a medium-size provider while HUA is seen as a small dataset producer. Table 2 provides an overall view of their characteristics (Ingwersen and Chavan 2011, p. 7).

For the large-scale US provider OBIS the analysis window is one month against 6 month for the two other providers. Comparisons should hence not be carried out them in between. The *Usage Ratio* signifies the number of records downloaded over number of records searched during the same period. The higher the ratio the more searched records are also subsequently downloaded and imply a kind of *social attractiveness* of the datasets in question.

The table shows that regardless of length of analysis window the numbers of *Searched Records* and *Download Frequency* were quite substantial in 2009, supporting the conception of a DUI. *Download Events* were very low compared to the number of *Search Events* across all three publishers and periods. Three years later the GBIF portal seems well established in the mind of the global research community, Fig. 5, with a *Download Event* score during the six-month period February–August 2013 for HUA raised to 4,226 events and with a *Download Density* reaching 196.6 against 15,205 *Search Events* with a corresponding much lower *Density* of 17.6 (Biodiversity data: Herbarium of University of Aarhus 2013).

The *Usage Balance* between *Download* and *Search Events* was quite low in 2009: only approx. 1–2% of the search events lead to direct downloading for the providers; for HUA less than 1%. In 2013, for one HUA dataset, the *Usage Balance* reaches 28%, implying that for each 4 search events there is one pure download event taking place, signifying that searchers seem more familiar with the dataset contents and do not require constantly to search and investigate the set prior to actual usage. This coincides with the *Usage Ratio*, or social attractiveness score, which for HUA during the six month in 2013 reaches 3.1 signifying that more than three times the searched records are actually downloaded.

According to Ingwersen and Chavan (2011, p. 7) the *Interest* and *Usage Impact* factors inform about the average number of times each record stored by a dataset publisher has been searched or actively downloaded. In both metrics a value greater than 1.0 implies that in principle all the dataset records on average have been searched or downloaded at least once during the analysis period. The two time slots, Table 2 (2009a, b), may illustrate the developments for a dataset provider like HUA during the entire year 2009, i.e., showing a slight decrease in *Usage Impact* (from 3.1 to 2.8) and a strong increase in *Interest Impact* (from 8.9 to 28.3). In contrast, during the recent six-month period in 2013 HUA's *Usage* and *Interest Impact* values are 7.4 and 2.4 respectively[1]. The *Usage Impact* has increased substantially while the *Interest Impact* has noticeably dropped. This is due to a strong increase in downloads and much less searching and viewing activity during the later period, in accordance with the *Usage Balance* and *Ratio* scores.

Aside from the DUI indicators, Table 2, the event logs may in addition produce data on the most popular objects, i.e., the species in the dataset that are most searched and viewed during the selected analysis period. Such data constitutes the *usage profile* for a particular dataset and changes can be monitored over time.

These absolute DUI metrics can be turned into relative indicators, e.g. by relating single datasets to their provider's cumulated properties or associating several providers to the national aggregation for particular indicators. The HUA *Usage Impact Factor* for 2009b relative to Denmark (U-IF/DK) is thus 2.77/0.32 = 8.65. The corresponding U-IF (DanBIF) is 0.53. Examples of relative DUI indicators and all formulas are shown in (Ingwersen and Chavan 2011).

Concluding Remarks

The presentation demonstrates the feasibility of establishing a framework for academic crediting of dataset production, searching and usage. The Dataset Usage Index signifies a step forward towards such a dataset management framework. The reason that the DUI is appropriate lies in the rank distribution properties which, among other characteristics, follow the pattern of power laws in proximity of Bradford distributions. Further, the distributions make it feasible to point to the most popular or socially attractive datasets, providers or species, monitored over time, and to apply such evidence in dataset management decisions as well as for retrieval purposes. The latter perspective reaches into types of recommendation systems commonly applied to other kinds of social media (Bogers and van den Bosch 2011). Because of their usage dimension biodiversity datasets, as well as other scientific datasets may be seen as particular kinds of cooperative filtering information systems.

In addition, a range of absolute as well as relative usage indicators has been defined and exemplified. Biodiversity datasets and their records seem to display some similar characteristics as journals and articles published in such journals. It is thus

---

[1] The number of records in the one HUA dataset available in August 2013 is 111,525.

very likely that information management traits that have been found appropriate for academic journals and journal articles in repositories and libraries are equally useful for biodiversity and other scientific datasets. Similarly, a DUI is likely to serve as a convenient complement to traditional citation-based research monitoring, in particular with respect to institutional evaluations since the biodiversity datasets constitute a substantial workload otherwise not made visible in traditional research monitoring schemes.

Open Access This chapter is distributed under the terms of the Creative Commons Attribution Noncommercial License, which permits any noncommercial use, distribution, and reproduction in any medium, provided the original author(s) and source are credited.

References

Biodiversity occurrence data published by: Danish Biodiversity Information Facility (Accessed through GBIF Data Portal, data.gbif.org, 2010-01-01)

Biodiversity occurrence data published by: Danish Mycological Society (Accessed through GBIF Portal, data.gbif.org, 2013-08-16)

Biodiversity occurrence data published by: Herbarium of University of Aarhus (Accessed through GBIF Portal, data.gbif.org, 2010-01-01; 2013-08-16)

Biodiversity occurrence data published by: Ocean Biogeographic Information System (OBIS) (Accessed through GBIF Portal, data.gbif.org, 2010-01-01)

Björneborn L, Ingwersen P (2004) Toward a basic framework for webometrics. J Am Soc Inf Sci Technol 55(14):1216–1227

Bogers T, van den Bosch A (2011) Fusing recommendations for social bookmarking websites. Int J Electron Commer 15(3):31–72

Chavan VS, Ingwersen P (2009) Towards a data publishing framework for primary biodiversity data: challenges and potentials for the biodiversity informatics community. BMC Bioinformatics 10(Suppl 14):11 s

Garfield E (1979) Bradford's law and related statistical patterns. current comments; essays of an information scientist 1979–1980, May 7 1979. pp 5–11

GBIF. http://data.gbif.org/

Green T (2009) We need publishing standards for datasets and data tables. White paper OECD Publishing; 2009, 9–11. doi:10.1787/603233448430

Ingwersen P, Chavan V (2011) Indicators for the Data Usage Index (DUI): an incentive for publishing primary biodiversity data through global information infrastructure. 15 Dec. 2011. BMC Bioinformatics 12(Suppl 15):S3, s. S3. 10 s

Ingwersen P, Järvelin K (2005) The turn: integration of information seeking and retrieval in context. Springer

Kurtz M, Bollen J (2010) Usage bibliometrics. Ann Rev Inf Sci Technol 44:3–64

Moed HF (2005) Citation analysis in research evaluation. Springer, Dordrecht

Moritz T, Krishnan S, Roberts D, Ingwersen P, Agosti D, Penev Y, Cockerill M, Chavan V (2011) Towards mainstreaming of biodiversity data publishing: recommendations of the GBIF Data Publishing Framework Task Group. 15 Dec. 2011. BMC Bioinformatics 12(Suppl 15):S1, 10 s

Thelwall M, Vaughan L, Bjorneborn L (2005) Webometrics. Ann Rev Inf Sci Technol 39:81–135

Knowledge Discovery of Complex Networks Research Literatures

Fei-Cheng Ma, Peng-Hui Lyu and Xiao-Guang Wang

Abstract Complex network research literatures have increased rapidly over last decade, most remarkable in the past four years. This paper attempted to visualise the research outputs of complex network research in a global context for the purpose in knowledge discovery on the world research progress and quantitative analysing on current research publication trends. The scientometric methods and knowledge visualization technologies are employed with a focus on global production, main subject categories, core journals, the most productive countries, leading research institutes, publications' most used keywords as well as the most cited papers, and the knowl-

---

Fei-Cheng Ma is a senior professor and doctoral supervisor, and currently the director of Centre for the Studies of Information Resources (CSIR) at Wuhan University. He is both the Editor-in-Chief of an information journal and international editor for several journals of information science. His major research lies in information resource management and planning, theory and methodologies of information science, and information economics. He can be touched at fchma@whu.edu.cn

Peng-Hui Lyu, as the corresponding author of this contributuoin, is an assistant researcher in Research and Development Centre for Smart City and also a Ph. D candidate in CSIR at Wuhan University. He is one of academic committees for the journal of Advanced Management Science, and the international reviewer for the journals of PLoS One and Water Resources Management. His academic interest involves in knowledge management, knowledge networks and knowledge city, especially in quantitative research for science information. He can be touched through lvph@whu.edu.cn.

Xiao-Guang Wang is a professor of the School of Information Management, Wuhan University. He has published in many international journals such as Journal of Information Science, *Journal of Knowledge Management and Scientometrics.* His research interests are in the areas of knowledge network analysis, digital assets management and semantic publishing. He can be contacted at wxguang@whu.edu.cn.

P.-H. Lyu (✉)
Centre for the Studies of Information Resources, Wuhan University, Wuhan, China
e-mail: lvph@whu.edu.cn

F.-C. Ma
Centre for the Studies of Information Resources, Wuhan University, Wuhan, China
e-mail: fchma@whu.edu.cn

X.-G Wang
School of Information Management, Wuhan University, Wuhan, China
e-mail: wxguang@whu.edu.cn

C. Chen, R. Larsen (eds.), *Library and Information Sciences,*
DOI 10.1007/978-3-642-54812-3_9, © The Author(s) 2014

edge basement. The keywords cluster analysis is used to trace the hot topics from the research literatures in this field. Research outputs descriptors suggested that the research in this domain has mainly focused on the dynamics, model and systems for complex networks. All the publications have been concentrated in two journals such as *Physical Review E* and *Physica A*. The USA is the leading country in complex network research field since it has both the world research centres and most of the top scientists worldwide. The research trend in complex network research are involved in complex routing strategy, models complex networks social as well as scale free percolation efficiency. Complex networks, dynamics, model and small-world networks are highly used keywords in the literatures from the main scientific database.

Keywords Complex Networks · Knowledge Discovery · Publication Trend · Citation Analysis · Knowledge Base · Subjects Category · Keywords Plus · Co-Citation

Introduction

Complex networks, attracting the attention of computer scientists, biologists, mathematicians and physicists et.al, are thoroughly studied in more and more evolved research fields now. As an effective reflection contacting the real world and theoretical exploration, it was initially come from the domain of chaos theory and fractal studies. Two pioneering works, small world network and scale-free network, encouraged an instantly wave of international research concerning complex networks by the end of the twentieth century. Small-world networks explored by Watts and Strogatz, which can be highly clustered and have small characteristic path lengths (Watts and Strogatz 1998), can portray biological, technological and social networks better than the networks completely regular or completely random. In many large networks it was found that the property that the vertex connectivity followed a scale-free power-law distribution (Barabasi and Albert 1999) by Barabási A.L and Albert R. Counting from this emergence, complex networks have gone through its first research decade.

In the early twenty-first century, the discovery of small world effect and scale-free property in the real network largely provoked the publications boom of complex networks. Initial research on complex networks focused on the analysis and modelling of network structure at large, such as degree exponents (Dorogovtsev and Goltsev 2002), dynamical processes (Yang et al. 2008), network growth (Gagen and Mattick 2005), link prediction (Zhou et al. 2009) and so on. Then Strogatz S.H tried to unravel the structure and dynamics of complex networks from the perspective of nonlinear dynamics (Strogatz 2001). The statistical mechanics of network as topology and dynamics of the main models as well as analytical tools were discussed (Albert and Barabasi 2002), the theory of evolving networks was introduced in Albert R and Barabasi A.L's work.

The developments of complex networks, including several major concepts, models of network growth, as well as dynamical processes (Newman 2003) were discussed in Newman MEJ's paper. The basic concepts as well as the results achieved in the study of the structure and dynamics of complex networks (Boccaletti et al. 2006) were summarized. The error tolerance was displayed only

Knowledge Discovery of Complex Networks Research Literatures 121

in scale-free networks, and it showed an unexpected degree of robustness (Albert et al. 2000). Network motifs and patterns of interconnections to uncover the structural design principles of complex networks was defined (Milo et al. 2002). The way in which self-organized networks grows into scale-free structures, and the role of the mechanism of preferential linking were investigated (Dorogovtsev and Mendes 2002). A number of models demonstrating the main features of evolving networks were also presented. Mixing patterns in a variety of networks were measured (Newman 2003) and technological as well as biological networks were found disproportionally mixed, while social networks tend to be assorted. It was pointed out that scale-free networks catalysed the emergence of network science (Barabasi and Oltvai 2004). The number of driver nodes is determined primarily by the network's degree distribution was also found, and the driver nodes tend to avoid the high-degree nodes (Liu et al. 2011). The control of degrees on complex networks was carefully studied later (Egerstedt 2011). The fragility of interdependency on complex networks was also studied hence (Vespignani 2010).

With the continuous development of complex networks, in addition to the theoretical and technical research on the complex network itself, scholars have also focused on the network function. Barabasi A.L and Oltvai Z.N indicated that cellular networks offer a new conceptual framework for biology and disease pathologies (Barabasi 2009), which could potentially revolutionize the traditional view. An approach which not only stresses the systemic complexity of economic networks was pointed out (Schweitzer et al. 2009), it can be used to revise and extend traditional paradigms in economic theory which is urgently needed. A biologically complex multistring network model was designed to observe the evolution and transmission dynamics of ARV resistance (Smith et al. 2010).

The current situation is that the complex network research was not only limited to the study of the theory and methods, but has become a new research direction of multi-disciplinary and a powerful tool in multi-disciplinary research. Nowadays complex network have been applied in many different areas including spread (Yang et al. 2008), network synchronization (Motter et al. 2005), transports (Wang et al. 2006), game theory (Perc and Szolnoki 2010), physics (Newman 2002), computer science (Guimera and Amaral 2005), biochemistry or molecular biology (Jeong et al. 2000), mathematics (Guimera and Amaral 2005), engineering (Olfati-Saber et al. 2007), cell biology (Rosen and MacDougald 2006). These research directions took us more and more productions and publications in recent years.

Most important it was known to all that the methods of complex networks are used more and more for scientomtrics and informetrics research in information science. For example the complex networks analysis was employed for co-citation or co-occurrence network to get the knowledge structure as well as scientific cooperation performance for a specific filed. While in these studies, the metric data is the base of all complex networks analysis. Traditional bibliometrics research was widely applied to acquaint information from the scientific or technical literatures, and for further study the complex networks method could also help.

In this study the records of literature were analysed with scientometric methods via several aspects. This effort will provide a current view of the mainstream research on complex networks as well as clues to the impact of this hot topic.

In addition, this study also attempted to analyse the significance of the complex networks production patterns, especially in the way of co-authors and authors' keywords study originally acted from WoS database. The main body of this article includes scientometric analyses in production, subject category, and geographical distribution of WoS data. Moreover, appropriate statistical tests were used in the authors' keyword yearly to predict the developing trend of complex networks research.

Data and Method

This study is based on the metadata analysis of the articles from the authoritative scientific and technical literature indexing databases such as SCI-E, SSCI and CPCI. The impact factor of SCI & SSCI journals with the latest data available in 2012 was determined by Journal Citation Reports (JCR) of Thomson Reuters, which was operated by Thomson Scientific, Philadelphia, PA now (Proudfoot, McAuley et al. 2011). The statistical analysis tool is Thomson Data Analyser (TDA) and the drawing tool is Aureka and MS Office Excel 2010.

Date Source

The data source was come from WoS database offered by Thomson Reuters, and the publishing time span was last updated in Dec 28th, 2013. Data in this study was acquired on December 30th, 2013 using the topic= "complex* network*" selecting "all the years" within the metadata including publication's title, keywords and abstract. In total, 10,832 articles were retrieved from the database of Web of Science (WoS). Precision retrieval strategy used in this paper make the ability of the search term to minimize the number of irrelevant records retrieved. As an abstract database, WoS offered only the metadata, certainly if given the chance to extract information from the full text of all paper the results may be more accurate.

Methodology

In this scientometrics study, the annual publications, subjects' category, core journals, productive countries, fruitful institutes, main authors and keywords of the papers was deeply studied using the quantitative analysis methods. In this study comparative analysis was also used to analyse the data by putting the SCI and SSCI data into the same figure so that a direct and vivid result can be gotten from the figures and as much as possible information obtained.

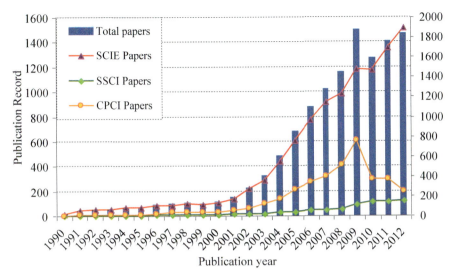

Fig. 1 Papers record indexed in WoS from 1990 to 2012

Results Analysis

In this section, figures and tables are employed to describe the production and the development trends of complex networks research in both science and social science fields. Publications (as indicator for scientific performance) are commonly accepted indicators for quantitative analysis on innovation research performance (Garfield 1970). Papers from SCI as well as SSCI were studied together in this paper with scientometric analysis to explore the knowledge discovery.

Production Trend

As seen in Fig. 1 the complex networks publications increased dramatically in the last two decades. From 1990 to 2001, the complex networks' research were just begun and its publications were relatively low and there were not more than 200 papers in the WoS database. After 2001, the research outputs increased rapidly from less than 200 in 2001 to more than 2000 in 2009 and then stabilized changed in recent. The complex networks research came into its fast growth stage in twenty-first century and may enter the mature period of its publish life cycle in the next decade.

Subjects Category

The complex networks related research was distributed in the subjects of physics, computer science, biochemistry & molecular biology, mathematics and engineering. Most complex networks outputs were produced under the subject of physics due to

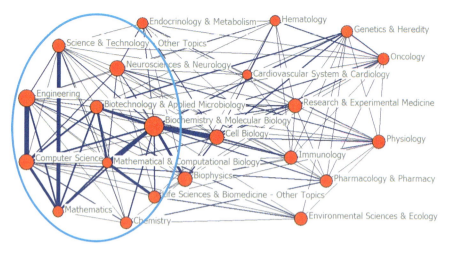

Fig. 2 Subjects co-occurrence networks of SCI&SSCI papers

it is a branch of theoretical physics originally. As time went by, this approach was used in bioscience or engineering to solve many problems as a migrating concept, which proved its superiority for many disciplines from the metadata of SCI & SSCI papers. Through the subject co-occurrence networks it can be known that the complex network is based on the mathematics and computer science, and be successfully used in engineering and related sciences, which is shown in Fig. 2. Bio-related sciences such as biochemistry, biophysics, biotechnology, and cell biology are the best domains in which complex networks being well developed. In future, there will be more and more bio-scientists put their attention into complex networks research.

Journals Analysis

The complex networks research was published mainly in physics related journals such as *Physical Review E* and *Physica A,* which published most complex networks papers in all journals from the SCI&SSCI database. *PLoS One* produced 217 papers and ranked third, *European physical journal B* with 205 papers in forth and *Chaos* with 205 papers in fifth for publications in the complex networks research. The American journals *PNAS* and *Physical Review Letters* were two journals with the highest impact factor in 2011. The annual publications distribution about complex networks papers are shown in Fig. 3. The research in this field attracted the most attentions from scientists far in the year 2001. *Physical Review E* was the main publisher of complex networks in the last decade, while *Physica A* reached the publication level of *Physical Review E* in 2007 once. Other journals kept a stable publication state in the past decade with about 30 papers per year in SCI&SSCI database; *PLoS One* (Full name of *Public Library of Science One*) was the only exception with a dramatically increasing rate in recent three years.

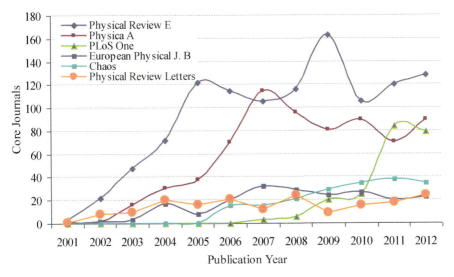

Fig. 3 Annual SCI&SSCI journals outputs distribution during 2001–2012

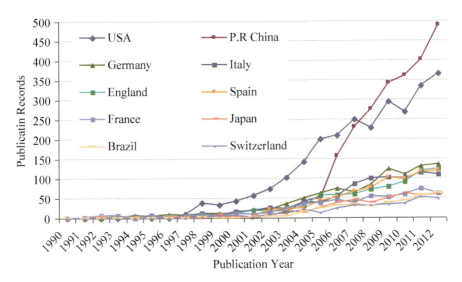

Fig. 4 Annual country record distribution in the complex networks study

Countries Analysis

In all complex networks publications, the United States of America and the People's Republic of China contributed the most parts as shown in Fig. 4. Hence the research centre was located in these two countries at present. However, the USA started

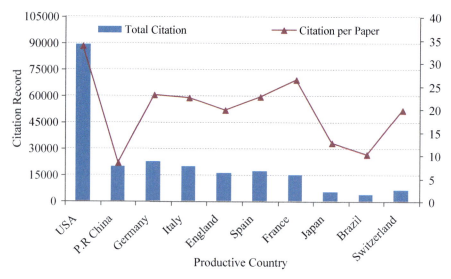

Fig. 5 Citation distribution of global SCI&SSCI papers

complex networks research as early in 1997 but dropped behind P.R. China in productions after 2007. Other countries such as Germany, Italy, England and Spain produced less outputs with a stable increasing rate in complex networks related publications. While in total these European countries published more papers than former other countries.

Active degree is defined as the outputs number in recent three years to all years' publication number in general bibliometric research. P.R. China had the highest active degree of 52.3% in all countries in the world, indicating that the research of complex networks was treasured much and in fact such activity as the Conference for Chinese Complex Networks (short for CCCN) was held for eight times already in recent years in P.R. China (Fig. 5).

The SCI&SSCI papers' citations results were shown in Fig. 4. From this figure it can be found that the USA obtained the most citations, which attested its high level in the field of complex network research. The highest citation per paper was from European countries such as England and Germany. P.R. China's average citation was relatively lower than most European countries and Brazil or Japan, but not far behind the USA with less total citations.

In the international collaboration of papers of complex networks, the USA, Germany and P.R. China are located in the central positions which can be seen in Fig. 6. It is also clear that USA is in the centre of collaborating activities. Other countries such as England, France, Italy, Spain and Switzerland had less cooperation in complex networks research in SCI&SSCI publications. The cooperation network between top productive countries reflected the knowledge transmission in the field of complex networks research in the world.

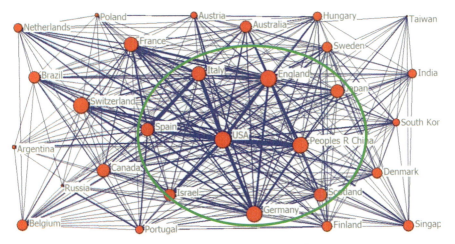

Fig. 6 The international collaboration network of complex networks

Institutes Analysis

The top productive institutes with an accumulative paper quantity of more than 40 are ranked in Fig. 6. The Harvard University published 70 papers in total, ranking first, followed by University of Science and Technology of China (USTC, 69) and CNR from France with an output of 63 papers. Other institutes produced many papers as the former ones did in complex networks, which reflecting their overall strength like these American and Chinese agencies.

For most productive institutes, the time span during 2005 to 2007 was the best years with most publications. The Harvard University from USA as well as University of Science and Technology of China produced the most complex networks research papers accumulatively before, far more than all the institutes in world organizations. After 2008, all top productive institutes published less paper for about five years while Boston University not. The production came into a former maturity stage in its publish cycle then (Fig. 8).

It can be seen from as shown in Fig. 7 that the Northwestern University has the most total citations as well as citations per paper in the world, which proved their priority in complex networks research. The Harvard University had the second most total citations and citations per paper. Compared with the University of Science and Technology of China, North western University and Harvard University has the highest citations per paper and most total citations. US agencies have the best research in complex networks research in the world.

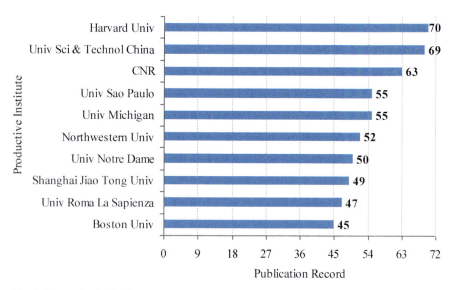

Fig. 7 Top productive institutes of SCI&SSCI papers published

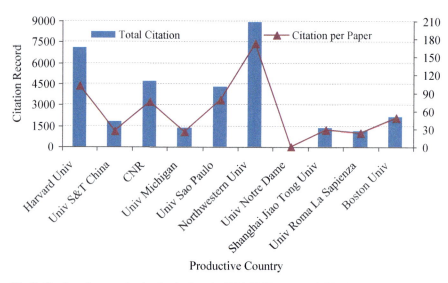

Fig. 8 Citation of top productive institutions in SCI&SSCI papers published

Keywords Analysis

All the high frequency keywords plus more than 200 are listed in Table 1. The complex networks related hotspots were mainly distributed in the dynamics, model and systems research as we can see from Table 1. What's more, the research of Small

Table 1 Keywords plus distributions of SCI&SSCI Publications

Keywords Plus	Complex Networks	Dynamics	Model	Systems	Small-World Networks
Records	4004	1428	823	785	680
Keywords Plus	Internet	Evolution	Organization	Scale-Free Networks	Synchronization
Records	507	481	453	409	341
Keywords Plus	Topology	Stability	Expression	Community Structure	Gene-Expression
Records	331	324	303	285	283
Keywords Plus	Graphs	Metabolic Networks	Web	Escherichia-Coli	Models
Records	283	257	249	236	234

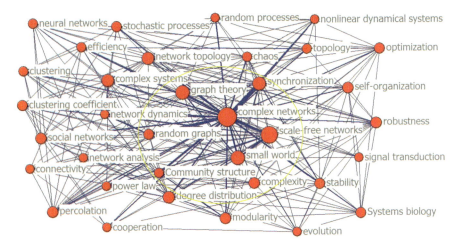

Fig. 9 Annual number of keywords plus of SCI&SSCI papers published

World networks, the internet and evolution were also the high frequency key words that emerged in research papers. Scale-Free Networks as well as organizations became the hot words only less than words plus listed above.

The annual keywords plus distribution was drawn in Fig. 9. The main retrieval word of complex networks was turned up in 2001 and with a fast increasing trend in the past decade. Scholars paid little attentions in the dynamics research before 2000, while they were interested in it during 2001 to 2007 so that the number of this word increased sharply from then. In the year 2006, almost all the research of systems, internet and Small-World Networks maintained a fast increase in papers production.

The complex networks research co-words map was drawn for the hotspot analysis in this paper as Fig. 10. All the words were extracted from the title, author keywords and abstracts of the publications automatically by the Aureka software and then clustered in the knowledge map to trace the research trends. The complex

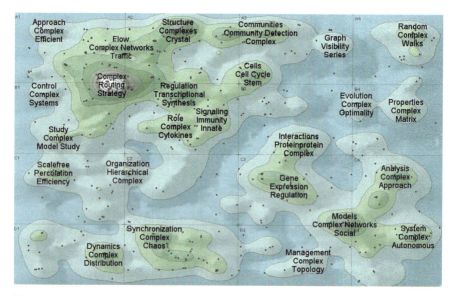

Fig. 10 Cluster and co-words map of SCI&SSCI papers published

routing strategy is the most popular research domain in all outputs for complex networks research. And such fields as models complex networks social as well as scale free percolation efficiency were less popular than the complex routing strategy research in recent years.

Citation Analysis

The most frequently cited papers are key literatures link the research of complex networks for years so the top SCI&SSCI papers with most citations are listed in Table 2. In the top 10 high influence research papers, six of which came from the USA and the remainders were produced by European countries. The paper "Statistical mechanics of complex networks" written by Albert R and Barabasi A.L from Notre Dame University was the most frequently cited paper in the world. These two famous scientists also wrote other three most cited papers under the topics of error and attack tolerance, network biology and metabolic networks before.

Figure 11 shows all the reference year of the complex networks related publications. Most complex networks outputs cited the papers published after 1998, the citation account before and after 1998 were at a huge difference. One reason was that the complex network research started at this time span, and the other was that the published papers attracted more and more attentions from this time point. In fact, the most important works published in 2000–2002 gained so much citation as can be seen from Table 3. While the new published papers, especially after

Knowledge Discovery of Complex Networks Research Literatures

Table 2 Top 10 SCI&SSCI papers with Most Citations

No.	Time Cited	Authors	Title	Journal	Institute	Country	Year
1	5775	Albert, R; Barabasi, AL	Statistical mechanics of complex networks	Reviews of Modern Physics	Univ Notre Dame	USA	2002
2	4117	Newman, MEJ	The structure and function of complex networks	Siam Review	Univ Michigan	USA	2003
3	2390	Strogatz, SH	Exploring complex networks	Nature	Cornell Univ	USA	2001
4	2048	Boccaletti, S; Latora, V; Moreno, Y; Chavez, M; Hwang, DU	complex networks: Structure and dynamics	Physics Reports-Review Section of Physics Letters	CNR	Italy	2006
5	1999	Albert, R; Jeong, H; Barabasi, AL	Error and attack tolerance of complex networks	Nature	Univ Notre Dame	USA	2000
6	1990	Barabasi, AL; Oltvai, ZN	Network biology: Understanding the cell's functional organization	Nature Reviews Genetics	Univ Notre Dame	USA	2004
7	1948	Jeong, H; Tombor, B; Albert, R; Oltvai, ZN; Barabasi, AL	The large-scale organization of metabolic networks	Nature	Univ Notre Dame	USA	2000
8	1660	Milo, R; Shen-Orr, S; Itzkovitz, S; Kashtan, N; Chklovskii, D; Alon, U	Network motifs: Simple building blocks of complex networks	Science	Weizmann Inst Sci	Israel	2002
9	1315	Dorogovtsev, SN; Mendes, JFF	Evolution of networks	Advances In Physics	Univ Porto	Portugal	2002
10	1039	Thiery, JP; Sleeman, JP	complex networks orchestrate epithelial-mesenchymal transitions	Nature Reviews Molecular Cell Biology	CNRS	France	2006

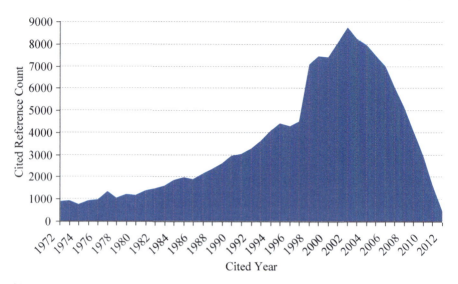

Fig. 11 Cited Reference Distribution of SCI&SSCI papers published

2010, were cited not much as the papers before due to their values not known by most scholars. The citation time window is of the normal distribution, with little citation in the former and later years and much citation in the middle location of the figure.

The reference account reflected the influence in the local domain, which is listed in Table 3. In the top 10 high influence research papers, most of them came from the USA and the remainders were produced by European countries. Those papers published in famous journals such as Science, Nature, and PNAS (Proceedings of National Academy of Sciences in USA). The paper wrote by Albert R in Review Modern Physics also attracted lots of attentions in the domain of complex networks' research. The results are accordance with the citation rank in Table 3.

Co-citation Analysis

Figure 12 give a vividly picture of the journals co-cited by the complex networks domain. Those journals co-cited by one given research topic are usually considered as the knowledge base, and they provided the original citations. In complex network domain, those journals such as Science, Nature, PNAS, Cell, Physica A, and Review Modern Physics, Physics Review E, New England Journal Medicine, Physics Review Letter, PLoS One are in the center location of the ci-citation network. Naturally, many other journals including Social Networks, Nature Physics, Physica D, Chaos, New Journal of Physics et.al also provided lots of knowledge base for complex networks' research development.

Table 3 Top 10 papers cited by all published papers

No	Time Cited	Authors	Article No. (DIO)	Journal	Country	Year
1	3,262	Albert R	10.1103/RevModPhys.74.47	Rev Mod Phys	USA	2002
2	2,808	Barabasi AL	10.1126/science.286.5439.509	Science	USA	1999
3	2,501	Watts DJ	10.1038/30918	Nature	USA	1998
4	2,449	Newman MEJ	10.1137/S003614450342480	Siam Rev	USA	2003
5	1,433	Boccaletti S	10.1016/j.physrep. 2005.10.009	Phys Rep	Italy	2006
6	1,336	Strogatz SH	10.1038/35065725	Nature	USA	2001
7	974	Albert R	10.1038/35019019	Nature	USA	2000
8	902	Dorogovtsev SN	10.1080/00018730110112519	Adv Phys	Portugal	2002
9	663	Girvan M	10.1073/pnas.122653799	P Natl Acad Sci USA		2001
10	658	Pastor-Satorras R	10.1103/PhysRevLett.86.3200	Phys Rev Lett		2002

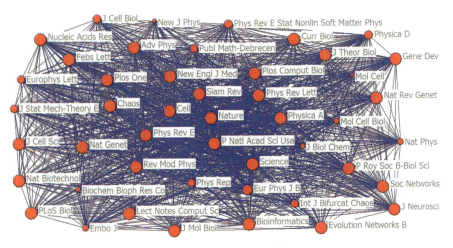

Fig. 12 Cluster and co-words map of SCI&SSCI papers published

Conclusion

As a strictly selected academic thesis abstract database, Web of Science (WoS, including SCI and SSCI) has been long recognized as the useful tool that can cover the most important science & technology, social science research productivities. SCI & SSCI citation search systems are unique and significant, not only from the perspective of literature cited but also from the academic assessment of the value in articles or from cooperation networks to research references. So all the papers published in this database were carefully studied to get the publication pattern and production orderliness.

The methods of complex networks are used more and more in other research such as in information science. The complex networks analysis was employed for co-citation or co-occurrence network to get the knowledge structure as well as scientific cooperation performance for a specific scientific filed often. Hence traditional scientometrics research was widely applied to acquaint information from the scientific or technical literatures, this will lead us a new direction for complex networks method in future as this research do.

Hence in this study, the impact of global complex networks literature has been studied with scientometric methods and the research history has been recalled firstly according to the complex networks research literatures. The publications history started from 1990 and boosted in recent four or five years. From 1990 to about 2001, the complex networks research stepped into its infancy stage and then began a fast increasing stage in growth, and now in the former stage of maturity in its life cycle. In near future the publications in this field will still keep going larger and larger for quite a long time as can be predicted.

Complex networks research are mainly in the subjects of physics. All the output concentrated in two journals such as *Physical Review E* and *Physica A* in SCI&SSCI database. The research papers were mainly completed by several authors according to network theory aggregation nodes in a power law correlation, and the multiple-authors made up an increasingly larger ratio to form a group size measured using papers. So the co-authored papers in the complex networks research were the mainstream of complex networks research and it formed a complex collaboration networks about complex networks research.

Complex networks related papers were distributed unevenly over all countries. The USA, China and Germany were the top productive countries of SCI&SSCI papers. Some Europe countries such as Italy and Germany published top influence paper than those productive countries. The complex networks research centre was located in the USA in the last few decades according to the metadata from countries and institutes analysis. Harvard University and USTC produced most SCI papers and some USA institutes such as University of Michigan and University of Notre Dame contributed most influence SCI articles.

Research on the fields of complex networks research focused on complex routing strategy, models complex networks social as well as scale free percolation efficiency. From the analysis of author keywords, except "complex networks", "dynamics", "model" and "small-world networks" were highly used key words plus in the scientific database. It is clear that complex networks research will be a hot spot in the complexity science field in the future. With scientometric and informetric method, the findings of this study can help scientific researchers understand the performance and central trends of complex networks research in the world, and therefore suggest directions for further research.

Acknowledgments This work is supported by the Natural Science Foundation of China (Grant No. 71173249: Research on Formation Mechanism and Evolution Laws of Knowledge Networks). The authors are grateful to Xiang Liu, Xiao Han and Gerard Joseph White for their helpful discussions and suggestions. And our special thanks also go to Professor Xiaojuan Zhang for her valuable comments on this research work.

Knowledge Discovery of Complex Networks Research Literatures

Open Access This chapter is distributed under the terms of the Creative Commons Attribution Noncommercial License, which permits any noncommercial use, distribution, and reproduction in any medium, provided the original author(s) and source are credited.

References

Albert R, Barabasi AL (2002) Statistical mechanics of complex networks. Rev Mod Phys 74(1):47–97

Albert R, Jeong H et al (2000) Error and attack tolerance of complex networks. Nature 406(6794):378–382

Barabasi AL (2009) Scale-free networks: a decade and beyond. Science 325(5939):412–413

Barabasi AL, Albert R (1999) Emergence of scaling in random networks. Science 286(5439):509–512

Barabasi AL, Oltvai ZN (2004) Network biology: understanding the cell's functional organization. Nat Rev Genet 5(2):101–U115

Boccaletti S, Latora V et al (2006). Complex networks: structure and dynamics. Phys Rep-Rev Sect Phys Lett 424(4–5):175–308

Dorogovtsev SN, Goltsev AV et al (2002) Pseudofractal scale-free web. Phys Rev E 65(6)

Dorogovtsev SN, Mendes JFF (2002) Evolution of networks. Adv Phys 51(4):1079–1187

Egerstedt M (2011) Complex networks degrees of control. Nature 473(7346):158–159

Gagen MJ, Mattick JS (2005) Accelerating, hyperaccelerating, and decelerating networks. Phys Rev E 72(1)

Garfield E (1970) Citation indexing for studying science. Nature 227(5259):669–671

Guimera R, Amaral LAN (2005) Functional cartography of complex metabolic networks. Nature 433(7028):895–900

Jeong H, Tombor B et al (2000) The large-scale organization of metabolic networks. Nature 407(6804):651–654

Liu YY, Slotine JJ et al (2011) Controllability of complex networks. Nature 473(7346):167–173

Milo R, Shen-Orr S et al (2002) Network motifs: simple building blocks of complex networks. Science 298(5594):824–827

Motter AE, Zhou CS et al (2005) Network synchronization, diffusion, and the paradox of heterogeneity. Phys Rev E 71(1)

Newman MEJ (2002) Assortative mixing in networks. Phys Rev Lett 89(20)

Newman MEJ (2003) The structure and function of complex networks. SIAM Rev 45(2):167–256

Olfati-Saber R, Fax JA et al (2007) Consensus and cooperation in networked multi-agent systems. Proc IEEE 95(1):215–233

Perc M, Szolnoki A (2010) Coevolutionary games-A mini review. Biosystems 99(2):109–125

Proudfoot AG, McAuley DF et al (2011) Translational research: what does it mean, what has it delivered and what might it deliver? Curr Opin Crit Care 17(5):495–503

Rosen ED, MacDougald OA (2006) Adipocyte differentiation from the inside out. Nat Rev Mol Cell Biol 7(12):885–896

Schweitzer F, Fagiolo G et al (2009) Economic Networks: the new challenges. Science 325(5939):422–425

Smith RJ, Okano JT et al (2010). Evolutionary dynamics of complex networks of HIV drug-resistant strains: the case of San Francisco. Science 327(5966):697–701

Strogatz SH (2001) Exploring complex networks. Nature 410(6825):268–276

Vespignani A (2010) Complex networks the fragility of interdependency. Nature 464(7291):984–985

Wang WX, Wang BH et al (2006) Traffic dynamics based on local routing protocol on a scale-free network. Phys Rev E 73(2)

Watts DJ, Strogatz SH (1998) Collective dynamics of 'small-world' networks. Nature 393(6684):440–442

Yang R, Zhou T et al (2008) Optimal contact process on complex networks. Phys Rev E 78(6)

Zhou T, Lu L et al (2009) Predicting missing links via local information. Eur Phys J B 71(4):623–630

Bibliometrics and University Research Rankings Demystified for Librarians

Ruth A. Pagell

Abstract In the six years since I first researched university research rankings and bibliometrics, much of the world suffered an economic downturn that has impacted research funding and open access journals, research institution repositories and self-published material on the web have opened up access to scholarly output and led to new terminology and output measurements. University rankings have expanded beyond the national end-user consumer market to a research area of global interest for scientometric scholars. Librarians supporting scholarly research have an obligation to understand the background, metrics, sources and the rankings to provide advice to their researchers and their institutions.

This chapter updates an article in Taiwan's *Evaluation in Higher Education* journal (Pagell 2009) based on a presentation at Concert (Pagell 2008). It includes a brief history of scholarly output as a measure of academic achievement. It focuses on the intersection of bibliometrics and university rankings by updating both the literature and the rankings themselves. Librarians should find it relevant and understandable.

Keywords Bibliometrics · Universities · Rankings · Higher Education · Research · International · Librarians

Introduction

One result from the internationalization of the education industry is the globalization of university rankings, with a focus on research output. Governments, intergovernmental organizations and funding bodies have shown a growing concern for

---

Adopted from Pagell, Ruth A., "University Research Rankings: From Page Counting to Academic Accountability" (2009). Research Collection Library. Paper 1.http://ink.library.smu.edu.sg/library_research/1; 高教評鑑3:1(June 2009):33–63

Ruth A. Pagell has extensive international experience, writing and speaking on topics such as international business, bibliometrics and information literacy. After working in US libraries, she was founding librarian for the Li Ka Shing Library, Singapore Management University. She currently teaches in the LIS program at University of Hawaii. Email: rpagell@hawaii.edu

---

R. A. Pagell (✉)
University of Hawaii, Honolulu, USA
e-mail: rpagell@hawaii.edu

C. Chen, R. Larsen (eds.), *Library and Information Sciences,*
DOI 10.1007/978-3-642-54812-3_10, © The Author(s) 2014

research accountability which has moved the university rankings from a national to a worldwide playing field.

This chapter examines three different research streams underlying today's university research rankings and demonstrates their impact on today's university rankings to help readers understand "… how an arguably innocuous consumer concept has been transformed into a policy instrument, with wide ranging, intentional and unintentional, consequences for higher education and society" (Hazelkorn 2007).

National, Regional and International Policy and Accountability

The increased ability to measure and analyze scholarly output has increased the involvement of governmental and funding agencies in the rankings arena. They seek methodologies that will measure universities' accountability to their funding sources and their constituencies. Government concern about the spending and impact of its research monies is not new. In 1965, U.S. President Johnson (1965) issued a policy statement to insure that federal support "of research in colleges and universities contribute more to the long run strengthening of the universities and colleges so that these institutions can best serve the Nation in the years ahead.

A growing number of countries have initiated research assessment exercises, either directly or through evaluation bodies such as the benchmark United Kingdom Research Assessment Exercise (RAE) initiated in 1992 which used peer review. The newer initiatives by the Higher Education Funding Council for England incorporates bibliometric measures of research output and considers measurements of research impact (van Raan et al. 2007; Paul 2008; HEFCE 2013) An OCLC pilot study (Key Perspectives 2009) looks at five specific countries, the Netherlands, Ireland, United Kingdom, Denmark and Australia, who have taken different approaches to assessment. Hou et al. (2012) examine the higher education excellence programs in four Asian countries, China, Korea, Japan and Taiwan.

Other active agencies are the Higher Education Evaluation and Accreditation Council of Taiwan (HEEACT 2013) University Grants Committee of Hong Kong (2013) and the Australian Research Quality Framework (Excellence in Research 2013). Most of these incorporate some form of bibliometrics into their evaluation methodology. Italy introduced performance related funding in 2009 (Abbott 2009), establishing the National Research Council (CNR 2013). In conjunction with the new Italian initiative is a series of articles examining many aspects of rankings and productivity (Abramo et al. 2011a, b, 2012, 2013a, b).

Europe has been active in tracking academic rankings at a multi-national level. A group of experienced rankers and ranking analysts, who met first in 2002, created the International Ranking Expert Group (IREG 2013), now called the International Observatory on Rankings and Excellence. In 2006, the Group met in Berlin and issued the Berlin Principles for ranking colleges and universities. The UNESCO-European Centre for Higher Education in Bucharest, Romania and the Institute for

Higher Education Policy (IHEP), an independent group based in Washington D.C., co-hosted the meeting. The four categories for the 16 Berlin Principles for rankings and league tables include:

A. Purposes and Goals of Rankings
B. Designing and Weighting Indicators
C. Collection and Processing of Data
D. Presentation of Ranking Results

The guidelines aim to insure that "those producing rankings and league tables hold themselves accountable for quality in their own data collection, methodology, and dissemination (Bollag 2006; IHEP 2006). As a follow-up, IHEP (2007) issued an evaluation of various existing ranking systems.

The key findings of the proceedings of the three assessment conferences are in the UNESCO-CEPES publication, *Higher Education in Europe*:("From the Editors," 2002; Merisotis and Sadlak 2005) and("Editorial," 2007).

The OECD Feasibility Study for the International Assessment of Higher Education Learning Outcomes (AHELO)gauges "whether an international assessment of higher education learning outcomes that would allow comparisons among HEIs across countries is scientifically and practically feasible. Planning began in 2008 and the final results are presented in several publications (OECD 2013) 17 countries, representing 5 continents are included in the study.

Incorporating both the Berlin Principles and the AHELO learning outcomes, the European Commission, Directorate General for Education and Culture, issued a tender to "look into the feasibility of making a multi-dimensional ranking of universities in Europe, and possibly the rest of the world too' (European Commission 2008). A new system U-Multirank, scheduled for launch in 2014, is the outcome of the feasibility study. (van Vught and Ziegele 2011).

At the university level, rankings have been viewed as a game (Dolan 1976; Meredith 2004; Henshaw 2006; Farrell and Van Der Werf 2007). University administrators play the game by making educational policy decisions based on what will improve their standings in those rankings that are important to them. 63 % of leaders/ university administrators from 41 countries who responded to a 2006 survey under the auspices of OECD reported taking strategic, organizational academic or managerial actions in response to their rankings. The results of this survey are available in variety publications (Hazelkorn 2008).

Historical Literature Review

The appearance in 1983 of U.S. News and World Report ratings of U.S. colleges based on a survey of college presidents (Solorzano and Quick 1983) marked the beginning of the modern era in rankings, with a shift in emphasis from small studies in scholarly publications to a national comparison for a general audience. By 1990, the magazine's rankings included university provided student and faculty measures to go along with the initial "reputational " survey of college presidents, Governments and scholars had been publishing quality or research rankings for over 100 years. Salmi and Saroyan (2007) examine rankings and public accountability and also identify statistical annual reports published by the Commission of the US Bureau of Education from 1870–1890 that classified institutions.

Pagell and Lusk (2002) discuss a series of early scholarly business school rankings. The earliest work they cite, Raymond Hughes' "A Study of Graduate School of America", published on behalf of the America Council of Education., rated 19 graduate departments in the U.S., primarily Ivy League private universities and the major mid-western state universities. All but three of his initial 19 do not appear on one of this article's list of top 30 worldwide universities today (See Table 8 below). Magnoun (1966) compares additional studies using Hughes methodology and analyzes the consistencies and changes during the 40 year interval. He emphasizes the importance of the rankings to university administration and the importance of quality graduate programs to the country as a whole. Other studies that Pagell and Lusk examine focus on individual departments and they count pages, publications and weighted page counts. The American Educational Research Association sponsored research rankings in the 1970s (Blau and Margulies 1974; Schubert 1979). Kroc introduces citation analysis for schools of education and analyzes early challenges using Social Science Citation Index (SSCI), many of which persist today (Kroc 1984).

These earlier rankings focused on specific departments in a limited number of U S universities. While scholarly rankings in today's higher education environment are global, individual disciplines continue to use their own rankings. For example, Jin published two studies on economic rankings in East Asia relying on Econlit and page counts(Jin and Yau 1999; Jin and Hong 2008). The economics open access repository RePEc contains numerous rankings using multiple metrics, based on authors' deposits in the repository (IDEAS 2013).

No one ranking is "correct". However, there is a consistency across top rankings. In the scholarly surveys this paper cites, spanning 1925 to 2014, employing peer review and a variety of counting methodologies across different subject categories, a limited number of schools are number one with Harvard leading the way.

Using Bibliometric Methodology

Pritchard (1969) coined the term "bibliometrics" to mean the quantitative analysis and statistics to scholarly outputs, such as journal articles, citation counts, and journal impact. September 1978 marked the debut of the journal Scientometrics. This broader concept refers to the quantitative features and characteristics of science and scientific research and is attributed to Vaissily V Nalimov by Hood and Wilson (2001). They examine the similarities and differences among bibliometrics, scientometrics and also infometrics and informetrics. Webometrics is now considered a different approach to research rankings. Originally coined by Almind and Ingersen (1997), it applies bibliometric techniques to new web metrics. Webometrics entered

Bibliometrics and University Research Rankings Demystified for Librarians

Table 1 Institutions and Countries Ranked by Number of Articles on Bibliometrics from 1980–2013 (WOS General Search, Topic Bibliometric* searched 11 September, 2013)

Institutions	Articles	Citations	Countries	Articles	Citations
Leiden Univ	151	3936	USA	837	10698
Consejo Superior de Investigaciones Cientificas(CSIC)	150	1248	Spain	548	3633
Univ Granada	101	805	England	329	3530
Indiana U	75	1751	Netherlands	263	5167
Hungarian Academy of Sciences	74	1642	Germany	249	2275

the mainstream with the December 2004 special issue of *Journal of the American Society for Information Science and Technology*. Table 1 tracks the leading universities and countries producing bibliometric literature. 1969 marked the first year that WOS included articles on bibliometrics and the number has increased every year since. Papers on "bibliometrics and university rankings" are about 10 % of all bibliometric papers.

Since the first article on bibliometrics appeared in 1969, there were 4474 articles in WOS and 5760 in SCOPUS with almost 34000 citations in WOS and 54800 in Scopus by October 2 2013 (using Biblometric* as a topic in WOS and a keyword in SCOPUS). Fig. 1 illustrates growth by decades.

No matter what term is used, the rankings are only as good as one's understanding of the underlying measurements described below. Anyone using a ranking should check the documentation and methodology. The earlier rankings used peer review, now referred to as "reputation" and countable output such as journal articles in a group of "top" journals, proceedings, number of actual pages, number of normalized pages based on characters per page or doctoral degrees by school (Cleary and Edwards 1960). Some give full credit to each author, some distribute a percent per school by author; a few just use first author. Peer review may cover one to three years; other output measures cover one year to decades. Article counts may include book reviews, editorials and comments. All of these methods have their strengths and weaknesses. In order to select the international research university ranking that reflects an organization's needs today, it is necessary to understand the bibliometrics that are used.

The appearance of *Science Citation Index* in 1955 laid the groundwork for the change from qualitative and manually countable scholarly output to the new era of citation metrics. When Eugene Garfield (1955) launched Science Citation Index, he originally positioned citation indexes as a subject approach to literature and a way to check the validity of an article through its cited references. In 1963, he wrote about the value of using citation data for the evaluation of publications (Garfield and Sher 1963). By 1979, in an article in volume one of *Scientometrics* he raised concerns about using citations as an evaluation tool that are still being examined by today's researchers such as negative and self-citations; counting of multiple authors and disambiguation of authors names (Garfield 1979).

Today bibliometrics is a primary tool for organizations, such as universities and government bodies, to measure research performance. Widespread use of

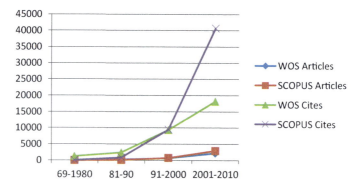

Fig. 1 Growth of Bibliometric Articles and Citations. (Searched October 2 2013)

bibliometrics is possible with easy access to articles, citations and analytical tools in both Thomson-Reuters Scientific Web of Science (WOS) and Elsevier's Scopus. Many individuals turn to Google Scholar.

Measurement in today's academic environment is evidence-based and as noted by Leung (2007) "There is now mounting pressure all over the world for academics to publish in the most-cited journals and rake in as many citations to their work as possible".

Individuals, researchers, departments, universities and outside bodies are all counting output. Departments employ bibliometrics to evaluate faculty for hire, tenure and promotion decisions, using number of publications and citation counts, journal impact and additional tools such as an H-Index. Academic output such as articles and citations provide the data for internal and external benchmarking. Universities are using more bibliometrics for government and stakeholder reporting of output. Country level benchmarking and comparisons use bibliometrics as well.

International data in any field poses problems involving standardization and cross country comparisons. University research rankings using both quality measures such as peer review and metrics compound these issues. Usher (2009) notes that "as rankings have spread around the world, a number of different rankings efforts have managed to violate every single one of "rankings principles. (Federkeil (2009) adds that "The only field typified by valid international indicators is research in the natural and life sciences...." He also notes that there is no "valid concept for a global ranking of teaching quality..."

Even if rankers agree to use a standard source for tracking articles or citations, there is no consensus on how to count multiple authors. Abramo et al. (2013b) studied the multi-author issue and suggested a further weighting based on how much each author contributed to the research. Other counting questions arise over authors who have changed universities and on whether to use a total figure, which favors large institutions or a per faculty count favoring smaller institutions. However, a per-faculty definition has issues of its own in whom to count as a faculty and how to calculate FTE.

Bibliometrics and University Research Rankings Demystified for Librarians 143

Table 2 Standard Bibliometrics Used in Rankings. (© Pagell 2008, updated 2013)

METRIC	MEASUREMENTS	SOURCES
Publications	Number of articles	Web of Science
	Number of pages	Scopus
		Google Scholar
		Individual databases and websites
Citations	Number per article	Web of Science & Essential Science
	Number per faculty	Indicators
	Number per university	Scopus
	Highly cited papers	Google Scholar
		Individual databases (Science Direct, EBSCO, JStor, Proquest)
		Scholarly websites (Repec, ACM Portal)
H—Index	The number of papers with citation numbers higher or equal to the number of citations (Hirsch 2005)	Web of Science
		Scopus
		Individual calculations
Journal Quality	Journal Impact Factor	Journal Citation Reports
	Eigenfactor	Eigenfactor.org
	SNIP	SCImago
	SJR	Leiden

It is necessary to understand the strengths and weaknesses of each of the bibliometric tools when analyzing and applying them to real world situations. It is important to check the methodology, including definitions and weightings, when comparing rankings or doing time series comparisons with the same tool. Table 2 organizes the most commonly used bibliometrics for research assessment by what they measure and which sources use them.

The H-Index is a measure of quality relative to quantity based on papers and citations within the given database. For example, if an author has 44 papers in SCOPUS with 920 citations and the 16th paper has 16 citations the H-Index is 16; if the same author has 36 papers in WOS with 591 cites and the 13th paper has 13 citations, the H-Index in WOS is 13. That same author created an author ID in Google Scholar, which tracks articles and citations. The author has 65 publications, 1921 citations and the 21st article has 21 citations for an H-index of 21.

Other approaches use weighted averages or scores, output per capita and output by subject or country norms. They may also adjust for multiple authors from different organizations. Metrics should be stable and consistent in order to measure changes over time and be replicable for user input.

One of the most controversial metrics is Journal Impact Factor from Thomson-Reuter's Journal Citation Reports (Werner and Bornmann 2013). Concern about the over-use of this metric in the evaluation of faculty, from publishers, editors and researchers led to DORA, the San Francisco Declaration on Research Assessment, (San Francisco 2013) the outcome of the December 2012 meeting of the American Society for Cell Biology. Not only is there concern for the misuse of the impact factor as a rating instrument but also for its impact on scientific research. Alberts (2013) notes that impact factor encourages publishers to favor high-impact disciplines such as biomedicine and discourages researchers from taking on risky new work, which take time for publication.

JCR is being challenged by newer measures of journal quality which are appearing in university ranking scores. These include the eigenfactor, SNIP and SJR all of which are freely available on the web. The Bergstrom Lab (2013) at the University of Washington developed the eigenfactor, where journals are considered to be influential if they are cited often by other influential journals. The eigenfactor is now incorporated into Journal Citation Reports. SNIP, Source Normalized Impact per Paper, from Leiden's CTWS measures contextual citation impact by weighting citations based on the total number of citations in a subject field. The impact of a single citation is given higher value in subject areas where citations are less likely, and vice versa. SCImago's SJR2 recognizes the value of citations from closely related journals (Journal M3trics 2012).

New tools using webometrics and altmetrics which incorporate social media question the old model of scholarly impact (Konkiel 2013). The growing body of literature around "Webometrics" and Altmetrics expand the scope of this article. Björneborn and Ingwersen, in a special webometrics issue of *Journal of the American Society for Information Society and Technology* warned against taking the analogy between citation analyses and link analyses too far (Björneborn and Ingwersen 2004). However, we can no longer ignore the role of the web in academic research.

Despite the rise of alternative measures of scientific output, Web of Science (WOS) and Scopus remain the two major English language commercial bibliographic sources used by the research rankings. WOS is the current iteration of the original Science Citation Index. The entire suite of databases may include Science Citation Index (SCI-e from 1900), Social Science Citation Index (SSCI from 1900) and Arts & Humanities Citation Index (A&HCI from 1975). Other databases include Conference Proceedings and Books in Sciences and Social Sciences. An institution can subscribe to any or all of the databases, for as many years as they can afford. WOS has two search interfaces: General Search and Cited Reference Search. General Search includes only those articles that WOS indexes. Each article has the references in the article and the times the article is cited by other WOS publications. It is used at an institutional level for the rankings. Users can create their own rankings using analysis tools for authors, institutions or journals and rank output by number of articles by subject area, document type, leading authors, source titles, institutions and countries. Each author's information (institution, country) receives one count. Not all articles include addresses. An H-Index is also calculated. The Cited Reference Search includes all citations in the WOS articles from any reference source and is primarily used for data on individual researchers. Until the end of 2011, Thomson provided a listing of highly cited papers also used in international rankings. This is now part of *Essential Science Indicators*, a separate subscription service. Thomson-Reuters publishes *Science Watch*, covering metrics and research analytics (Thomson-Reuters 2013). Registration is required

Elsevier's SCOPUS began in late 2004. It includes citations received since 1996. The subscription includes all subject areas and document types for all the years that information is available. The subscription includes four broad subject areas: Health

Sciences, Physical Sciences, Life Sciences and Social Sciences. Added features are author and affiliation searches and analysis of citing journals, authors and institutions and an H-Index. Elsevier publishes *Research Trends* a quarterly newsletter which provides insights into research trends based on bibliometric analysis with a range of articles on different aspects of ranking, from assessing the ARWU (Shanghai Rankings) to explaining the soon to be released U-Multirank (Research Trends 2008).

Google Scholar is the third and most controversial source of citations. The search engine has improved since authors, such as Peter Jacsó, exposed all of the errors that limited the use of Google Scholar for comparative evaluation purposes (Jacsó 2008). Today's Scholar has an advanced search feature to search by author's name. It has improved its ability to differentiate dates from numbers; it added the ability to download to bibliographic software; it has its own metrics for measuring journal quality and it is now linking to article citations on publisher pages. It still lacks the editorial control of WOS and Scopus, the controlled vocabulary with subject terms and any information on how articles and citations are included. Meho and Yang (2007) discuss the impact of data sources on citation counts and provide a balanced review, while pointing out the thousands of hours required for data cleansing using Google Scholar.

All three systems have mechanisms for authors to identify themselves, their affiliations and their publications if they chose to do so. Researchers may also create one unique ID through ORCID (http://orcid.org)

WOS and SCOPUS understate the number articles and citations, especially for universities that are not strong in the sciences and SCOPUS, because it only includes citations from articles written after 1995, also understates the citations for older authors. Google Scholar is not a viable alternative for quality university rankings. Table 3 compares features in WOS, SCOPUS and Google Scholar.

WOS or SCOPUS offer quality and standardization. However, they are slower to reflect changes in scientific communication

Factors Limiting the Number of Articles and Citations

Scientific disciplines are the strength of WOS and SCOPUS. This is especially obvious in rankings such as SIR that include research and medical institutes. Subject matter, language, country of origin and format understate the scholarly output in social science and humanities and put pressure on authors to publish in high impact journals at the expense of local research. Local journals or books publish scholarly output in these fields in the local language. In an article published in *Scientometrics* and summarized in *Nature*, Van Raan et al. (2011) reported that the language effect is important across multiple disciplines for articles published in German and French. While rankers now include separate listings for social sciences and humanities universities, these rankings are still based on the WOS or SCOPUS publications.

Table 3 Comparison of Key Sources ((Pagell 2008), updated 2013)

	WOS Thomson Reuters *	SCOPUS Elsevier	GOOGLE SCHOLAR
Cost	Multiple subscription options	One subscription	Free
Coverage	>16000 selected scholarly journals; conference proceedings & books: 55 million records	>21,000 selected scholarly journals, conference proceedings; books 50 million records	Articles, books, papers.??
Time	Varies by subscription (1900-)	1 1996 for citations ((started in 2004) articles back to 1800s	Not stated
Strengths	History of quality and scholarly applications; Date range; Scientific coverage; Cited Reference Search; Analytical tools	Conference proceedings; Ease of use; Flexible software; Scientific coverage; Prepub articles; One subscription; Non-English publications	Widest coverage of materials not found in peer reviewed sources
Weaknesses	Western focus; Scientific bias; Cost	Date Range; Scientific bias	No quality control; Numerous errors; Time consuming (Meho and Yang 2007)
Users	Top tier institutions; funding agencies	Scientific institutions; usage growing	Individuals
Rankings Applications	Governments; Research Institutions; Shanghai Jiao Tong; THE; HEEACT; HEFCE	QS; SCImago & Webometrics	
Quality Control	Peer reviewed Publications	Peer reviewed publications	None
Citations	Citations included from non-WOS journals in cited references; cumulated counts	Only citations from SCOPUS articles Cumulated counts	Not stated; web harvesting; must use manual counting for author totals

Table 3 (continued)

	WOS Thomson Reuters *	SCOPUS Elsevier	GOOGLE SCHOLAR
Name Identity	Building Name Authority Self-Registration ResearcherID	Building Name Authority automatically; needs clean-up but good start; encourages ORCID	Authors can self-identify; no way to deal with common names
Add-ons	Analysis tools; ESI, JCR	Analysis tools; SNIP SJR, Altmetric add-on	Harzing's Publish orPerish
Notes:	EXCLUDES in General Search:, theses, working papers, reports "*"Thomson-Reuters was unwilling to provide any updated materials.	EXCLUDES cites from publications not covered within SCOPUS content	INCLUDES:, non-reviewed articles; best for; individual use with extensivedata cleansing

Table 4 Journal Impact Factors for Selected Fields. (Extracted from JCR, September 2013)

FIELD	Total Cites	Median Impact	Aggregate Impact	Aggregate Cited Half-Life	# Journals
Neuroscience	1787981	2.872	3.983	7.5	252
Medical Research	562580	2,263	3.307	6.9	121
Zoology	291515	1.059	1.521	>10	151
Telecommunications	149916	0.962	1.335	6.3	78
Sociology	129174	0.829	1.054	>10	139
Economics	450167	0.795	1.193	>10	333
History	11787	0.231	0.344	>10	69

Table 4 displays impact factors for selected fields from the 2012 *Journal Citation Reports*

The most ranked journal from this selection, *Nature Review in Neuroscience* has an aggregate impact score of 35.9 and most highly ranked in the social sciences area, *Journal of Economic Literature* has an aggregate impact score of 10.160. JCR is transparent, showing the calculations for the metrics. Worldwide rankings generally use Essential Science Indicators, which is a sub-set of Web of Science and a separate subscription.

A user can download the entire SNIP and SJR dataset (with minimal registration), allowing an analyst to sort by scores, general topic, field or country but it lacks the underlying methodology. In the 50 most impactful journals using SJR, only three were exclusively in the Social Sciences.

Table 4 in Pagell's original version (2009) includes data on Chinese social science and humanities articles published abroad from the Information Network of Humanities and Social Sciences in Chinese Universities. That data have not been updated and the Chinese Social Science Citation database ceased a couple of years ago. Table 5 provides data retrieved from WOS and SCOPUS on the same universities. Data estimate the total number of articles in social sciences and humanities in these databases and the number published in Chinese.

The situation for Asian institutions is more positive in the sciences. The U.S. National Science Board tracks the growth of non-U.S. science and engineering (including social science) output in *Science and Engineering Indicators.* Below are some of the 2012 data (Academic Research 2012)

- "The United States accounted for 26% of the world's total S&E articles in 2009, down from 31% in 1999. The share for the European Union also declined, from 36% in 1999 to 32% in 2009.
- In Asia, average annual growth rates were high—for example, 16.8% in China and 10.1% in South Korea. In 2009, China, the world's second-largest national producer of S&E articles, accounted for 9% of the world total.
- Coauthored articles grew from 40% of the world's total S&E articles in 1988 to 67% in 2010. Articles with only domestic coauthors increased from 32% of all articles in 1988 to 43% in 2010. Internationally coauthored articles grew from 8 to 24% over the same period.

Bibliometrics and University Research Rankings Demystified for Librarians

Table 5 Chinese Universities Publishing Social Science Articles in WOS and SCOPUS

University	Total Number of Articles WOS	Total Number of Articles In Chinese WOS	Total Number of Articles SCOPUS	Total Number of Articles in Chinese SCOPUS
Peking U	4488	48	2993	307
Zhejiang U	3521	98	2085	197
Fudan U	2243	30	1324	62
Wuhan U	1263	49	3411	1304
Renmin U	1230	60	4079	430
Xiamen U	906	21	968	56
TOTAL	13651	306	14860	2356

About 6% of all articles in SCOPUS have a Chinese address and 30% of those are in Chinese. 4% of all articles in WOS are from a Chinese address and only 5% of those are in Chinese. Web of Science and Scopus, searched 30 September, 2013

- U.S.-based researchers were coauthors of 43% of the world's total internationally coauthored articles in 2010."

The appendix to the report includes data by region, country and broad discipline, but not by university.

Jin and Hong (2008), in their article ranking economics departments in East Asian universities, note that "when journal quality and sample periods were adjusted favorably to East Asian schools, the current research productivity of top-tier East Asian universities was found to be close to that of major state universities in the United States a decade ago"

Figure 2 displays the calculations for the percent of articles in WOS for four Asian-Pacific countries. It shows the rapid growth of articles from Taiwan and Korea and the much slower growth for English language Singapore and New Zealand. The number and percent of Chinese articles in WOS is growing annually and is up to almost 4%, similar to the number of articles in Japanese, French and German. Growth of peer reviewed articles from Asia-Pacific as indicated in data from WOS and Science and Engineering Indicators will have a positive impact on the number of Asian-Pacific universities appearing in the research rankings.

Contemporary International University Rankings or League Tables

Many countries publish national rankings which are tools for their own students, faculty and funding bodies. An example is the ranking of top Chinese universities from Research Center for Chinese Science Evaluation (RCCSE) at Wuhan University and the Network of Science & Education Evaluation in China (www.nseac.com). ARWU's Resource page provides a listing of local rankings from 28 different countries. With the internationalization of education at an organizational level, institutions and even countries compete for students and researchers and not surprisingly, this

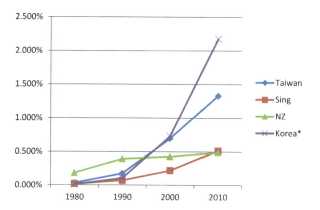

Fig. 2 Growth of Asian-Pacific Articles in Web of Science from 1900–2010. (Extracted from Web of Science, August 2013)

has led to international ranking systems. Commercial sources, universities, evaluation authorities and scientometric research organizations compile today's university rankings. The rankings may incorporate bibliometric data from Thomson-Reuters or Scopus, peer review or "reputational surveys". Some research institutions are creating new algorithms from bibliometric sources or from web metrics.

Some of the better-known rankings include:

- ARWU (Academic Ranking of World Universities) from 2003;
  Center for World-Class Universities at Shanghai Jiao Tong University (Center, 2013)
- National Taiwan University Rankings, "Performance Rankings of Scientific Papers of World Universities" from 2012-; formerly HEEACT (2007–2011); (National, 2012-)
- THE World University Rankings from 2011 (Times, 2013 – 14)
- Leiden Rankings from 2008; Center for Science and Technology Studies (CWTS, 2013)
- SIR (SCImago Institutional Rankings) from 2009—(SCImago, 2013)
- QS World University Rankings from 2004 (Quacquarelli Symonds 2013) (republished by US News and World Reports as World's Best Colleges and Universities from 2008-)

The University of Zurich (2013) presents a clear overview of the rankings listed above. Chen and Liao (2012) statistically analyze the data and calculate correlations among the rankings, especially ARWU, HEEACT (now NTU) and THE.

Shanghai Jiao Tong's Center for World-Class Universities produces Academic Rankings of World Universities (ARWU). It has the World's Top 500 and top 200 in five fields and five subjects. Nobel Prize winners in two indicators, Thomson Reuters bibliometric data and articles from *Nature* and *Science* comprise the rankings for all but those schools strongest in social sciences (Liu and Cheng 2005). The Academic Ranking of World Universities (ARWU) is published and copyrighted by Shanghai Ranking Consultancy, which is not affiliated with any university or government agency. Billaut et al. (2010) take a critical look at ARWU while DoCampo (2011) examines ARWU relative to university systems and country metrics.

Similar to, but not as well known as ARWU, is the former HEEACT(Higher Education Evaluation and Accreditation Council of Taiwan) ranking which is now published by the National Taiwan University and renamed NTU Ranking. It presents a worldwide ranking for 500 universities and rankings by six fields and 14 subjects. All the rankings are based on data from Thomson Reuters *Essential Science Indicators.*

CWTS at Leiden and SCImago expand the measurements used for rankings by experimenting with new metrics. Leiden University's Center for Science and Technology Studies (CWTS) developed its own ranking system using bibliometric indicators from Thomson Reuters to measure the scientific output of 500 major universities worldwide. It uses no reputational data or data collected from the universities themselves. The researchers modify the existing data to create normalized scores and continue to experiment with new measures. The web site provides an overall ranking and the user can select field, region, country and indicator. These rankings receive little attention in the international press but the researchers from Leiden publish the most papers about "bibliometrics" based on searches in WOS and SCOPUS (searched 10 September, 2013).

SIR, SCImago's Institutions Rankings, uses metrics from SCOPUS. It ranks over 2700 organizations including research and medical institutions. Ranking are worldwide, by region and by country. Measures include output, percent international collaboration, normalized citations and the percent of articles published in the first quartile of their categories using SJR, SCImago's own journal impact score. SCImago claims that SIR reports are not league tables and the goal is to provide policy makers and research managers with a tool to evaluate and improve their research results. Reports are all in PDF format.

THE and QS have broader target markets, with a focus beyond the research community. Originally published as part of the QS rankings, THE began publishing its own rankings, powered by Thomson Reuters in 2010–2011. It ranks 400 worldwide universities. Its ranking metrics include teaching, research, knowledge transfer and international outlook. There are rankings by region and broad subject area and separate rankings by reputation and for universities less than 50 years of age.

QS continues to publish its rankings, with less emphasis on evidence based bibliometrics and more emphasis on qualitative "Academic reputation". Recognizing the need to internationalize the market for North American college–bound students, *U.S. News and World Report* began republishing the then THE-QS in 2008 and it continues to republish the QS rankings. According to Robert Morse (2010), *U.S News* is working together with QS. A noticeable difference in the QS rankings is that 20 out of the top 50 universities are from Commonwealth or former Commonwealth countries.

The Berlin Principles emphasize the importance of accountability for the rankers, not only the institutions they are ranking. Enserink (2007), in his article in *Science* "Who Ranks the University Rankers", examines the various international rankings. Other authors from such prestigious journals as *Chronicle of Higher Education, Nature* and *Science* have examined the effect of rankings on university behavior (Declan 2007; Labi 2008; Saisana et al. 2011).

Table 6 Comparison of Methodology of Two Research Rankings

Academic Ranking of World Universities (Thomson-Reuters)	SCImago Institutions Rankings (Scopus)
Quality of Education 10%	Output: Total number of journals publishing in SCOPUS
Alumni (with any degree winning Nobel prize or Fields Medals **Quality of Faculty/Staff**	**% International Collaboration**
Winning Nobel Prize or FieldMedals 20%	**Normalized Impact** (at an article level)
Highly Cited 20% **Research Output 50%**	**% High Quality Publications** (top quartile of SJRII)
Articles in *Nature* and *Science* (20%)**	Specialization Index
Articles in SCI and SSCI prior year (20%)	% Excellent (Highly Cited)
Articles per capita (10%)	% Lead (first author)
**For institutions social sciences and humanities universities, *Nature* and *Science* points are reallocated	% Excellence in Leadership
	No weightings are given
	A similar rankings is created for Ibero-American Institutions
	Includes research and medical institutions
September 2013	September 2013
http://www.shanghairanking.com/ARWU-FIELD-Methodology-2012.html	http://www.scimagoir.com/pdf/SCImago%20Institutions%20Rankings%20IBER%20en.pdf

Table 7 Comparison of THE and QS. (© Pagell 2009; updated 2013)

THE World University Rankings (Thomson Reuters)	THE—QS WorldUniversity Rankings (and U.S. News)*
Citations, Research Influence (30%)	Academic Reputation 40%
Research, Volume, Income and Reputation (30%)	Survey (current response past 3 years)
Reputation (18%)	**Employer reputation 10%**
Income (6%)	Global survey
Papers published* (6%)	**Student-faculty-ratio 20%**
Teaching: The Learning Environment(30%)	**Citations per Faculty 20%**
Invitation Only Reputation Survey* (15%)	**International Faculty Ratio 5%**
Staff/Student Ratio (4.5%)	**International Student Ratio 5%**
Doctorate/BA (2.25%)	
Doctorate awards (6%)	
Income/Staff (2.25)	
International Outlook (7.5%)	
Industry Income (2.5%)	

U.S. News uses THE-QS methodology

Tables 6 and 7 summarize the methodologies of selected international ranking, as described above. They illustrate the differences in metrics and weights of the various indicators. More information on methodology is available from the websites in the last row of the table.

QS modifies its metric weightings for rankings by subject and field, putting even more weight on reputation for social science and humanities.

In addition to modifications of existing metrics from Thomson-Reuters and Scopus by Leiden and SCImago, the use of web data is now receiving serious

Bibliometrics and University Research Rankings Demystified for Librarians

consideration. Consejo Superior de Investigaciones Científicas (CSIC)first issued the semi-annual Ranking Web of Universities in 2004. CSIC claims that it is an independent, objective, free, open scientific exercise for the providing reliable, multi-dimensional, updated and useful information about the performance of universities from all over the world based on their web presence and impact. Built from publicly available web data, it includes almost 12,000 institutions arranged by world, region, and country' Rankings are based on impact (external links to…), presence openness, including repositories, on the one bibliometric element, excellence, the top 10% of scholarly output with data from SCImago available from about 5100 institutions weighted at about 17%. (CSIC http://www.csic.es).

Comparing a variety of rankings and ranking criteria clarify the importance of understanding the different metrics and weightings.

Table 8 uses 2013 Shanghai Jiao Tong (ARWU) as the basis for the top ten, and compares them to the top ten from the 2013 rankings from THE, QS, SCImago, Leiden and Webometrics and the 2012 rankings from NTU.

18 universities make up the top 10 on the four main lists (ARWU, NTU, THE and QS). Harvard, Stanford, MIT and Oxford are top ten on all of them; Harvard leads the pack across all the rankings. It is interesting to note the similarities and differences among the schemes and between the international lists and Hughes original 1925 rankings. Of Hughes Top 10 in 1925, only one school, University of Wisconsin, was not in the top ten in one of the selected rankings and 16 of the 19 are on at least one top 30 list. Internationalization brings UK universities into the top 20 and time has shifted the U.S. balance away from public institutions in the mid-west. Two top technology universities are in the top tier.

Another interesting factor in the tables is the difference in the SCImago and Leiden rankings for top papers, highlighting differences between the contents of SCOPUS and WOS.Webometrics top four are the same top four as ARWU's research rankings

The evaluating bodies list universities by their rank, based on an underlying scoring system. Table 9 shows the importance of checking underlying scores to get a better understanding of what it means to be one or 100. It shows the scores for universities one, two and 100 and the percent of separation from 1st to 100th. For example, in the QS rankings the first and 100th universities show a 31.6% difference while in the NTU rankings the first and 100th universities are over 79% apart.

Only U.S. and U.K. universities are in the top ten lists. The number of Asian universities in the top 100 has been growing. Table 10 lists Asia's top ten from four bibliometric rankings and Webometrics. There are a total of 24 universities on the list and the majority is now ranked in the top 100 in world. The strongest showings are from Japan and China.

An interesting, specialized addition to scholarly rankings comes from *Nature* which is publishing a rolling year's ranking for Asia-Pacific institutions and countries based on its own publications. The ranking includes only total publications and uses two calculations for giving an institution credit when there are multiple authors. University of Tokyo is the standout in the *Nature* ranking for Asia which is comparable to those listed above but includes more countries, (Nature 2013).

Table 8 World Rankings

University	ARWU	NTU 2012[a]	THE	QS	SCImago[b] NI	%Q1	Leiden top 10%	Webo-metrics Composite	Hughes
Harvard	1	1	2	2	2	12	5	1	2
Stanford	2	3	4	7	4	72	3	3	14
UC Berkley	3	8	8	25	10	115	7	4	9
MIT	4	10	5	1	1	173	1	2	
Cambridge	5	15	7	3	26	103	24	20	
CalTech	6	34	1	10	20	160	8	41	
Princeton	7	52	6	10	5	70	4	19	6
Columbia	8	13	13	14	9	39	19	12	3
U Chicago	9	30	9	9	8	17	16	23	1
Oxford	10	9	3	6	18	68	30	18	
Yale	11	14	11	8	31	24	10	15	5
Cornell	13	21	19	15	48	78	32	8	10
Johns Hopkins	17	2	15	16	12	43	36	33	7
U Tokyo	21	17	23	32	102	400+	330	63	
U Michigan	23	6	18	22	36	81	40	7	8

Other top 10 on 2 lists, Imperial College; on one list: Yale, UCLA, U Washington, Johns Hopkins, UC San Francisco, University College London and U Michigan

[a] NTU Rankings due out later in October

[b] Rankings for normalized impact and top quartile

Bibliometrics and University Research Rankings Demystified for Librarians

Table 9 Scoring Differences among Ranking Schemes for Universities 1, 2 and 100. (Extracted from rankings 2 October 2013)

RANK/Score	1	2	100	% from 1–2	% from 1–100
THE	94.9	93.9	52.6	1.05%	44.57%
ARWU	100	72.6	24.3	27.40%	75.70%
QS	100	99.2	68.4	0.80%	31.60%
NTU/2012	96.36	51.2	19.85	46.87%	79.40%

Table 10 Top 10 Asian Universities (ex. Israel) in 2013

RANK	ARWU 2013	THE 2013	NTU (HEACT) 2012	QS 2013	Webometrics 2013
1	Tokyo	Tokyo	Tokyo	NUS	NUS
2	Kyoto	NUS	Kyoto	U Hong Kong	Tsinghau
3	Osaka	U Hong Kong	Osaka	Tokyo	Tokyo
4	Hokaido	Seoul National	Seoul Ntl U	HKUST	NTU Taiwan
5	Kyushu	Peking	NUS	Kyoto	Peking
6	Nagoya	Tsinghau	Tohuku	Seoul	Zhejaing
7	NUS Singapore	Kyoto	Peking	Chinese U (HK)	Wuhan
8	Ntl U Taiwan	KAIST	Tsinghau	NTU Singapore	Shanghai Jio Tong
9	Seoul Ntl U	HKUST	NTU Taiwan	Peking	Fudan
10	Tokyo Inst Tech	Pohang U of Science and Technology	Zhejaing	Tsinghau	Seoul Ntl U
Top 100	3	All	8	All	8
Overlap	6	8	9	8	7

Extracted from sources in Table 7

Beyond Bibliometrics

The European Union's new U-Multirank and the web-based Altmetrics deserve a mention in any 2013 discussion of global university rankings and metrics. U-Multirank is the outcome of the EU's Feasibility study mentioned above. It differs from most existing rankings since there is no one overall score. According to an overview article in *Research Trends* (Richardson 2011) it is user-driven and designed to encourage diversity. The ranking components include research, education, international orientation, knowledge exchange and regional engagement. The 2014 U-Multi rank will be based on 500 universities worldwide who have agreed to be included. The League of European Research Universities and most US and Chinese universities declined (Rabesandratana 2013). The complete study is available from CHERPA (Consortium for Higher Education and Research Performance Assessment). It is based on the CHE methodology used to rank German universities. (van Vught and Ziegele 2011).

Fig. 3 An example of Altmetrics (Downloaded from Scopus 5 October 2013)

Altmetrics, which uses social media and web content, is currently embedded in results for SCOPUS and an Altmetric box will pop up for articles with a score. It is unclear if it will be incorporated into global rankings but it does add another dimension to impact.

Figure 3 is the Altmetric for a 2013 article on Altmetrics from PLoS One in SCOPUS.

Conclusion

Today's university rankings combine a variety of methodologies, including the traditional research output data and peer review and faculty or student input data as well as non-bibliometric measures such as contribution to industry, employers reputation and international orientation. Researchers are also looking for new and different measures that are available from the web and social media.

Existing research rankings are as narrow as a few journal titles in a discipline or as broad as all publications in Web of Science or Scopus or all links to universities and research institutions on the web. Countries have their own national rankings. International organizations are seeking new approaches to measure learning outcomes and research impact.

Government organizations and funding bodies require measures that evaluate quality of scholarly output as well as quantity. Commercial and academic publishers and faculty researchers are creating new and more complex measuring tools to meet these needs. A higher level of accountability is expected from the research producers. A higher level of accountability is also needed by the consumers of the metrics used to evaluate the outputs.

Librarians need to be aware of the different measures, not only to use as evaluation tools for collection development but also to be able to explain the meaning of these rankings to their researchers and institutions and assist them in interpreting the growing mass of rankings and research in the field.

Despite the different methodologies, the external pressures and internal maneuvering, there are two somewhat conflicting conclusions: Many of the historical best continue to dominate the top of the rankings; and many new faces, including a growing presence from Asia are joining the elite.

Open Access This chapter is distributed under the terms of the Creative Commons Attribution Noncommercial License, which permits any noncommercial use, distribution, and reproduction in any medium, provided the original author(s) and source are credited.

References

Abbott A (2009) Italy introduces performance-related funding. Nature 460(7255):559. doi:101038/460559a

Abramo G, Cicero T, D'Angelo CA (2013a) The impact of unproductive and top researchers on overall university research performance. J Informetr 7(1):166–175. doi:10.1016/j.joi.2012.10.006.

Abramo G, D'Angelo C, Cicero T (2012) What is the appropriate length of the publication period over which to assess research performance? Scientometrics 93(3):1005–1017. doi:10.1007/s11192-012-0714-9

Abramo G, D'Angelo C, Di Costa F (2011a) National research assessment exercises: a comparison of peer review and bibliometrics rankings. Scientometrics 89(3):929–941. doi:10.1007/s11192-011-0459-x

Abramo G, D'Angelo C, Di Costa F (2011b) A national-scale cross-time analysis of university research performance. Scientometrics 87(2):399–413. doi:10.1007/s11192-010-0319-0

Abramo G, D'Angelo CA, Rosati F (2013b) The importance of accounting for the number of co-authors and their order when assessing research performance at the individual level in the life sciences. J Informetr 7(1):198–208

Academic Research and Development (2012) Science and engineering indicators www.nsf.gov/statistics/seind12/c5/c5s4.htm. Accessed 23 Sept 2013

Alberts B (2013) Impact factor distortions. Science 340(6118):383

Almind TC, Ingwersen P (1997) Informetric analyses on the World Wide Web: methodological approaches to 'Webometrics'. J Doc 53(4):404–426. doi:10.1108/EUM0000000007205

Bergstrom Lab (2013) Eigenfactor.org: ranking and mapping scientific knowledge. http://www.eigenfactor.org/. Accessed 1 Oct 2013

Björneborn L, Ingwersen P (2004) Toward a basic framework for webometrics. J Am Soc Inf Sci Technol 55(14):121

Billaut JC, Bouyssou D, Vincke P (2010) Should you believe the Shanghai Rankings? Scientometrics 84(1):237–263

Blau PM, Margulies RZ (1974) A research replication: the reputations of American professional schools. Change Winter(74–75):42–47

Bollag B (2006) Group endorses principles for ranking of higher-education. The Chronicle Daily News, 9 June 2006. http://chronicle.com/article/Group-Endorses-Principles-for/25703. Accessed 25 Sept 2013

Center for World-Class Universities at Shanghai Jiao Tong University (2013) Academic Rankings of World Universities—ARWU (2013). http://www.shanghairanking.com/index.html. Accessed 29 Sept 2013

Chen K, Liao P (2012) A comparative study on world university rankings: a bibliometric survey. Bibliometrics 92(1):89–103

Cleary FR, Edwards DJ (1960) The origins of the contributors to the A.E.R. during the 'fifties. Am Econ Rev 50(5):1011–1014

CNR (Consiglio Nazionale delle Richerche) (2013) http://www.cnr.it/sitocnr/Englishversion/Englishversion.html. Accessed 25 Sept 2013

CWTS (2013) Leiden Rankings. http://www.leidenranking.com/. Accessed 29 Sept 2013

Declan B (2007) Academics strike back at spurious rankings. Nature 447(7144):514

DoCampo D (2011) On using the Shanghai ranking to assess the research performance of university systems. Scientometrics 86(1):77–92

Dolan WP (1976) The ranking game: the power of the academic elite. pp 121. Retrieved from ERIC: ED 129 131

Editorial (2007) Higher Education in Europe 32(1):1–3

Enserink M (2007) Who ranks the university rankers? Science 317(5841):1026–1028

European Commission (2008) Ranking Europe's Universities, European Commission—IP/08/1942 11/12/2008. http://europa.eu/rapid/press-release_IP-08-1942_en.htm. Accessed 25 Sept 2013

Excellence in Research for Australia (ERA) initiative (2013) http://www.arc.gov.au/era/default.htm. Accessed 25 Sept 2013

Farrell EF, Van Der Werf M (2007) Playing the rankings game. Chron High Educ 53(38):A.11

Federkeil G (2009) Ranking—New developments in Europe 3rd International Symposium on University Rankings, 2009 (February 26). http://www.mediabank.leidenuniv.nl/ppt/ics/2009/federkeil.ppt

From the Editors (2002) Higher Education in Europe 27(4):359

Garfield E (1955) Citation indexes for science. Science 122(3159). doi: http://www.jstor.org/stable/1749965

Garfield E (1979) Is citation analysis a legitimate evaluation tool? Scientometrics 1(4):359–375. doi:10.1007/BF02019306

Garfield E, Sher IH (1963) New factors in the evaluation of scientific literature through citation indexing. Am Doc 14(3):195–201

Hazelkorn E (2007) OECD: consumer concept becomes a policy instrument. University World News. http://www.universityworldnews.com/article.php?story=20071108144018483. Accessed 25 Sept 2013

Hazelkorn E (2008) Learning to live with league tables and ranking: the experience of institutional leaders. High Educ Policy 21(2):193–215

HEEACT (2013) Higher Educations Evaluation Accreditation Council of Taiwan. http://www.heeact.edu.tw/mp.asp?mp=4. Accessed 25 Sept 2013

HEFCE (2013) Higher Education Funding Council for England—Research. http://www.hefce.ac.uk/research/. Accessed 25 Sept 2013

Henshaw JT (2006) The ratings game: overall measurement and rankings in Does measurement measure up? How numbers reveal and conceal the truth. Johns Hopkins University Press, Baltimore

Hirsch J (2005) An index to quantify an individual's scientific research output. Proceedings of the National Academy of Science 102(15569)

Hood WW, Wilson CS (2001) The literature of bibliometrics, scientometrics and informetrics. Scientometrics 52(2):291–314

Hou ATC, Ince M, Chiang CL (2012) A reassessment of Asian Pacific excellence programs in higher education: the Taiwan experience. Scientometrics 92(1):23–24

Hughes RM (1925) A study of the graduate schools of America. Miami University, Oxford, Ohio

IDEAS Rankings (2013, updated monthly) http://ideas.repec.org/top/. Accessed 1 Oct 2013

IHEP (Institute for Higher Education Policy) (2006) Berlin principles on ranking of higher education institutions. http://www.ihep.org/assets/files/publications/a-f/BerlinPrinciplesRanking.pdf. Accessed 25 Sept 2013

IHEP (Institute for Higher Education Policy) (2007) College and university ranking systems: global perspectives and American challenges. April 2007 p 67. http://www.ihep.org/Publications/publications-detail.cfm?id=11. Accessed 25 Sept 2013

IREG Observatory on Academic Ranking and Excellence (2013) http://www.ireg-observatory.org/. Accessed 25 Sept 2013

Jacsó P (2008) Google scholar revisited. Online Inf Rev 32(1):102

Jin JC, Hong JH (2008) East Asian rankings of economics departments. J Asian Econ 19(1):74–82

Jin JC, Yau L (1999). Research productivity of the economics profession in East Asia. Econ Inq 37(4):706

Johnson LB (15 September 1965) 514—Statement by the President to the Cabinet and Memorandum on Strengthening Academic Capability for Science. American Presidency Project. http://www.presidency.ucsb.edu/ws/index.php?pid=27257. Accessed 4 Nov 2009

Journal M3trics (2012) Research analytics redefined. http://www.journalmetrics.com/about-journal-metrics.php. Accessed 1 Oct 2013

Key Perspectives Ltd. (2009) A comparative review of research assessment regimes in five countries and the role of libraries in the research assessment process. Report commissioned by OCLC Research. http://www.oclc.org/research/publications/library/2009/2009-09.pdf. Accessed 25 Sept 2013

Konkiel S (2013) Altmetrics: a 21st century solution to determining research quality. Online/Searcher, July August 2013 11–15

Kroc RJ (1984) Using citation analysis to assess scholarly productivity. Educ Res 13(6):17–22

Labi A (2008) Obsession with rankings goes global. Chron High Educ 55(8):A.27

Leung K (2007) The glory and tyranny of citation impact: an East Asian perspective. Acad Manag J 50(3):510–513

Liu NC, Cheng Y (2005) The academic ranking of world universities. High Educ Eur 30(2):127–136

Magoun HW (1966) The Cartter Report on quality in graduate education: institutional and divisional standings compiled from the Report. J High Educ 37(9):481–492

Meho LI, Yang K (2007) Impact of data sources on citation counts and rankings of LIS faculty: Web of Science, Scopus, Google Scholar. J Am Soc Inf Sci Technol 58(13):2105–2125

Meredith M (2004) Why do universities compete in the ratings game? An empirical analysis of the effects of the U.S. News and World Report college rankings. Res High Educ 45(5):443–461

Merisotis J, Sadlak J (2005) Higher education rankings: evolution, acceptance, and dialogue. High Educ Eur 30(2):97–101

Morse R (2010) The world's best just got bigger and better. Morse Code: Inside the college rankings. http://www.usnews.com/education/blogs/college-rankings-blog/2010/02/25/the-worlds-best-just-got-bigger-and-better. Accessed 2 Oct 2013

Morse R, Space J (1990) What's behind the rankings? U.S. News & World Report 108(11):48–49

National Taiwan University (2012) NTU Ranking. http://nturanking.lis.ntu.edu.tw/Default.aspx. Accessed 29 Sept 2013

Nature Publishing Index Asia Pacific (2013) Monthly. http://www.natureasia.com/en/publishing-index/asia-pacific/. Accessed 30 Sept 2013

OECD Directorate for Education (2013) Measuring learning outcomes in higher education. (AHELO). http://www.oecd.org/site/ahelo/. Accessed 25 Sept 2013

Pagell RA (2008) Bibliometrics: From Bean counting to academic accountability. Paper presented at CONCERT. http://library.smu.edu.sg/aboutus/Bibliometricscomplete.pdf. Accessed 25 Sept 2013

Pagell RA (2009) University research rankings: from page counting to academic accountability. Eval High Educ 3(1):71–101. http://ink.library.smu.edu.sg/library_research/1. Accessed 25 Sept 2013

Pagell RA, Lusk EJ (2002) Benchmarking academic business school libraries relative to their business school rankings. J Bus Financ Librariansh 7(4):3

Paul RJ (2008) Measuring research quality: the United Kingdom Government's Research Assessment Exercise. Eur J Inf Syst 17(4):324–329

Pritchard A (1969) Statistical bibliography or bibliometrics? J Doc 25:348–349

Quacquarelli Symonds (2013) QS world university rankings. http://www.topuniversities.com/qs-world-university-rankings. Accessed Sept 2013

Rabesandratana T (2013) 'Brussels ranking' of universities off to a rocky start, Science 339(6118):383

Research Trends (2008) Quarterly newsletter. http://www.researchtrends.com

Richardson M (2011) A "democratization" of university rankings: U-Multirank, Research Trends (24) 9

Saisana M, d'Hombres B, Saltelli A (2011) Rickety numbers: volatility of university rankings and policy implications. Res Policy 40(1):165–177

Salmi J, Saroyan A (2007) League tables as policy instruments: uses and misuses. High Educ Manag Policy 19(2):31–68. http://www.oecd.org/edu/imhe/45380007.pdf#page=33. Accessed 25 Sept 2013

San Francisco Declaration on Research Assessment. http://am.ascb.org/dora/. Accessed 30 Sept 2013

Schubert WH (1979) Contributions to AERA annual programs as an indicator of institutional productivity. Educ Res 8(7):13–17

SCIMago Research Group (2013) SIR reports. http://www.scimagoir.com/#. Accessed Sept 2013

Solorzano L, Quick BE (1983) Rating the colleges: exclusive national survey. U.S. News & World Report 95:3

Times Higher Education (2013) The world university rankings. http://www.timeshighereducation.co.uk/world-university-rankings/. Accessed 2 Oct 2013

Thomson-Reuters (2013) Science watch. http://sciencewatch.com/. Accessed Sept 2013

U-Multirank (2013) http://www.u-multirank.eu/. Accessed 3 Oct 2013

University Grants Committee (2013). http://www.ugc.edu.hk/eng/ugc/about/about.htm. Accessed 25 Sept 2013

University of Zurich (2013) How international rankings work. http://www.uzh.ch/about/portrait/rankings/top_en.html. Accessed 29 Sept 2013

Usher A (2009) Rankings 2.0: the new frontier in institutional comparisons. Aust Univ Rev 51(2):87–89

Van Raan AFJ, Moed H, van Leeuven TN (2007) Scoping study on the use of bibliometric analysis to measure the quality of research in UK higher education institutions. 131 pp. http://webarchive.nationalarchives.gov.uk/20100202100434/; http://www.hefce.ac.uk/pubs/rdreports/2007//rd18_07/rd18_07.pdf. Accessed 30 Sept 2013

Van Raan T, van Leeuwen T, Visser M (2011) Non-English papers decrease rankings. Nature 469:34. doi:10.1038/469034a

Van Vught F, Ziegele F (eds) (2011) U-Multirank: Design and testing the feasibility of a multi-dimensional global university rankings published by CHERPA network, 183 p. http://ec.europa.eu/education/higher-education/doc/multirank_en.pdf. Accessed 25 Sept 2013

Werner M, Bornmann L (2013) Journal impact factor: "the poor man's citation analysis" and alternative approaches. Eur Sci Ed 39(3):62–63

Part V
Development of World Libraries

The Development of East Asian Libraries in North America

Eugene W. Wu

Abstract The development of East Asian libraries in North America is of recent history. Prior to World War II there were only some half dozen East Asian collections in the United States and Canada. But that number began to increase rapidly after the War. With the establishment of new East Asian collections at universities, problems concerning collection development, cataloging, and personnel began to be a common concern. A series of efforts led by the American Library Association (ALA), the Library of Congress (LC), and the Association for Asian Studies (AAS) led to the developing of national cataloging standards for East Asian materials, and the eventual founding of the Committee on East Asian Libraries (later renamed Council on East Asian Libraries, CEAL) of the Association for Asian Studies to better coordinate cataloging, collection development, and personnel training, and later on the introduction of automation in East Asian libraries. This essay is an attempt to trace that development by stage, with tributes paid to two pioneers in that development: Dr. A. Kaiming Chiu, the founding Librarian of the Harvard-Yenching Library of Harvard University, and Dr. Mary C. Wright, the founding Curator of the Chinese Collection at the Hoover Institution, Stanford University. Some comments are also made on the application of technology in East Asian libraries.

Keywords CEAL · ALA · AAS · LC · RLG · OCLC · CCRM · East Asian libraries · A. Kaiming Chiu · Mary C. Wright

---

This address was delivered before the Plenary Session of the Council on East Asian Libraries, Association for Asian Studies, at its Annual Meeting on March 8, 2000 in San Diego, California, and published under the title "CEAL At the Dawn of the 21st Century" in the *Journal of East Asian Libraries*, no. 20 (June 2000). It has been revised and updated, with endnotes, for republication here.

Eugene W. Wu was founding Curator of the East Asian Collection at the Hoover Institution at Stanford University in 1961, and later Librarian of the Harvard-Yenching Library at Harvard University from 1965–1997. Email: Ewwu@aol.com

---

E. W. Wu (✉)
Harvard-Yenching Library, Harvard University, Cambridge, USA
e-mail: Ewwu@aol.com

C. Chen, R. Larsen (eds.), *Library and Information Sciences,*
DOI 10.1007/978-3-642-54812-3_11, © The Author(s) 2014

The Beginning

The development of East Asian libraries in North America is of recent history. Prior to World War II there were only some half dozen East Asian collections in the United States and Canada. But that number began to increase rapidly after the war, and problems concerning management and operation became a matter of common concern. In 1948 a group of concerned scholars and librarians gathered at the annual meeting of the American Library Association (ALA) in Atlantic City to discuss these problems.[1] Although it was an informal meeting, the discussion that began at that time eventually led to a concerted organizational movement that made possible the phenomenal growth of East Asian libraries in North America, particularly in the United States, in the last six decades.[2]

This library development followed closely the spread of East Asian Studies in North America in the postwar years. Before that time a few universities had offered some courses on East Asia (then referred to as the Far East), but full-fledged study of East Asia, in all the disciplines of the humanities and social sciences, did not develop until after the end of the Second World War. The war in the Pacific, the transformation of Japan into a democracy, the communist revolution in China, and the Korean War contributed to a heightening of American awareness of the importance of East Asia in a changing world, and of the need for better understanding of their histories and civilizations. The universities, with generous foundation and government support, responded by expanding their teaching and research programs on East Asia, and today, after sixty years, East Asian studies in the United States is probably the largest and most comprehensive in the Western world. A concomitant development in this academic enterprise was the building of library resources. Although several American libraries had begun collecting in the East Asian languages long before World War II (the Library of Congress began as early as 1869, Yale started in 1878, Harvard in 1879, UC-Berkeley in 1896, Cornell in 1918, Columbia in 1920, Princeton in 1926, and Chicago in 1936), they all experienced their greatest growth after 1945. A number of today's major collections, such as those at Michigan, Stanford (incorporating the former collections of Hoover Institution), University of Washington, and UCLA, came into being only in the late 1940s; and others such as Illinois, Indiana, and Wisconsin, in the 1960s.

With the establishment of new East Asian collections at universities, problems concerning acquisitions, cataloging, and personnel began to be a common concern. That was the reason for the 1948 Atlantic City meeting. Those present were looking

---

[1] Elizabeth Huff, "The National Committee on Oriental Collections, 1948–1952,": Library Resources on East Asia: Reports and Working Papers for the Tenth Annual Meeting of the Committee on American Library Resources on the Far East, Association for Asian Studies, Inc., at the Palmer House, Chicago, March 21, 1967 (Zug, Switzerland: Inter Documentation Company AG, 1968) pp. 16–17. Also, Edwin G. Beal, "The Committee on East Asian Libraries: A Brief History," *Committee on East Asian Libraries Newsletter*, no 41 (Sept. 1973), Appendix I, pp. 42–43.

[2] According to 1957 statistics, the earliest available data on East Asian libraries, 20 libraries reported a total holding of 2,490.000 volumes. Those numbers increased to 50 libraries with a total holding of 17,900.000 volumes, not including serial titles or materials in electronic format. For detailed annual statistics from 1957 seehttp://lib.ku.edu/ceal/stat/

for cooperative solutions to these problems. A decision was made at that meeting to create an informal committee, to be named the National Committee on Oriental Collections in the U.S. and Abroad, to explore possible ways to achieve that purpose. It is instructive to note that the problems they discussed – acquisitions, cataloging, and the training of personnel—are still among our concerns today, albeit in a different context from that of sixty years ago. In all likelihood we will continue discussing them for years to come. This reminds us once again that the basic mission of the library—building collections and providing service—never changes, only the way that mission is carried out. The informal committee created in Atlanta was replaced a year later, in 1949, by an official Joint Committee on Oriental Collections, sponsored by the Far Eastern Association (the predecessor of the Association for Asian Studies) and the American Library Association (ALA).[3] This was the first time in the history of American libraries that an official body was established by the library and the scholarly communities to address the problems associated with East Asian library collections in the United States. The significance attached to this new development can be seen in the composition of the Joint Committee, which comprised three members appointed by the Far Eastern Association and three by the American Library Association. Representing the former were Arthur H. Hummel, Chief of Orientalia Division, Library of Congress; Osamu Shimizu, Head of Japanese Section, Orientalia Division, Library of Congress; and Elizabeth Huff, Head of East Asiatic Library, UC-Berkeley. The latter was represented by Warner G. Rice, Director of the University of Michigan Library; Charles H. Brown, Director of Library, Iowa State College; and Robert B. Downs, Director of the University of Illinois Library and UI's Library School. Howard Linton, Curator of the East Asian Library at Columbia University, who belonged to both associations, became the executive secretary. It was an auspicious beginning. Among the salient accomplishments of the Joint Committee in its three-years of existence was the agreement by the Library of Congress to reproduce for purchase unedited Chinese and Japanese catalog cards sent in by cooperating libraries under a new program named Oriental Card Reproduction Project. It was not cooperative cataloging, to be sure, but a mechanism for catalog card exchange, as it were, which did not exist before.[4] The Joint Committee ceased to function in 1952, but the recognition that no meaningful cooperative development of East Asian libraries in the United States would be possible without a satisfactory solution of one of its basic functions of a library, namely cataloging, prompted ALA to appoint in 1954 a Special Committee on Cataloging Oriental Materials under its Cataloging and Classification Division. In 1957 the name was changed to Special Committee on Cataloging Far Eastern Materials of the American Library Association because the Special Committee was spending most of its time working on problems involving materials in the Far Eastern languages. Because of the importance of its work this Special Committee was made in 1958 a standing committee of ALA under the name Far Eastern Materials Committee.[5] In the same

---

[3] Huff, *op. cit* p. 42.

[4] *ibid.*

[5] G. Raymond Nunn, "Development of Cooperative Cataloging and Resources for East Asian Collections, 1954–1963," *Library Resources on East Asia: Reports and Working Papers for the Tenth Annual Meeting of the Committee on American Library Resources on the Far East...*p. 18.

year, the Association for Asian Studies (AAS), at the urging of East Asian libraries, also established a Committee on American Library Resources on the Far East (CALRFE).[6]

Developing National Cataloging Standards for East Asian Materials

The Far Eastern Materials Committee was chaired by G. Raymond Nunn, then Head of the Asia Library, University of Michigan. (He was succeeded as chair by Charles E. Hamilton of the East Asiatic Library of the University of California in Berkeley.) Its members were mostly heads of large East Asian libraries with cataloging experience. This committee occupies a very special place in the history of the development of East Asian libraries in North America, as it was under its and LC's leadership a set of national standards for cataloging East Asian materials was established for the first time. It was the result of four years of intensive collaborative work, from 1954 to 1958, by this committee and LC's Oriental Processing Committee (OPC). These two bodies, in the most meticulous fashion, worked through the twin American standards for cataloging—*ALA Cataloging Rules for Author and Title Entries* and *Rules for Descriptive Cataloging in the Library of Congress*—and amended every rule that had implications for cataloging East Asian materials. The result was a major series of amendments to the two sets of rules, which were then approved by both ALA and LC and adopted as national standards. They remain so today, with modifications as incorporated in the *Anglo-American Cataloging Rules II (AACRII)*.[7] This was a significant milestone in the history of East Asian libraries in North America, for in those days not only were there no computers, there were even no national standards for cataloging Chinese, Japanese, or Korean materials. Every library was on its own, using its own format and following its own rules, although many opted for the Harvard-Yenching Classification Scheme. No library used subject headings (a few maintained a classified catalog) and there was little or no authority work. There was even disagreement as to whether the main entry should be by author or title. So, what the two committees accomplished under those circumstances was indeed epoch-making. There is a Chinese saying: "People before us planted trees, we can now enjoy the shade." We will always be indebted to these two committees for their lasting contributions to our profession. In this connection we should remember in particular the leadership provided to the work of the two committees by G. Raymond Nunn, Lucile Morsch, C. Sumner Spalding, and Charles H. Hamilton. Ray Nunn was an indefatigable workhorse, and he guided the work of the Special Committee with that spirit. Lucile Morsch and C. Sumner

---

[6] *ibid.* p. 19. Also, Beal, *op. cit.*

[7] Edwin G. Beal, Jr. "Discussion of Tsuen-Hsuin Tsien's paper. "East Asian Collections in America," in Tsuen-Hsuin Tsien and Howard Winger, ed., Area Studies and the Library, The Thirtieth Annual Conference of the Graduate Library School, May 20–22, 1965 (Chicago & London: The University of Chicago Press, 1965), pp. 75–76.

The Development of East Asian Libraries in North America 167

Spalding, who were successive chairs of the OPC in their capacity as chief of LC's Descriptive Cataloging Division, were incisive and always willing to meet us halfway. Charles Hamilton, chief cataloger at the East Asiatic Library of UC-Berkeley, who had the rare ability to discern linkages among seemingly disparate rules and their potential impact on cataloging East Asian materials, and his arguments often revealed our ignorance of the subtlety in the intent of some of the rules. It can be safely said that without his participation, the work of amending the rules would have been much more difficult.

The adoption of the amended rules as national standards did not mean, however, the end of East Asian libraries' cataloging problems. The new challenge was implementation, and there was great hope that everyone's dream of shared cataloging might come true at last. Toward that end LC established in 1958 a Far Eastern Section in the Processing Department under the direction of Warren Tsuneishi, who would later become Chief of the Orientalia Division and the first director of the Area Studies Department at LC. The purpose of the new section was to introduce a cooperative cataloging program for East Asian publications, patterned after what LC had been doing for decades for publications in other languages. Unfortunately, this program did not work as expected, and it was soon terminated mainly because of insufficient manpower at LC to do the editing that was required to bring cataloging copies from the participating libraries up to the very strict LC standard. The demise of this short-lived program notwithstanding, the drive toward some sort of shared cataloging did not lose its momentum altogether. It survived in part and in a different form when LC established a Japan office under its National Program of Acquisitions and Cataloging (NPAC). The purpose of NPAC was to insure both adequate coverage of current publications LC was acquiring from around the world and the speedy availability of bibliographical records for them for general use. The NPAC Japan office, under the direction of Andrew Kuroda, Head of the Japanese Section of LC's Orientalia Division, did just that for Japanese publications for a number of years. It was a very useful program. Unfortunately, it had to be dismantled for budgetary reasons. At the time the NPAC Japan office was established, discussion began on establishing a similar program for Chinese-language materials, perhaps in Hong Kong, both within and without the Library of Congress. (This was in the early 1970s, and there were no diplomatic relations between Washington and Beijing. It was impossible even to think of setting up a NPAC center on the China mainland at that time.) However, the discussion never went very far. Since libraries in those days all looked to LC to get things done, East Asian libraries thought it best to wait for LC to come up with a solution to deal with the Chinese acquisitions and cataloging problems for everyone, and they made a point of engaging LC in the discussion they were having among themselves. The Harvard-Yenching Library took the lead and invited twelve large East Asian libraries and the Library of Congress to a series of meetings on Chinese cooperative cataloging, the first in New York in 1972, followed by a second in Chicago in 1973, and a third in Boston in 1974. An Ad Hoc Committee on Chinese Cooperative Cataloging was set up at the first meeting to investigate the feasibility of establishing such a program. The subsequent deliberations centered on several related issues: the slowness in LC's distribution of its printed Chinese catalog cards; the exclusion from the *National Union Catalog* published by LC of records in any East Asian language, resulting in the costly duplication of cataloging efforts among East Asian libraries. In response, LC proposed the compilation of a new publication to be called *Chinese Cooperative Catalog* which would include all cards submitted by participating libraries. There were some misgivings about the LC proposal, the main concern being the likelihood that once the *Chinese Cooperative Catalog* was published, cataloging cards for East Asian publications may be permanently excluded from the *National Union Catalog.* This whole matter was turned over to the Committee on East Asian Libraries (CEAL), which at that time had appointed a Subcommittee on the National Union Catalog, and the Ad Hoc Committee was dissolved. The CEAL Subcommittee continued the discussion on the LC proposal, but there was insufficient support for it among the East Asian libraries, and the matter was dropped. East Asian libraries had to wait for a decade until the mid-1980s before a truly national and international shared cataloging program was in place, thanks to technology that brought us online cataloging and the services of the Research Libraries Group (RLG) and the Online Computer Library Center (OCLC).

The Birth of the Committee on East Asian Libraries

It is appropriate to mention at this point the creation of the Committee on East Asian Libraries (CEAL) and the vital role it played in the development of East Asian libraries in North America. Before 1967 there was no national organization of East Asian libraries. All developmental activities were carried out under the name of committees. The above-mentioned CALRFE came close to being a quasi-national organization, but in spite of its many accomplishments, CALRFE operated without a charter setting forth its functions, membership requirements, or voting procedures. It was run almost single-handedly by a chairperson, appointed by the Board of Directors of the Association for Asian Studies (AAS), who was also responsible for putting out a newsletter. The arrangement was not satisfactory, especially when the number of East Asian libraries was increasing rapidly. So, in 1963 CALRFE was reorganized with an Executive Group of seven members, also appointed by the Association for Asian Studies (AAS), in addition to the chairperson.[8] At the CALRFE annual meeting in 1967 East Asian libraries approved a set of *Procedures* proposed by the new Executive Group setting forth CALRFE's objectives, functions, and operating procedures, and it was at this time the name Committee on American Library Resources on the Far East (CALRFE) was changed to Committee on East

---

[8] Tsuen-Hsuin Tsien T-H "Report of CALRFE Programs and Activities for 1966–1967," Library Resources on East Asia: Reports and Working Papers for the Tenth Annual Meeting of the Committee on American Library Resources on the Far East...p. 28.

The Development of East Asian Libraries in North America 169

Asian Libraries (CEAL) of the Association for Asian Studies (AAS)[9] The *Procedures* became the basic operating document for CEAL. It was amended several times later, most significantly in 1980 by the requirement that all officers of CEAL, including the chair, members of the Executive Group as well as the chairs of the subcommittees be elected rather than appointed by AAS. It was a change welcomed by all East Asian libraries, and it has served the Easy Asian library community well over the years. In 1995 the name Committee on Ease Asian Libraries was changed to Council on East Asian Libraries (still known as CEAL) and it remained under the Association for Asian Studies.[10]

Issues in Collection Development

As already mentioned, many universities introduced teaching and research programs on East Asia in the post-World War II years, and new East Asian collections came to be established at those institutions. The collection development needs of these newly established libraries were somewhat different from those at the older libraries. The newer ones had to start from the ground up while the older ones, having already established core collections of the basic materials, had the advantage of being able to concentrate on current publications. Building a new East Asian collection where there was none presented a daunting challenge, even when there was adequate financial support, as was the case in the 1960s. The problem was that there simply were not that many sources of supply of older publications needed by the new collections, particularly in Chinese, which was what most of the newly established collections were concentrating on. Nor was the procurement of current Chinese publications an easy task. The volume of publications from the People's Republic of China at that time was limited, and the Chinese government did not allow direct purchases by foreign libraries. Every book had to be acquired in Hong Kong or Japan. The number of new publications in Taiwan was also small, and the publishers did not aggressively engage in export. A number of them were busily engaged in reprinting block-print editions of centuries ago, exactly what was needed

---

[9] Edwin G. Beal, Jr., "The Committee on East Asian Libraries: A Brief History," Committee on East Asian Libraries Newsletter, no. 41 (Sept. 1973), p. 48. For the full text of the Procedures, see Committee on East Asian Libraries Newsletter, no 40 (June 1973), pp. 35–37, reprinted in no. 49 (Mar. 1976), pp. 53–54.

[10] A report on the discussion of the revised Procedures before its adoption at the CEAL Plenary Session, held in Washington, D.C. is available in the Committee on East Asian Libraries Bulletin, no. 82 (June 1980), p. 3. The full text of the Procedures, as amended in 1984, is reproduced in Committee on East Asian Libraries Bulletin, no. 74 (June 1984), pp. 81–83.

When the Committee on East Asian Libraries was renamed the Council on East Asian Libraries in 1995, the designation "subcommittee" was replaced by that of "committee." At present there are nine standing committees: Committee on Chinese Materials, Committee on Japanese Materials, Committee on Korean Materials, Committee on Library Technology, Committee on Technical Processing, Committee on Public Services, Committee on Publications, Committee on Membership, and committee on Statistics.

170 E. W. Wu

by the newly established East Asian libraries in the United States; but these reprints were mostly to satisfy Taiwan's own needs, and the publishers seemed oblivious of the overseas market. So, in 1963 CALRFE submitted a proposal to AAS for the establishment, under AAS auspices, of a Chinese Materials and Research Aids Service Center in Taipei for the benefit of American libraries. The purpose was to coordinate and reprint out-of-print titles needed by the Chinese studies community in the United States. With AAS approval and with initial grants from it, as well as from the American Council of Learned Societies (ACLS) and the Council on Library Resources (CLR), the Taipei Center was set up and began operation in the fall of 1964. Robert L. Irick, a Harvard Ph.D. in Chinese history, was appointed as director. Since then the Taipei Center, which later became independent under the name, has reprinted thousands of out-of-print titles and helped fill the shelves not only of American libraries, but also of foreign libraries that collect Chinese-language publications.[11]

Meanwhile, current Chinese publications also demanded attention, particularly those from the People's Republic. As just mentioned, American libraries were not allowed to buy directly from China in the 1960s, and exchange was possible only with the National Beijing Library. Buying indirectly from Hong Kong or Japan was at best a poor substitute, as the supply was limited and many titles were not available at all because the Chinese government did not allow their export. At the time AAS was setting up the Taipei Center, an effort was also made to open up additional sources of supply of contemporary Chinese publications, especially those from the mainland. The Joint Committee on Contemporary China (JCCC), of the American Council of Learned Societies (ACLS) and the Social Science Research Council (SSRC), took the lead in this in hopes that the fast-growing teaching and research programs on contemporary China in the universities could be better supported. Toward that goal JCCC thought it important to find out how institutions in other countries were dealing with the problem of sources, especially contemporary publications, and see what we could learn from them. In 1964 I was commissioned by JCCC to conduct a survey and submit a report with recommendations. The survey was a year in the making, including visits to the major research and library centers in Chinese studies in Western and Eastern Europe, Scandinavia, the Soviet Union, India, Japan, Taiwan, Hong Kong as well as those in the United States. I found that a number of libraries in the Soviet Union and Eastern Europe, and to a lesser degree in Western Europe and Japan, were receiving research materials originating in the PRC in ways that were not available to us, and most of these libraries were receptive to the idea of exchange with American libraries. And so in the report submitted to JCCC, I recommended that a national service center for East Asian libraries be established to identify, procure (through interlibrary loans and exchanges), and reproduce for distribution contemporary Chinese publications unavailable to us and other hard-to-find research materials on 20th-century China available only in a very few American libraries. JCCC adopted this recommendation, and a not-for-profit organization, the Center for Chinese Research Materials (CCRM), was launched in 1968

---

[11] Committee on American Library Resources on the Far East Newsletter, no. 6 (Sept. 1964), p. 4.

under the auspices of the Association of Research Libraries (ARL) in Washington, D.C., with a generous Ford Foundation grant. P. K. Yu, a Lecturer in History at the University of Hong Kong and owner of the prestigious Long Men Book Company in Hong Kong, was recruited as director. Additional grants from the Andrew Mellon Foundation, and the National Endowment for the Humanities made it possible for CCRM to become an academic publisher in a very short period of time. For more than three decades CCRM, now independently incorporated but still a not-for-profit organization under the directorship of Pingfeng Chi, has made available to libraries world-wide a great many once hard-to-find research materials on 20th-century China. It has become one of the most important support facilities for modern and contemporary China studies in the world, and Chinese collections in libraries everywhere would be much poorer today if not for CCRM.

In collecting PRC publications East Asian libraries have also benefited from significant and timely help from the American government. In the early 1960s when no Chinese local newspapers were available for subscription or purchase by foreign libraries, the government released to the Library of Congress its holdings of some 1,200 such papers published between 1949 and 1957.[12] While the great majority of them were incomplete files, and many were very fragmentary (some containing only a few issues), the significance of this release cannot be overemphasized, as none of the publications was available elsewhere at that time. (Now we can read many of the local newspapers online free of charge!) The release of the Red Guard tabloids in 1967 by the State Department to the academic community was another case in point. Soon after the start of the Cultural Revolution in 1966, normal publishing in China was supplanted by the issuing of millions of copies of the *Quotations of Chairman Mao* and *The Selected Works of Mao Zedong*, and vendors in Hong Kong and Tokyo had little else to offer. So when reprints of a number of Red Guard tabloids began to appear in Hong Kong, they became instant best sellers. Although most of these publications were highly polemical, they contain a great deal of information and documentation taken from government archives which were not available elsewhere. The rarity and importance of these new sources made them must-have items overnight, and libraries from around the world competed with one another to acquire them, pushing the already high price charged for them even higher. The Joint Committee on Contemporary China (JCCC) (Chairman: John H. Lindbeck) was again asked for help. JCCC approached the State Department with the request that it consider sharing its collection of Red Guard materials with the academic community. The State Department responded in the affirmative, and invited JCCC to send a representative to Washington, D.C. to evaluate what they had and determine whether their release would indeed be helpful to the academic community as believed. JCCC asked that I undertake that mission. After examining samples of the materials made available to me by the State Department, I had no doubt about their research value and urged their immediate release. The materials

---

[12] The content of this release is published as A List of China Mainland Provincial and Local Newspapers Held by the Library of Congress, 1949–1957 by the Orientalia Division of the Library of Congress, 1964. eld by Hed.

thus released formed the bulk of the 20-volume *Red Guard Publications* issued by CCRM in 1975. This kind of government-academe cooperation is to be encouraged. It may be mentioned in this connection that CCRM has since collected from other sources many more Red Guard publications and has reprinted them in a total of 132 folio volumes for research purposes. This collection – published in 1975 (20 volumes), 1998 (20 volumes), 2001 (40 volumes), and 2005 (52 volumes) – is probably the largest publicly available Red Guard publications in the world.

I have dwelled on issues in Chinese collection development because they were the most pressing to the East Asian libraries in the 1960s and the 1970s. This is not to say that there were no problems in Japanese or Korean collection development work. Indeed, there were. Generally speaking, the Japanese case was not been a matter of availability but of cost. South Korea was like Japan in that respect; and there was a great resemblance between North Korea and China, at least in the early years, in terms of the difficulties involved in acquiring publications from them. The establishment of the National Coordinating Committee on Japanese Library Resources (NCC), funded by the Japan-U.S. Friendship Commission and the Japan Foundation, and of the Korean Collections Consortium of North America, funded by the Korea Foundation were two important milestones in the development of Japanese and Korean collections in American libraries.

Technology in East Asian Libraries

While general American research libraries were seriously exploring in the 1960s and the 1970s the use of technology to improve operations, East Asian libraries were still occupied with the more mundane problems of cataloging standards and how to build or strengthen collections. Automation was far from everyone's mind and not on East Asian libraries' agenda. A 1975 statement CEAL was invited to submit to the Ford Foundation on the "Priorities for the Development and Funding of Library Programs in Support of East Asian Studies" made no reference to the role that emerging technology could play in East Asian library development. This was not East Asian libraries' fault. No serious work was being done on East Asian character codes in the United States at that time, and computers could not handle any of the East Asian languages. But the various needs outlined in the 1975 CEAL statement to the Ford Foundation were both urgent and persuasive, and in the same year the Ford Foundation urged the American Council of Learned Societies (ACLS) to appoint a Steering Committee for a Study of the Problems of East Asian Libraries. The Steering Committee was composed of the following persons:

George Bechman, Professor of Asian Studies and Dean, College of Arts and Sciences, University of Washington (Chairman)
Albert Feuerwerker, Professor of History and Director, Center for Chinese Studies, University of Michigan

The Development of East Asian Libraries in North America · 173

Herman H. Fussler, Martin A. Ryerson Distinguished Service Professor, Graduate Library School, University of Chicago
Hanna H. Gray, Provost, Yale University
Warren J. Haas, Vice President for Information Services and University Librarian, Columbia University
William F. Miller, Provost and Vice President, Stanford University
Warren Tsuneishi, Chief, Orientalia Division, Library of Congress
Eugene Wu, Librarian, Harvard-Yenching Library, Harvard University

As a guide to its work, the Steering Committee commissioned a series of papers, a number of them written by CEAL members, including Karl Lo (University of Washington), T. H. Tsien (University of Chicago), Weiying Wan (University of Michigan), Raymond Tang (University of California—Berkeley), Thomas Kuo (University of Pittsburg), Thomas Lee (University of Wisconsin), Richard Howard (Library of Congress), Warren Tsuneishi (Library of Congress), and Eugene Wu (Harvard University). The Steering Committee made its report in 1977 under the title: "East Asian Libraries: Problems and Prospects" with recommendations for bibliographical control, collection development and access, and technical and personnel matters.[13] The report attracted significant national attention, and in the following year ACLS, joined by the Social Science Research Council (SSRC), co-sponsored a Joint Advisory Committee to the East Asian Library Program in order to continue the work begun by the Steering Committee. The following persons were appointed to the Joint Advisory Committee:

Patricia Battin, Vice President and University Librarian, Columbia University
Charles Churchill, Dean of Library Services, Washington University (for 1980–1981)
Hideo Kaneko, Curator, East Asian Collection, Yale University Library
W. Mote, Professor of East Asian Studies, Princeton University
Robert E. Ward, Director, Center for International Studies, Stanford University
Eugene Wu, Librarian, Harvard-Yenching Library, Harvard University
John W. Haeger (ex-officio), Director, ACLS-SSRC-ARL East Asian Library Program

It was the work of this committee that eventually led to online cataloging in East Asian libraries. In its report on "Automation, Cooperation, and Scholarship: East Asian Libraries in the 1980s,"[14] the Joint Advisory Committee stated that "after a decade of unprecedented growth along a course linked primarily to foreign area studies programs rather than to the development of research libraries in general.... East Asian libraries were at a crossroad," and with the lessening of federal and foun-

---

[13] *East Asian Libraries: Problems and Prospects, A Report and Recommendations*, prepared by the Steering Committee for a Study of the Problems of East Asian Libraries (Washington, D.C.: The American Council of Learned Societies, 1977).

[14] *Automation, Cooperation and Scholarship: East Asian Libraries in the 1980's, Final Report of the Joint Advisory Committee to the East Asian Library Program* (Washington, D.C.: The American Council of Learned Societies, 1981).

dation funding, they ought to embark upon a new course of sharing work, materials, and access, and of relying "on automation as a principal planning and management tool." The keystone to this, according to the report, "is the capability to input, manage, store, transmit, display and output bibliographic records containing East Asian vernacular characters in exactly the same automated systems already created to perform similar functions for Western language materials and general research libraries." This basic reorientation of the course of development of East Asian libraries in North America, as advocated in the report, would fundamentally change the way East Asian libraries operated, but it was welcomed by all concerned.

The immediate result of the Joint Advisory Committee's recommendation was the decision by the Research Libraries Group (RLG) to introduce in 1983, with Ford Foundation support, the CJK enhancements to the Research Libraries Information Network (RLIN), RLG's operating arm. This move made possible for the first time the creation of cataloging records at one library which could then be copied by other libraries and also viewed by researchers everywhere. In 1986 the Online Computer Library Center (OCLC) also established a similar CJK bibliographic utility. The rest, of course, is history.

Remembering the Pioneers

As we reminisce about our past, it is important that we honor the pioneers in our profession. I would like to salute two of them in particular, as I knew them the best: A. Kaiming Chiu (1898–1977) and Mary Clabaugh Wright (1917–1970). Dr. Chiu was the first Librarian of Harvard-Yenching Library and served in that position with great distinction for thirty-eight years, from 1927 to 1965. Dr. Wright was the first Curator of the Chinese Collection at the Hoover Institution, Stanford University, for eleven years, from 1948 to 1959. I had the singular honor of succeeding both of them, Mary Wright in 1959 when she was appointed a professor of history at Yale University, and Kaiming Chiu in 1965 when he retired from Harvard-Yenching Library.

Dr. Chiu's name has long been synonymous with East Asian librarianship in the United States. He was the very first person to be appointed Librarian of an East Asian library at an American university, and his tenure of almost four decades at the Harvard-Yenching Library remains to this day the longest among the nation's East Asian librarians. But his legacy lies elsewhere. He will be remembered for his Harvard-Yenching Classification Scheme, the first such work for cataloging Chinese, Japanese, and Korean books in the Western world. The scheme was adopted for use by the major East Asian libraries in the United States and several leading East Asian collections in Europe and Australia until the 1970s and the 1980s. He will also be remembered for putting romanization along with the vernacular script on the catalog card, something we take for granted today, and for introducing separate catalogs and shelving by language. Dr. Chiu was also a great mentor. A number of people he trained at the Harvard-Yenching Library later achieved prominence, among them were James S. K. Tung, who became Assistant University Librarian

The Development of East Asian Libraries in North America 175

and Curator of the Gest Library and Oriental Collections at Princeton; Fang Chao-ying and Tu Lien-che, known for their impeccable scholarship on Ming and Ch'ing history, who collaborated with Dr. Arthur H. Hummel and Professor L. Carrington Goodrich respectively in the compilation of *Eminent Chinese of the Ch'ing Period* and *Dictionary of Ming Biography,* two publications of lasting importance to Chinese studies; Tien Hung-tu, who became Librarian of Yenching University Library; Teng Yen-lin, who served as the Reference Librarian at the National Library of Peking, and Chen Hung-shun) who taught at the Department of Library Science at Peking University after 1949. Of course, his greatest legacy is the collection he built at the Harvard-Yenching Library. He was a giant in this respect, as he succeeded in building from almost nothing one of the greatest libraries for East Asian research in the Western world. It is unlikely that his accomplishments will ever be duplicated. In the words of the Trustees of the Harvard-Yenching Institute who paid him tribute upon his retirement, he was "a scholar who exemplifies the best in the traditions and accomplishments of both East and West."[15]

Prof. Mary C. Wright was another legendary library builder. Trained as a historian at Harvard, she was with her husband, Arthur Wright, in Peking when Pearl Harbor came. Subsequently they were interned by the Japanese in Wei Xian in Shandong for the duration of the War. When the War ended, she accepted an offer from the Hoover Institution at Stanford University to collect materials for a Chinese Collection that was being planned at Hoover. Since Hoover's main interest was, and still is, in modern and contemporary affairs under the rubric of "War, Peace, and Revolution," Mary Wright was asked to focus on her acquisitions work accordingly. This she did, with entrepreneurial energy, skill, resourcefulness, and imagination. She traveled to all the major cities in China, sought advice from eminent scholars and bibliographers, badgered government agencies for their publications, and negotiated exchange agreements with major libraries and universities. Her painstaking efforts resulted in tons of materials, including a large number of journals, newspapers, and other ephemeral materials that are essential to social science research and which up to that time had not been systematically collected by most other libraries. Mary Wright did not confine herself to the ordinary channels in her collecting activities. In 1947, having wangled a seat on a U.S. military transport, she flew to Yenan, the base of the Chinese Communist Party, where she succeeded in obtaining a large group of Chinese communist publications issued there and in other communist-controlled "border areas". Such publications were not even available elsewhere in China at that time. The almost complete set of the *Jiefang Ribao* (Liberation Daily), the official organ of the Chinese Communist Party, she acquired on this excursion remains to this day the only original copy in the Western world. Following her return to the United States in late 1947, she managed to acquire the Harold Issacs Collection, a group of underground Chinese communist publications of the late 1920s and early 1930s collected by Mr. Issacs in Shanghai in the 1930s when he was editor of the *China Forum.* Soon after wards she reached

---

[15] For a chronological biography of Dr. Chiu, see 程焕文编, 《裘开明年谱》, 哈佛燕京图书馆学术丛刊第九种。桂林:广西大学出版社, 2008.

agreement with Nym Wales (Helen Snow) for the sale to Hoover of the Nym Wales Collection, containing Chinese communist and other related publications and documents of the mid- and late 1930s collected by Edgar Snow and Nym Wales when they visited Northwest China. The Harold Issacs and Nym Wales Collections together provided the basis for much of the subsequent research on the early history of the Chinese Communist movement by scholars from all around the world—a task theretofore impossible for lack of documentation.[16] As a scholar and library-builder, Mary Wright left us with a lifetime of work rich in insight and inspiration. As a pioneer in East Asian librarianship, she provided vision and ingenuity in her collection-building efforts. She supplied the necessary perspective as a scholar and active library user on what a research library should be and how it should function, and then went about creating such a library.[17] (It may be mentioned in this connection that Hoover's collection of the primary documentation for the early history of the Chinese Communist Party was made complete by the acquisition of the Jiangxi Soviet Government documents, commonly known as the Chen Cheng Collection which I microfilmed in Taipei in 1960.)[18]

The Future

It is often said that only fools make predictions. And so I will make none here as to where East Asian libraries will be in another ten, twenty or fifty years. But I do want to say a few words about technology and East Asian libraries as we enter a new millennium. High technology has done wonders. It has made it possible for libraries to do things that were hardly imaginable ten or twenty years ago. Libraries can now manage much more efficiently and serve their users much more effectively. Information is now available at our fingertips. We can search the catalog in a university library or view a museum collection in China, Japan, Korea or anyplace else. We have access to digitized databases, and their number is growing rapidly. We can read journals and newspapers online and order copies. We have tens of thousands, perhaps hundreds of thousands of specialized web sites that provide information

---

[16] The most important items in the Harold Issacs Collection and the Nym Wales Collection are annotation by Prof. Chun-tu Hsueh and published under the titles *The Chinese Communist Movement, 1921–1937* and *The Chinese Communist Movement, 1937–1949. The Hoover Institution Bibliographical Series* VIII and XI (Stanford: The Hoover Institution on War, Revolution, and Peace, 1960 and 1962).

[17] See also Eugene Wu, "Mary Clabaugh Wright: A Memorial," *China Quarterly*, no. 43 (July-September 1970), pp. 134–135.

[18] The Jiangxi Soviet documents, totaling approximately 1,500 items, are on 21 reels of microfilm. A selection of 670 of them was annotated by Prof. Tien-Wei Wu and published under the title, *The Kiangsi Soviet Republic, 1931–1934, A Selected and Annotated Bibliography of the Chen Cheng Collection. Harvard-Yenching Library Bibliographical Series* III. (Cambridge, Mass.: Harvard-Yenching Library, Harvard University, 1981) The content of the entire microfilm collection is listed at the end of the publication by the microfilm reel number and then by the title of the document.

of every kind. And the list goes on. High technology will undoubtedly continue to develop, and libraries and library users will all benefit. Although the unprecedented contribution high technology has made to libraries and scholarship has been huge and most likely will be even greater in the future, we must be mindful that technology is but the means to achieve an end, and not the end itself. While we continue to employ new technology in the service of scholarship, we must also continue our efforts to build collections as we have in the past. For in the final analysis, what scholarship demands of libraries is the substance of information, and that substance can only come from what libraries are able to collect. In the words of the great American naturalist, Henry David Thoureau, who made Walden Pond famous, we cannot afford to have "improved means to an unimproved end." It will serve us well as librarians to remember these words as we proceed with digital libraries and apply more technology to our work.

Open Access This chapter is distributed under the terms of the Creative Commons Attribution Noncommercial License, which permits any noncommercial use, distribution, and reproduction in any medium, provided the original author(s) and source are credited.